T0265740

Y2K

For my family, whose support
helped me begin this book,

and for Lyle, whose support
helped me complete it

"Maybe someday you will
rejoice to recall even this."

—VIRGIL, *AENEID*

Contents

Author's Note

THIS IS A WORK OF NONFICTION. THE EVENTS AND experiences detailed here are all true and have been faithfully rendered as I have remembered them, to the best of my ability. Some names, identities, and circumstances have been changed, and some composite characters have been used, in order to protect the privacy of the individuals involved. Some events are condensed for narrative clarity. Though conversations are written based on my keen recollection of them, they are not written to represent word-for-word documentation; rather, I've retold them in a way that evokes the real feeling and meaning of what was said, in keeping with the spirit of the event.

Introduction

WHEN I WAS ELEVEN, I BEGGED MY MOM TO BUY me an inflatable silver chair from Target. The year was 1999, and I had just started middle school and puberty. I saw it advertised on a piece of junk mail that hadn't yet made it to the recycling bin, in among deals on tissues and backpacks and Halloween decorations.

I had never seen anything like it. A chair filled with air like a pool float? I just knew my life would improve if I owned it. It was so shiny and futuristic, with its rounded edges, like it belonged on a spaceship or something. It looked like it came from the new millennium, which would arrive in just a few months. Y2K was practically all anyone talked about, at school and on TV and in magazines. I had to prepare! If I got the silver inflatable chair now, I'd be ready before the clock turned to midnight and the future arrived.

"Are you sure this is the chair you want?" my mom asked when I rushed over to her with the mailer. "What about something more practical?"

"Mom, it's really practical!" I insisted. "I'm gonna do all my homework in it!"

She paused, talked out her hesitations.

"I guess it's only twenty bucks," she reasoned.

"It's a really good deal!" I said. "And I swear, if you buy it I won't ask for anything else for a really, really, really long time."

She agreed that we could probably go to Target that weekend on the way back from swim practice.

"Yes!" I exalted, jumping up and down. "Thank you thank you thank you!"

The chair came in a box that my dad—ever the engineer—cut open with his X-Acto knife. Inside was some folded gray plastic that looked nothing like furniture. He read the instructions while I fiddled with the hand pump. There wasn't much to figure out, and pretty soon we were taking turns pushing the handle up and down. The chair was taking shape.

It was so lightweight that I carried it upstairs by myself. I put it in a corner of my room, where I had pale blue sheets with clouds on my bed and I slept under a gauze canopy that my mom (raised in a foreign service family in Afghanistan and Pakistan and Nigeria) recognized as mosquito netting when I had begged her to buy me that, too, at Bed Bath & Beyond.

"I guess it will come in handy if there's a malaria outbreak in Northern Virginia," she had said.

I loved that silver chair. When I first sat down it was cool to the touch, and my skin made little squeaking noises against it. When I wore shorts, the material stuck to my bare legs, and the seams left small red indentations. I sat in that chair while I talked on the phone with my best friend, Hannah, doodling with gel pens and balling up pieces of paper to toss in my purple Garbino trash can. I sat in that chair while I organized my Pokémon cards in a special binder. I sat in that chair while I played Smash Mouth's *Astro Lounge* on my silver Discman again and again and again. This, I thought, was the future.

A few months earlier, we made a Y2K time capsule at school. Outside in the warmth of the early June sun, we sat on folding chairs while our principal gave her remarks.

She said the new millennium would be full of innovation, of technologies we couldn't even imagine yet. We would all work collaboratively and celebrate multiculturalism, just like we were doing at school every day.

Beside her was the capsule. The three-foot-tall metal cylinder was filled with contributions from students, including letters from Mrs. Hathaway's fifth-grade class, the ones we all had to write looking a decade into the future. Where would we be in the year 2008?

2008 seemed so far away. I would be twenty, an age that sounded impossibly old. I would, presumably, have boobs—another seeming impossibility. How strange it was that I would leave behind childhood at the exact moment when America (and the world it led) would seem to slip the bonds of history. Though uncertain about its specifics, I knew the new millennium would be good—for me, for America, and for the world. And so I typed the following in ClarisWorks on our family's Power Macintosh:

In 2008 I will be in my third year of college at Stanford University in Palo Alto, California. They will have discovered a cure for AIDS by then and be close to a cure for cancer. By then most people will be watching their movies over the Internet. But the Internet will be even better than it is now. Instead of just viewing them on a normal computer that is about 1' 6" wide and 10" tall, we will view it on a big screen computer and it will have full sound and everything.

They will have fixed up the New York Avenue area in Washington, DC. It will have a huge shopping mall that will be famous all around the country and people-mover conveyor belts, like San Francisco Airport, so that people can get off at any shop they want without walking. They will also have escalators like we have today, but the shopping mall will be about eight stories high. Smoking will have been banned in all public places including parking lots and sidewalks. They will have new drugs to help people stop smoking.

The environment will have become a lot worse than it is today, but we will start to realize that we are destroying our environment so people will be getting in the process of banning power boats and stuff.

The popular artists will be using computer electronic music and you will rarely hear their real voices because it will be changed by the computer.

Bye!!!!!!:):):);):):);):)

I imagined a future fifth grader reading this in the cool bluish light of the new millennium, in a version of our elementary school where all the furniture had turned silver and white.

In 2018, I found a copy of it in a box at my parents' house. I was about to turn thirty, and my life was a mess. After a promising start, my writing career had stalled. I had recently gone through a bad breakup, and my ex was engaged to someone else. Donald Trump was the president, and nearly every month set a new climate record. As I read, the memories came flooding back: the time capsule, the ceremony, the jubilant turn-of-the-millennium anticipation. It occurred to me that I hadn't felt hope in years.

IN JULY 1997, THE cover of *WIRED* magazine read: "The long boom: we're facing 25 years of prosperity, freedom, and a better environment for the whole world. You got a problem with that?" The cover was bright yellow. A cartoon smiley-face globe held a flower in its lips: a callback to the 1960s, when the internet was born in California in a liaison between DARPA* and the counterculture.

The headline summed up the mood of the moment. In 1991, the Soviet Union collapsed and the Cold War ended. American-led capitalism versus Soviet-led communism had been the defining conflict of the twentieth century, and finally, capitalism had won. Capitalism's victory seemed to prove that it was the superior system, that its birthright was to take over the globe completely. Sure, there were some questions, but around the world everyone collectively exhaled, relieved to no longer live under the constant threat of nuclear annihilation. Political scientist Francis

---

* The Defense Advanced Research Projects Agency.

Fukuyama announced that we were at "the end of history" in a bestselling 1992 book of the same name.

In 1992, twelve countries in Europe signed the Maastricht Treaty and started the European Union. In this peaceful and collaborative new era, the trenches and the concentration camps and the Iron Curtain could all be forgotten. That same year back in America, Democratic presidential nominee Bill Clinton was elected on a "Third Way" platform of deregulation and privatization that borrowed heavily from Republicans. Why not? After all, history was over. In 1995 and 1997, his French and British counterparts Jacques Chirac and Tony Blair would bring the same type of post-politics to their countries. Poor nations, meanwhile, were transformed by free trade agreements, which brought manufacturing jobs outsourced from wealthy countries—a process which was broadly referred to as globalization. All these changes were part of the same single process: capitalism had, for the first time in its short history, taken over every part of the world and every aspect of life. It merged fully with politics, and it shaped how people saw themselves. In this, it was a psychological victory as much as an economic and political one. Nearly everyone—from public figures to regular people—operated under the assumption that we lived in the best of all possible worlds, that there could be no alternative.

Whatever you want to call it—the End of History, the New Economy, globalization, the neoliberal turn, the Washington consensus, the triumph of the capitalist world system, the end of politics—this process defined the 1990s. But what I will call the Y2K Era started around 1997 and lasted until 2008. The Y2K Era was defined by two things: the End of History and the rise of the internet. Like the End of History, the rise of the internet revolutionized politics, social relations, and our own individual self-perception. And both the End of History and the rise of the internet were fundamentally forward-looking. Together, they made the era feel ecstatic, frenetic, and wildly hopeful.

The Y2K Era was bounded by two economic bubbles. It opened, in 1997, with the dot-com bubble and it closed, in 2008, with the housing bubble. Both relied on stories about frontiers and endless growth, old stories that go back to foundational American thinkers like Thomas Jefferson. These stories looked only to the future, blinding us to warnings from the past.

The dot-com bubble lasted from 1995 through 2000 (though it really took off around 1997, the year *WIRED* printed its "long boom" issue). It fused the techno-optimism of the early internet with record-breaking stock prices. The internet, people thought, would not only connect the entire planet and let us buy kitty litter at home in our pajamas; it would launch stock values into the stratosphere, literally higher than they had ever been since good numbers became available in 1871.

All this wealth, it was assumed, would make everybody rich, even though labor protections had been dismantled and inequality had increased throughout the '80s and '90s. In the new millennium, we wouldn't need pensions or unions or labor laws. We could just invest our mutual funds in the stock market, which would, of course, go up forever. Alternately, we could found or invest in a dot-com startup. The IPOs of Netscape, Amazon, eBay, Google, and PayPal minted a large portion of our current billionaire class, and they were covered by the media in a way that suggested *anyone* could take this route and get rich overnight.[*]

With all this wealth everywhere, it seemed like there would be no more wars, no more conflict between labor and capital,

---

[*] I mean, technically they could, but it was highly unlikely, statistically.

no more racism, and no more sexism. Deindustrialization? Who cares! Since capitalism and the internet made everything so great for everybody, there was no longer a need for politics.

This mood shaped popular culture. In 1997—the same year *WIRED* published its "long boom" issue—Puff Daddy and Mase released the video for their song "Mo Money Mo Problems." The video, directed by Hype Williams, embodies the hopeful, futuristic aesthetic of the moment. Stylist June Ambrose dressed the rappers in half a dozen looks consisting of baggy, monochrome street wear: shiny red leather jeans and matching jackets, head-to-toe silver, high-visibility yellow and clear vinyl paired with matching goggles. They rap and dance and gesture into a fish-eye lens. They float in zero gravity on sets of white and chrome designed by artist Ron Norsworthy. Presumably in outer space, Puff Daddy and Mase have transcended history. The video is intercut with scenes back on Earth, with Puff Daddy transcending history in another way, by winning a golf tournament as a Black man, just like Tiger Woods really did at the Masters that year.[*]

Back then you couldn't turn on MTV without seeing videos like that. Rappers and pop stars and R&B singers all seemed to be living in the future and having a great time. They wore futuristic clothes, used real or fictional technology, existed inside video games, and rode around on spaceships. In "The Rain (Supa Dupa Fly)"—another Hype Williams/Ron Norsworthy/June Ambrose collab—the fish-eye lens goes in close on Missy Elliott, who wears a shiny black bodysuit resembling an inflated garbage bag and a glittery helmet with red sunglasses attached. She looks like a dignitary from an alien civilization. Timbaland's beats, too,

---

[*] Not only that, but he—like the stock market—broke record after record, winning a total of five Masters Tournaments and eighty-two PGA Tour titles.

sound like they came from outer space, or perhaps from a very sophisticated computer not yet available to the public. The year before, Timbaland and Missy produced Aaliyah's album *One in a Million*. She sings over a collection of digital bleeps and bloops. In her videos she looks like a teen cyberpunk: silver sunglasses, baggy pants, crop tops showcasing incredible abs. "Your love is one in a million," she sings. "It goes on and on and on."

Jennifer Lopez's 1999 video for "If You Had My Love" depicts a generically handsome man logging onto his computer, typing "Jennifer Lopez" into a search engine, and clicking on the singer's website. The viewer is then transported through the screen, in between 0s and 1s of binary code, to a minimal, silvery-blue room filled with surveillance cameras. The singer walks in wearing a flowing white ensemble and shimmery eyeshadow, waves at the viewer, and begins to perform. The video cuts between Lopez—in different rooms and different white and silver outfits—and the man from the beginning of the video, staring pruriently at his desktop. We then see other online viewers: a group of teenagers, a young girl, all watching Lopez mediated through computer screens, the camera lingering on the slightly pixelated interface.

That same year, TLC released an internet- and email-themed album called *FanMail*. In the album art, T-Boz, Chilli, and Left Eye are silver-tinged cyberbabes.* Some of the typeface gleams white; the rest looks like binary code. The three women appear pixelated, as if conjured online. The album opens with a stilted digital voice that producer Dallas Austin created using Macintosh text to speech.

---

* The women were, in fact, painted with silver body paint for the album photoshoot.

"Welcome," the voice says. "This is a journey into life, love, and the future of music."

The futuristic, intergalactic, and digital aesthetic permeated the entire music industry, from Whitney Houston, Cher, and Madonna to Destiny's Child, NSYNC, and the Backstreet Boys. Cher popularized autotune in her rave-inspired dance track "Believe," from 1998. The 1999 Backstreet Boys album *Millennium* featured the band members in matching white outfits against a pale blue digital backdrop. In a 2000 issue of *American Girl Magazine*, the album is listed as a good item to include in a millennium time capsule, alongside butterfly hair clips, a WNBA basketball, a bottle of glitter nail polish, and an i-Zone instant camera.

It wasn't just music. Between 1997 and 2001, more and more products and spaces were white or clear, neon or silver, bathed in white or blue light. Everything was blobby and fluid, in motion like droplets of water. There wasn't a sharp edge in sight. In the words of industrial designer Karim Rashid, whose self-described "blobjects" shaped so much of the era's look, "If freedom were a form, it would be a never-ending undulating boundless shape that is in perpetual motion." Rashid's ubiquitous, award-winning Garbino trash can debuted in 1996, all curves and lightweight translucent plastic. Another common household object was Rashid's Oh Chair, from 1999, made again of molded plastic, in white or hot pink or maybe lime green, with oval cutouts in the back and under the arms.

Round plastic iMacs were available in your choice of candy colors, ready to connect to the World Wide Web. First came Bondi Blue in 1998, then Strawberry, Blueberry, Lime, Tangerine, and Grape. The look of the iMac—rounded edges, translucent plastic, an array of colors—was taken up by every conceivable consumer good: PlayStation controllers, floppy discs, Game Boys, boom boxes, Tamagotchis, televisions, cameras, and memory cards.

Even clothes began to look this way. There were silver wraparound Oakleys and silver puffer jackets and translucent raincoats and translucent handbags and white ripstop bondage pants and white nylon vests with hoods. Japanese, Chinese, and Hindi characters were incorporated into graphic tees and mesh tops, as if to signify that globalization was here, and it was beautiful. Hair was spiked and separated and chunky, almost pixelated, or worn in space buns, shot through with bleach or colored dye. Eyeshadow was silver and ice blue and white. Body glitter shimmered like the underside of a CD. Even cars were part of the vibe. The Volkswagen New Beetle came out in 1998, available in Silver Arrow, Techno Blue, and—most iconically—Cyber Green, a shimmering peridot. Though its design pointed to the future, it called to mind the '60s, of course, and California.

Contra popular belief, a subsection of the hippies *had* won, and they gave us what appeared to be a capitalist techno-utopia. The future promised to us by the internet and the stock market and the fall of the Soviet Union and the turn of the millennium was one of seamlessness, of open borders and endless choice and perpetual motion. At the turn of the millennium, the future had no limits. Technology was fun. Technology was friendly. Technology was transparent. Its soft edges wouldn't hurt you.

ON AUGUST 25, 2001, Aaliyah died in a plane crash near the Bahamas, where she had just wrapped up filming the video for her single "Rock the Boat." She was only twenty-two. Her music had sounded like the future, and with her violent death, it seemed like a part of the future had died, too.

Her death seemed to foreshadow another plane-related tragedy that would happen just weeks later. On 9/11, hijacked jets sliced through the clear blue twenty-first-century sky, filling it with black smoke. It was a violent rebuke of everything that the blobject aesthetic and its accompanying ideologies stood for—the internet, globalization, free market capitalism. The possibility of a twenty-first-century utopia was over, and it had barely even begun.

Instead, American culture and public policy took an alarmingly atavistic turn. Flag buying became socially mandatory, radio stations banned songs that were not sufficiently patriotic, and the government openly celebrated its illegal 2003 invasion of Iraq, alongside torture and widespread domestic surveillance. A popular country song celebrated Americans collectively "put[ting] a boot in [the] ass" of, presumably, Osama bin Laden/terrorists in general, but also possibly just Muslims and/or Arabs in general.

The president told Americans to buy trips to Disney World. Other people told Americans to buy Viagra and Frappuccinos and Hummer H2s that got twelve miles per gallon, to buy issues of *Us Weekly* that said how fat or skinny Lindsay Lohan or the Olsen twins were getting, to buy McMansions, to buy Fiji Water. Jay-Z told us he was a hustler, baby, and Lil Scrappy said he had money in the bank and J-Kwon told us everybody in the club was getting tipsy. In New Orleans, a hurricane trapped families on roofs. In LA, Britney shaved her head when she could no longer stand the contradictions of trying to be a virgin and a sexy woman at the same time. This second half of the Y2K Era—2001 to 2008—was a kind of chauvinistic reverse of the optimism from 1997 to 2001.

It was in 2008—that fateful year I had attempted to predict for my school time capsule in fifth grade—when the Y2K Era truly came to a close. A decade of speculative investment in the American housing market resulted in the meltdown of the entire global economy. The Dow Jones Industrial Average dropped by 777.68 points—at the time, its biggest single-day point loss in history. US unemployment would reach 10 percent, and about 3.8 million American households would lose their homes in foreclosure. Around the world, pension funds lost 23 percent of their value. The Great Recession and its aftermath permanently altered the political economy and culture, in America and around the world. It ended the End of History.

In a post-2008 world, the future looks very different. It mocks instead of beckons. It looks hard instead of soft, sharp instead of round, solid instead of translucent. Between growing economic inequality, political breakdown, and escalating climate change, the future appears to get worse with each passing year. And the crises, particularly around the current and future habitability of Earth, appear not just bad but terminal. Temperatures rise over time, causing more breakdowns, in turn causing more breakdowns. This is, interestingly, very similar to how capital operates. The more debt you have, the more it generates compound interest over time, putting you deeper into debt. The more wealth you have, the more compound interest it generates, making you wealthier.

I'm sad about the state of the world, but I'm also disappointed with my own life trajectory. When I wrote that time capsule letter in 1999, it really seemed like I could have gone to Stanford. When I pictured "growing up," I imagined I'd become a surgeon, a movie director, a research scientist, a classical trumpet player, a CEO. I imagined I'd be married, with children of my own. At ten, I never imagined graduating into a recession, struggling to pay rent, or moving back in with my parents. I never imagined that it would be so difficult to piece together a career or feel financially secure enough to have kids.

"MEN MAKE THEIR own history," wrote Karl Marx in 1852. "But they do not make it just as they please; they do not make it under circumstances chosen by themselves, but under circumstances directly encountered, given and transmitted from the past."

I came across this quote around the same time I found the time capsule letter. It's about the return of a dictatorship in nineteenth-century France, but it feels relevant to just about any problem in the twenty-first century. It could also, I realized, apply to my own story. Try as I might to shape my life in a particular way, it has never been mine to shape. Much of adulthood has felt to me like an accumulation of disappointment and despair. It's historical, it's personal, and I'm not quite sure where the one ends and the other begins. And it hurts because, as Smash Mouth says, "The years start coming and they don't stop coming."

Amid all this, I've found myself drawn back to the Y2K past. I shop for lettuce hem micromesh tops on Depop and silver platform shoes on Poshmark. I paint my nails peridot. I peruse scanned fashion editorials from turn-of-the-millennium issues of *Vogue* and *Teen People*. Smash Mouth's *Astro Lounge* has become my most-listened-to album on Spotify. I stream *You've Got Mail* and *Sex and the City* and *Men in Black* and *10 Things I Hate About You* and *The Sopranos*. I play every video I loved on MTV all in a row on YouTube: TLC and the Goo Goo Dolls, Crazy Town and NSYNC, Limp Bizkit and Fiona Apple and Lil' Kim and Sugar Ray and Ludacris and Christina Aguilera and Destiny's Child and Sum 41 and Mýa. Here, I feel safe, like the future is still full of promise, like my whole life is still ahead of me.

I first began to seek out these old pleasures as a kind of critical project, to see what they might reveal about how the present came to be. But along the way I became a connoisseur. I began to love this stuff in a way completely divorced from the intellectual,

critical, and historical judgments I impose as an adult. I do his-
toricize *TRL* and *You've Got Mail* and the blobject aesthetic, but
this is kept separate from my true and genuine love for this stuff:
the love of a preteen girl.

I'm not alone. Turn-of-the-millennium nostalgia has been a
trend going on several years now. "Y2K" is a top search term
on social media and clothing resale sites. Self-funded internet archivists like the Consumer Aesthetics Research Institute
and Instagram accounts like @shes__underrated, @y2kdaily, and
@discontinuedmakeup painstakingly catalog images of editorials,
advertisements, consumer products, and video content from the
era. Celebrity memoirs from Britney Spears, Paris Hilton, Pamela
Anderson, and Jessica Simpson have topped bestseller lists. Ludacris did a State Farm ad. Gen Z kids who never lived through the
Y2K Era post TikToks of themselves in body glitter and butterfly
hair clips and low-rise flares. When I see this stuff, I see a marketing construct, as nostalgia runs on a twenty-to-thirty-year cycle
(the amount of time it takes for the people who lived through it
the first time around to become the adults who create culture).
But I also see a yearning for a more stable world: by those who
grew up in it, and by those younger generations who have only
known entropy.

Though I indulge in nostalgia, I am skeptical. Don't we all ideal-
ize our childhoods, whether we were kids in the '90s or the '50s or
the Justinian Period of the Byzantine Empire? The past will always
seem better because it always recedes from our grasp. For adults
like me who are entering middle age, so much of our yearning
comes from our sense of foreclosed possibilities, from our aging
bodies, from our accumulated bitterness about careers and relationships and money and death. When we say things were better
in our youth, what we often mean is that our parents were still

healthy and our hearts hadn't been broken and our backs didn't hurt. We mean that the future hadn't happened yet, that it could still be (in our minds, at least) whatever we wanted it to be.

While there is a timelessness to this yearning, it is also true that many things really *have* gotten measurably worse since my childhood: economic inequality, political instability, and, most of all, climate change. The costs of housing, health care, and education have gone up even when adjusted for inflation. There is a general sense of futurelessness pervading both politics and culture. It makes me want to reach for a tube of body glitter.

A FEW MONTHS after I persuaded my mom to buy it, a hole developed in my inflatable chair. It didn't pop dramatically. Rather, air slowly leaked out of a seam until I began to notice that it was no longer taut and shiny but wan and flaccid. I tried to fix it with duct tape but another hole appeared, so it ended up in the trash: a flattened heap of gray PVC, unrecognizable. I blamed myself for not being more careful with it, but the thing was made cheaply. The structural integrity was the problem; it wasn't made to last.

Only Shooting Stars Break the Mold

ALMOST EVERY SUMMER WE TOOK THE SAME FLIGHT: United Airlines nonstop, Dulles to SFO. I chewed watermelon Bubblicious to keep my ears from popping, but they always did as we descended over the bay. It was an unusually steep descent, and as the flight attendants put up the tray tables babies began, inevitably, to cry. I wanted to cry, too, but instead I chomped and chomped, watching the water glitter into view. Soon, I told myself, we would be in the place that I called paradise.

Uncle Paul was my mom's older brother, and he lived in the Bay Area with his wife, Aunt Caroline. When I was younger they lived in Los Gatos, a sleepy town in the southern part of Silicon Valley with a bunch of notable residents—most important, Steve Wozniak, the less-famous cofounder of Apple. Los Gatos consisted of a valley and dry Mediterranean hills where sequoias and eucalyptus and almond trees grew. Uncle Paul and Aunt Caroline lived in those hills, in a yellow stucco house with a red tile roof and a big sloped yard full of secret paths and bottlebrush trees. I ran through those paths barefoot until I got a sequoia needle splinter in the arch of my foot.

In 1996 Uncle Paul and Aunt Caroline sold their Los Gatos house for an apartment in San Francisco, on the top of Telegraph Hill. From the living room window you could see the Bay Bridge. Every evening the fog would roll in along the Embarcadero, and you could see it roll out the next day while you ate your cereal on the balcony. At night the cables on the Bay Bridge lit up like strings of pearls. You never needed a coat but you always needed a fleece.

Even then I understood that San Francisco was where it was all happening. It was California, yes, and therefore inherently special due to its comfortable climate and semitropical flora, plus the fact that you had to sit on a plane for nearly six hours to get there. But more important it was the headquarters of the internet. And the internet was where Uncle Paul worked.

His was a typical arc for a certain type of white middle-class boomer. He skipped two grades in school and got into Stanford at sixteen. At one point, Philip Zimbardo (of Stanford Prison Experiment fame) was his faculty dorm resident. But after a couple semesters Uncle Paul got bored. He got into smoking weed and experimenting with psychedelics.* He dropped out and lived in a van. He enrolled in an alternative college with no grades or majors to study music and two semesters of computer science. He learned to sail and took up aikido. He and a friend tried to navigate a sailboat from Georgetown, Guyana, to Miami, but ended up wrecking it in the Windward Islands. My uncle emptied his savings to buy a plane ticket home. After graduation, he toured the Pacific Northwest with his Americana band in between working odd jobs.

---

* Purchased, he tells me, from friends who worked in the research labs, which at the time were flooded with defense industry money for psychedelics research. In fact, Ken Kesey got turned on to LSD at the Menlo Park Veterans Administration Hospital when he volunteered as a test subject in an MK-ULTRA experiment.

Eventually, Paul got sick of the bohemian life. So, like former yippie Jerry Rubin, my uncle put on a suit, got a haircut, trimmed his beard, and got a job at Intel when it was a new company and he could get stock options. He began referring to himself as "a born-again capitalist." He moved up the corporate ladder. He bought a house and a convertible and took foreign vacations and managed his 401(k). He kept sailing and practicing aikido. And then he got into startup investing.

ON AUGUST 6, 1991—JUST a few months before the dissolution of the Soviet Union—the first website went live on the brand-new World Wide Web. It was published by a British computer scientist named Tim Berners-Lee at CERN, the European Organization for Nuclear Research in Switzerland. Berners-Lee's site explained what the World Wide Web was and how it worked, from HTML to URLs to hyperlinks. There were ten websites online the next year, and by 1994 this number had multiplied to three thousand.

But it was in 1995 when the internet inflection point truly arrived, even though only 36 percent of American households that year owned a personal computer. On August 9 (the same day Jerry Garcia died), the computer services company Netscape Communications had its initial public offering on NASDAQ following the successful debut of its web browser Netscape Navigator. Netscape hadn't made a profit yet, but by the closing bell, the company was worth $58.25 a share, with a market value of $2.9 billion.

"It was the spark that touched off the Internet boom," wrote Adam Lashinsky of the Netscape IPO. "More than any other company, [Netscape] set the technological, social, and financial tone of the Internet age. Its founders, Marc Andreessen and Jim Clark—

a baby-faced twenty-four-year-old programmer from the Midwest and a restless middle-aged tech pioneer who badly wanted to strike gold again—inspired a generation of entrepreneurs to try to become tech millionaires."

And inspire they did. The late '90s gave us eBay, Netflix (then a mail-order DVD rental service), PayPal, and Google. Amazon went public (though it was still primarily an online bookseller). These companies all seemed to be led by earnest, bootstrapping nerds and/or former hippies, a majority of whom were somehow affiliated with Stanford. People, in other words, like Uncle Paul.

By 1998, the dot-com sector was in a frenzy. It seemed like everyone—in the Bay Area especially—was trying to get a piece of the action. That year, online pet goods retailer Pets.com was founded. In 1999, the company was bolstered by an infusion of startup capital from Amazon, which obtained a 50 percent ownership stake. That November, Pets.com sponsored a float in the Macy's Thanksgiving Day Parade: a thirty-six-foot-tall balloon version of their mascot, a talking dog sock puppet. In January 2000 the company spent $1.2 million on a Super Bowl ad to drum up excitement about their impending February IPO. The dog mascot was voiced by comedian Michael Ian Black.

The dot-coms kept coming. There was Webvan (an online grocery delivery website), eToys (a web-based toy retailer), and Flooz (a website that sold noncash tokens that could be used at participating retailers like Tower Records). Former US surgeon general C. Everett Koop founded drkoop.com, which made $88.5 million at its June 1999 IPO and quickly became the number-one-ranked health care information site on the internet. Profits spilled over from tech into other ventures: CGI animation pioneers Pixar Studios, cosmetics company Urban Decay (famous for their bold, metallic nail polishes and eyeshadows), and the educational children's books company Klutz Press (famous for teaching kids to juggle and Hacky Sack in appropriate Bay Area fashion).

THE INTERNET CAME to my house in 1995 (we were among the 36 percent minority of computer-owning American households that year). One Friday night when I was in second grade (following our weekly viewing of Kevin Sorbo's *Hercules* and its spin-off series *Xena: Warrior Princess*) my mom brought me over to the computer.

"Let's go on the internet," she said.

"What's the internet?" I asked.

"It's a new way to get all kinds of information from around the world on your computer," she explained.

What information, I wondered, could I possibly need as a seven-year-old?

"We'll use our phone to connect to the World Wide Web," she added.

If this statement was intended to clarify, it had the opposite effect.

"Look," she said, clicking the CompuServe icon.

A window popped up. She clicked the button that said SIGN ON. There was a dial tone, followed by what sounded like someone pressing buttons on a phone. There were some terrible beeps and screeches and static, followed by more beeps and static. I covered my ears.

When we were finished logging on, she typed www.yahoo.com into the bar at the top of the screen.

"Pick a topic," she said. "Any topic."

"Maybe Xena," I said.

She typed "xena warrior princess" into the Yahoo search bar, and we waited. A list of bullet-pointed blue hyperlinks loaded on the screen. She clicked one. The computer whirred, and a bright yellow page with purple text began to load. **ALEX'S XENA FANPAGE**, it read. Below, a photo of the princess warrior herself began to blink into view, line by line. I clicked through the website's sections: **News, Photos, About Me**. After a while, my mom said, "I think that's enough internet for tonight," and logged me off. I had to admit, it *was* cool that I could look at pictures of Xena whenever I wanted.

As the dot-com bubble inflated, I spent more and more time online. Back then, with dial-up, you actually had to *log on*. I'm *going online*, people would say. I'm *surfing the web*. And then you would sit, as I had, through that thirty-second cacophony. If a parent or a sibling picked up the phone, you'd be immediately booted off. "Hang up!" you'd yell. "I'm on the internet!"

I loved sending emails. I would write to my uncle in California, my cousin in Canada, my friend in Pittsburgh. I went in chat rooms sometimes, where I met kids from Texas and Oregon and England. I visited Beanie Babies fan sites and Pokémon forums. I perused the clothes on limitedtoo.com. For a school project on the geography and culture of Japan, I used the internet for research, listing websites alongside books in my bibliography. By middle school, I was spending hours each day on AOL Instant Messenger, talking to my friends about boys or homework or what was on TV (often, I had MTV going while I was logged on, and I would provide commentary about each music video as it aired). It was AIM, more than anything, that got me excited about being online. It made me feel like I lived in the future.

IN 1999, WHEN I was in sixth grade, Nokia bought one of Uncle Paul's startups for $57 million.* That year for Christmas, he gave my brother and me $100,000† each of blue-chip Nokia stock. From a gift bag we produced two brown hats embroidered with the name of the company he sold.

"Oh," I said. My brother directed his attention back to his new Playmobil set.

"There's something else in there, too," my mom said with a smirk.

I fished around beneath the blue tissue and produced two pieces of paper. I saw our full legal names, and then I saw the number.

"Oh my GOD," I screamed, jumping up and down.

"That's a lot of zeros," my dad said.

At five, the significance of this moment was lost on my brother. Even the number meant nothing to him; he could only count to one hundred and he couldn't read yet. He returned again to Playmobil. But I felt my entire world rearranging. I thought of all the things $100,000 could buy: CDs, Pokémon cards, candy, inflatable furniture.

My parents had other ideas. It was deposited into my T. Rowe Price college fund to pay, they suggested, for Stanford. That wasn't the only place they wanted me to go: they showed me, too, the campuses of UVA and Georgetown; they suggested William and Mary, Reed, Amherst, and Berklee College of Music. But I specifically remember driving by Stanford's Palo Alto campus, with its matching red roofs and red-tailed hawks, my mom telling me that one day, maybe, I'd go there, too.

---

* Over $106 million in 2024 money.
† Over $187,000 in 2024 money.

Her logic made sense. I loved Uncle Paul, and he seemed like he had life all figured out. My idol Chelsea Clinton went to Stanford, as did this new golfer Tiger Woods who broke all the records. Stanford was where this new search engine called Google was invented, which my mom told me was the best one yet because, unlike Yahoo! or Ask Jeeves or Lycos, it used complex algorithms to give users better results. If I could afford it and if I could get in, why would I go anywhere else?

UNCLE PAUL RANG in the millennium in Bora Bora with his wife and a group of their tech friends. His friends took ecstasy under the Milky Way as the year 2000 arrived.* He retired at age forty-five, then took Aunt Caroline on long trips to Italy and Greece and London. He got multiple black belts in aikido. He went to art school. He was in talks with another guy about going halfsies on a private jet. He bought a second home in Sarasota, an eight-bedroom waterfront mansion that Aunt Caroline filled with antiques. The grown-ups were right, I thought. The new millennium really would change everything. If the internet could make Uncle Paul rich, the same thing must be happening to everyone.

These thoughts were not just the inferences of a child. Adults in positions of power were saying stuff like this in the media all the time.

"The US economy likely will not see a recession for years to come," said economist and MIT professor Rudi Dornbusch in 1998. "We don't want one, we don't need one, and, as we have

---

* He told me that later and said that he didn't partake, that he gave up MDMA at age eighteen.

the tools to keep the current expansion going, we won't have one. This expansion will run forever."

You see, insisted Dornbusch, if we just think positively, we can change how the economy works with our minds.

George Gilder—a prolific author, conservative think tank affiliate, and *Forbes* contributor whose arguments against welfare and economic regulation influenced the policies of Ronald Reagan and Bill Clinton—refashioned himself in the '90s as a New Economy tech booster. In his 1989 book *Microcosm: The Quantum Revolution in Economics and Technology*—a book about "the overthrow of matter"—Gilder argues that silicon chips would allow humans to transcend the laws of physics, that "the powers of mind are everywhere ascendent over the brute force of things."

There were books like *Dow 36,000: The New Strategy for Profiting from the Coming Rise in the Stock Market*, which argued that the Dow would reach 36,000 within three to five years, and that people who purchased blue-chip stocks could expect 300 percent returns on their investments. When the Dow crossed 10,000 for the first time ever on March 29, 1999, traders passed out hats on the floor that said *Dow 10,000*. New York City Mayor Rudy Giuliani and NYSE Chairman Richard Grasso wore them when they rang the closing bell. "1999 Goes Into the Record Book on Wall Street," reads an *L.A. Times* headline from January 1, 2000. It seemed like the stock market would keep going up forever and ever, and everyone would be rich if they could just get in on the action.

Some commentators had a more critical take, but they could be handily dismissed as losers and spoilsports. "The Californian Ideology," a 1995 essay by British theorists Richard Barbrook and Andy Cameron, falls into this category. It predicted the fervor of the dot-com economy when it was just beginning, along with many problems familiar to just about anyone living in the twenty-first century who isn't a tech billionaire.

"In American folklore, the nation was built out of a wilderness by free-booting individuals—the trappers, cowboys, preachers, and settlers of the frontier," they write. "For both the New Left and the New Right, the early years of the American republic provide a potent model for their rival versions of individual freedom. Yet there is a profound contradiction at the centre of this primordial American dream: individuals in this period only prospered through the suffering of others."

You know this old saw already: the racist, sexist, imperialist myth of the frontier. But it bears repeating, not only because it is true, but because less widely understood is the way that, at the turn of the last millennium, technology and the stock market *were* the frontier. And the promise of the frontier, of any frontier, is a promise of a radical break with history, of life without limits. Where else could this have happened *but* California?

It was on Telegraph Hill where I thought I could best see the future. It was, in the words of Y2K-Era industrial designer Karim Rashid, a never-ending undulating boundless shape in perpetual motion. In the new millennium, we could all invest in the stock market. We could all invest in startups and take a buyout and retire at age forty-five like Uncle Paul. We could all log onto the internet with our Bondi Blue iMacs and check our portfolios, then hop in our New Beetles and cruise Highway 1, a Smash Mouth CD on the stereo.

IN 1999, SMASH Mouth released their second album, *Astro Lounge*. That summer (the one between elementary and middle school) its lead single, "All Star," became a runaway hit. The San

Jose–based former ska band united around a tightly produced, layered pop sound, at once retro and futuristic; the late '90s does the '60s. There are theremins and Farfisa organs. One song is a cover of the Four Seasons' 1965 single "Can't Get Enough of You Baby." Another uses a riff nearly identical to the one in The Crystals' 1963 hit "Then He Kissed Me."

Astro Lounge was recorded in the same Los Gatos hills where Uncle Paul and Aunt Caroline had lived. The album is, implicitly and explicitly, about California, taking its melodies from surf music and '60s dance grooves. In the song "Radio," the band references being from San Jose. In the opening song, "Who's There," "a night out in California" at the movies is disrupted by the arrival of aliens.

This is the album's other recurring motif: outer space. This wasn't a particularity. During the late '90s, there was a cultural fascination with aliens, specifically green ones with lozenge-shaped heads and large eyes. I owned a necklace with a charm in this shape that glowed in the dark. My AIM screen name was LilAlien2. When our fifth-grade teacher, Mrs. Hathaway, asked us to vote on our class mascot, we elected to call ourselves the Aliens. Aliens were everywhere in the culture: *The X Files*, *Independence Day*, *Men in Black*, as well as less-remembered media properties like Nickelodeon's *The Journey of Allen Strange*. The United States Postal Service held an international contest called Stampin' the Future in 1998, in which kids designed stamps to commemorate the new millennium. All four winning images—which were printed on stamps you could actually buy at the post office—depict spaceships or planets. In the turn-of-the-millennium cultural imagination there was a connection among outer space, the future, and the cyber. It makes sense to me now: all three are frontiers.

Despite its sunny exterior, *Astro Lounge* contains a kernel of bitterness and defeat. It senses a darkness lurking as the millennium turns. In "Home," an eerie, reggae-inflected track near the end of the album, singer Greg Camp reflects on the state of the music industry, just a few years before Napster and Spotify would devastate it: "Lottery or poverty, you're a commodity, so what's it gonna be?"

In "I Just Wanna See," Camp examines the state of the economy more generally: "Sleeping on the sidewalk, a home they call, doctors and lawyers race for the ball."

That line made me think of summer 1998. Uncle Paul had walked me all over Chinatown and North Beach, showed me storefronts filled with pungent traditional medicines and tables where old ladies played mahjong and a café where—he claimed—you could get the best sfogliatella outside of Naples. He bought me one, and the crisp outer layers yielded to a sweet, citrus-flecked ricotta filling. I had no point of comparison—I had never been to Italy—but it was certainly one of the most delicious pastries I had ever tasted, I thought, crumbs flecking my shirt.

We found ourselves down along the Embarcadero. Behind us, a colonnade of palm trees lined the roadway. The bay lapped gently at the pilings a few feet below, scenting the air in a way I found comforting. The ground was littered with discarded sourdough bread bowls that Uncle Paul informed me had recently been filled with clam chowder and were eaten, he said, "by tourists." Now pigeons and seagulls swarmed, crumbs flying as they pecked. I had never seen anything like it. All that bread on the ground. A whole grocery store's worth of bread.

Paul started dribbling one of the bread bowls like a soccer ball.

"Look alive!" he said, kicking it my way.

I trapped it, dribbled it, laughed. He was always so silly, so fun. I passed it his way, he passed it back. I tried to juggle it on my knee like I had seen some of the kids who were really good at sports do in PE. I punted the bread bowl. It almost flew off over the railing into the water below, arcing a few feet short and lodging under a bench. I jogged over to retrieve it.

"What do you think you're doing?" said a man, coming closer.

"I . . . I dunno," I said, confused and surprised before I started to feel scared.

"Not everyone can afford to play with their food," he said, his voice rising.

Who was this man? Where did he come from? And why was he so angry at me?

"But I'm just a kid," I wanted to say, but didn't.

He was saying other stuff now, yelling it.

"Hey!" I heard Uncle Paul's voice. "Hey!"

He was right there, towering over this other man, tall and burly even by grown-up standards.

"Get out of here, okay, buddy?" Uncle Paul said.

The guy wandered off. Uncle Paul patted me on the back.

"You have to be careful in the city," he said. "Not everyone here is nice."

As we walked on, Uncle Paul explained that the guy was homeless and, he added, "probably crazy."

I didn't know it then, but there was a change underway in San Francisco, where people like my uncle were displacing people like that guy. I might have been just a kid, but to that guy, I represented the forces that put him out on the street. I didn't fully understand this until years later, but Smash Mouth did.

Even "All Star"—that ubiquitous, number-one hit played at parties and sporting events, eventually making its way into the soundtracks for *Rat Race* and *Shrek*—has pretty dark lyrics if you listen closely. There is, for instance, an entire verse that appears to be about climate change. And the chorus—with its talk of gold and getting paid, where *only shooting stars break the mold*—feels like it's about the New Economy. In the New Economy—as it was called by journalists and economists and President Clinton—we must all build our human capital and compete with each other on the free market. It is no longer enough to be good. You must be great, as well as very, very lucky. A shooting star, if you will.

THE DOT-COM BUBBLE began to burst in March 2000, triggering an eight-month recession in 2001. By October 2002, the majority of dot-com wealth had been erased. As it turns out, a rapid surge in asset prices is not sustainable over the long term, whether the assets are tulips or Pets.com stocks. I know Uncle Paul incurred losses, though I'm not sure of the extent. He seems to have fared well enough, though he later sold the waterfront mansion, and he never bought that private jet. Nokia retained blue-chip status throughout the 2000s. In 2007, the company had 51 percent of market share in mobile phones. That was the year Uncle Paul told us to liquidate our shares. The proceeds were put in another investment account and helped put my brother and me through college even as tuition rates surpassed inflation. By the skin of our teeth, we both graduated debt free, I in 2011 and my brother in 2016.

But I didn't graduate from Stanford. I'm disappointed in myself, though I've read enough history and theory to know better. The New Economy was a winner-take-all economy, where only shooting stars could break the mold. It wasn't enough to shine—you had to glow. Sure, I was relatively smart, and I had some talents, but I was never a shooting star. Most people aren't. Definitionally, most people *can't* be, no matter how good they are. At least I didn't end up like that guy on the Embarcadero.

Maybe it was better, the fact that I didn't go to Stanford. It is, after all, the flagship institution of tech futurism, and technology these days kind of sucks. Monopolistic social media companies have corralled users into a handful of addictive platforms filled with bots, misinformation, and violent threats. Streaming services have decimated artist revenue, ride-share services have destroyed the taxi industry, and self-driving cars plow into pedestrians. Google's vaunted search algorithm is now clogged with ads. Some tech billionaires pursue experimental life extension treatments, while others seek to colonize Mars (there's that frontier motif again). Many subscribe to some flavor of eugenics. The internet did, in fact, reshape the twenty-first century, just not in the way I assumed it would as a kid.

And California, instead of serving as a beacon of hope and progress, now catches fire annually. It is the hated home of the richest and most powerful people on the planet: your Thiels, your Zuckerbergs, your Musks. It is a place that spawned a cottage industry of nonfiction books–cum–streaming miniseries about venture capital scams. It is a place where the rapidly growing homeless population is corralled into brightly painted camps to keep them out of public view. California remains a vision of the future: not as utopia but as dystopia.

I don't know if I could have seen any of that from Stanford. I think I can only see it from here.

Global Village, Crying Eagle

T WAS LATE WINTER 2000 AND MY MOM WAS DRIVING ME back from a trumpet lesson. I was in sixth grade. The weather was mild. Her car was a 1987 Toyota Corolla, something I had only recently realized I should be embarrassed about. I had begun to notice that most of the other cars on the road had round edges. Even the other Corollas looked nothing like the one my mom drove, with its sharp angles that denoted shoulder pads and hair spray and the last days of the Reagan administration. Her car had a radio and a tape deck but no CD player. You had to crank a handle to roll down the windows.

My mom glanced at me.

"I've been thinking, maybe we should stop buying clothes made in sweatshops. I read this article in *Utne Reader* about how some people are doing that. They're boycotting Nike and the Gap for using sweatshop labor."

"Where would we buy clothes?" I asked, looking down at the swooshes on my sneakers.

"Well," she said. "Maybe we can start shopping at stores that don't use sweatshops."

"Like who? I guess I thought everybody did that."

"I think Ten Thousand Villages doesn't use them. Or maybe we could make our own clothes?"

"But you don't know how to sew," I said.

She started talking about borrowing Nana's sewing machine and I started to tune out. Would we also borrow a rubber vulcanizer to make our own sneakers? How bad would I look in those dorky, boxy clothes from Ten Thousand Villages, the ones made of linen that swished when you walked, that tied at your waist with a drawstring and emphasized your stomach fat? And how could my mom possibly expect me to stop shopping at Gap when it was my favorite store, followed by Old Navy, Limited Too, and the Brass Plum at Nordstrom?

This was so typical. Growing up on diplomatic outposts in Kabul, Karachi, Lahore, and Lagos, she was steeped in the virtues of foreign service culture—thrift, curiosity, resourcefulness. Her family had to buy all their clothes when they were posted stateside every couple of years, returning overseas with suitcases full of children's shoes in graduating sizes, because when the children outgrew their shoes there was nowhere to shop but the bazaar and the PX. For Uncle Paul's tenth birthday, Nana went down to the bazaar and bought him a donkey. According to a favorite family story, Uncle Paul went out in the yard a few days later to find the animal had died of dysentery.

How could someone like my mom possibly appreciate an American mall?

The mall was the cleanest place I knew, with its white marble floors and its mezzanines crisscrossed by escalators. During the day, sun poured down from the vaulted glass ceilings, and at night, little lights switched on like electric stars. I could go from store to store collecting bags: the ocean blue of Gap, the matte silver of Nordstrom, the psychedelic orange and pink of Limited Too, the trinket-sized Sam Goody with a Backstreet Boys CD inside. When I got hungry I could snack on Dippin' Dots, "the ice cream of the future," letting little pearls of strawberry dissolve on my tongue. When I got tired I could rest in the massage chairs at Sharper Image. I entered the mall with a crisp stack of twenties and I left as myself.

I felt I was speaking a shared language that transcended borders. When I wore a dark denim jacket and power bead bracelets and capris hemmed with metallic Indian ribbon, when I glossed my lips and sang "Larger than Life," I was participating in something with the other kids at my middle school, my cousin in Canada, and kids I would never meet in Brazil and Japan and Russia and South Africa and the Netherlands. It reminded me of this dorky poster on the wall at my old elementary school that showed different-colored children holding hands around a globe. The phrase I heard adults use was "globalization" or, more quaintly, "global village." There was world peace for real now. We were happily connected through computers. Shopping and mass media were our sacraments. My mom might have grown up around diplomats, but that was so last millennium. This was the real diplomacy now.

There was a specific look that coincided with globalization that the YouTuber VENUSSTADT (citing both the Consumer Aesthetics Research Institute and the work of scholars David Morley and Kevin Robins) calls "techno-orientalism." This look features Y2K futurism fused with motifs from East Asia and India. It's color-saturated mesh shirts decorated with Chinese characters, lotuses, Japanese ukiyo-e geishas, the Buddha, Hindu gods and goddesses.[*]

---

[*] The first designer to do this was probably Gaultier in 1994, but the look took a few years to really permeate retail fashion.

It's Gwen Stefani in a jeweled bindi and blue Bantu knots, Aaliyah in a belly chain, Sisqó in a red wet-look jacket embroidered with a Chinese dragon. It's Madonna reinventing herself with yoga and posing for David LaChapelle in bangles and a sari. It's tattoos: Chinese and Japanese characters, "tribal" armbands modeled on traditional designs from Polynesia. It's power bead bracelets and chopsticks as hair accessories and Chinese Laundry strappy satin platforms. It's a magazine ad for Maybelline's Cosmic Edge collection, which features the white model Josie Maran in purple eyeshadow, dark lipstick, and body jewelry, including a jeweled bindi like the one worn by Gwen. The ad promises "beauty nirvana for face and body" and "instant karma" with shimmery eyeshadow and "zen gems."

But globalization wasn't really about body jewelry and tribal tattoos and everybody holding hands around a giant planet Earth while singing along with the same pop music. It was about global economic organizations like the World Bank and the World Trade Organization setting new rules for the post–Cold War economy. And that was about teens in Indonesia and Bangladesh and Mexico stitching Gap T-shirts and gluing soles on Nike sneakers for $2 a day in subcontracted factories with no safety or environmental protections while unionized American garment workers got laid off. Globalization was shorthand for a new kind of colonialism in a supposedly postcolonial world.

Though globalization was often depicted as both consensus and inevitable, not everyone agreed with this new state of affairs. The anti-sweatshop movement my mom referenced in the car first emerged in the '90s, prompted by a series of high-profile exposés by activists. In 1992, *Harper's* published "The New Free-Trade Heel" by Jeff Ballinger, which examined Nike's use of low-wage labor at an Indonesian factory. Overnight, Nike's carefully designed brand became synonymous with sweatshops. In 1996, the labor activist Charles Kernaghan revealed that Kathy Lee Gifford's eponymous Walmart clothing line was being stitched by Honduran thirteen-year-olds working twenty-hour days. In response, President Clinton assembled a task force on sweatshops. Representatives from Nike were there, as was Kathy Lee herself. In 1997, they agreed to create a nonbinding list of minimum labor standards for apparel manufacturing.

The anti-sweatshop movement continued to grow. It was a coalition of domestic labor unions, human rights groups in the developing world, religious organizations, and student activists who operated under the banner of United Students Against Sweatshops (USAS). Starting in 1998, over two hundred chapters of USAS opened on campuses in the US and Canada, growing quickly thanks to new technologies like websites and email listservs. Student activists pressured their schools to divest from apparel manufacturers with poor labor practices.

November 30, 1999 was supposed to be the first day of the World Trade Organization's Ministerial Conference in Seattle. Normally, "the World Trade Organization's Ministerial Conference in Seattle" was the sort of boring phrase I would have heard Jim Lehrer say as my parents watched *NewsHour*. It would have gone in one ear and out the other. I would have been barely aware the event was even happening, let alone understood what it signified. It was all guys in suits who were like a million years old.

But things didn't go as expected that day. At least forty thousand organized protesters descended on the city. The crowd included the aforementioned anti-sweatshop activists, as well as environmental organizations, Indigenous rights groups, and black bloc anarchists. Protesters carried signs that said DON'T TRADE ON ME and WTO DESTROYS FORESTS and CORPORATIONS

HAVE BLOOD ON THEIR HANDS. Giant papier-mâché puppets towered over the crowd, bearing their own protest slogans. The Rainforest Action Network suspended a giant banner downtown with two horizontal arrows pointing in opposite directions. One pointed toward WTO, the other toward DEMOCRACY.

"The Battle in Seattle," as it would be called, was a kind of coming-out party for the alter-globalization movement that had been building throughout the '90s. There were permitted marches, street theater, and a dance party. The more radical protesters—mostly organized under the anarchist umbrella group Direct Action Network—chained themselves together, blocking intersections and preventing delegates from entering the conference. The opening ceremony was canceled. Secretary of State Madeleine Albright got trapped inside her hotel. For a few hours, it seemed like this ragtag coalition could bring the entire global financial order to a halt.

But it couldn't last. The meeting had to get going; President Clinton was set to fly in the following day.

"We will clear this intersection," announces a mustachioed Seattle police officer to a group of protesters in the 2000 documentary *This Is What Democracy Looks Like*. "We will clear it with chemical and pain compliance. If you do not move, you will be the subject of pain."

The camera pans out, shows a group of protesters sitting on the ground. They take turns fastening each other's gas masks and goggles, wetting each other's bandannas, awaiting the promised pain.

"Think about if you agree with what you're being told to do," announces a woman, seemingly to the police.

And then come the clouds of OC—pepper spray.

"You're shooting poison!" yells a man.

The protesters squirt bottled water in each other's swollen eyes. There are clouds of CS gas, and the flash of projectiles.

In another part of town, groups of black bloc anarchists fought the cops. They threw CS canisters back. They kicked in store windows, targeting the likes of Nike, Starbucks, and Nordstrom, leaving graffiti behind with messages like CORPORATE GREED SUX!

"For us to have to close our stores during the peak season, the holiday Christmas season just beginning, really is an injustice," Starbucks CEO Howard Schultz told a reporter.

The City of Seattle instituted a state of emergency, a curfew, and a fifty-block no-protest zone. Public transit was shut down, the purchase and possession of gas masks banned. The police pushed protesters into another neighborhood, where residents were tear-gassed along with everybody else. The WTO meeting ran its course, adjourned on its planned end date of December 3, and its delegates dispersed back to their countries of origin.

The Battle in Seattle was unprecedented, and it stayed in the headlines for weeks. The whole thing was a big middle finger to the End of History—and to the New Economy. At the turn of the millennium, the idea that a group of regular people would take to the streets and disrupt daily life to demand a say over closed-door economic negotiations seemed like a relic of a previous era. It was a big fat *no* to how everything had been going in recent years. Even President Clinton acknowledged that the protesters' concerns were legitimate, though he condemned their more aggressive methods.

My mom's anti-sweatshop musings never made it to the streets. She was too busy raising kids to fly out to summits and protest. Plus, we knew too many people who worked in global development. There was Papa, of course—her dad—who had been in the State Department for decades. Then there was our neighbor George, a soft-spoken Greek man who worked for the World Bank. He walked with a cane and his wife gave us paper plates of homemade baklava every Christmas. When protesters held up anti–World Bank signs at a summit in Prague the next year, I imagined them angry at poor old George.

My mom never even did the boycott she talked about—much to my relief. Her attitude about shopping remained the same as her stance on that era's popular culture and snack foods: skepticism, confusion, derisive commentary, then modest capitulation to the multimillion-dollar marketing budgets of multinational corporations. She abstained as much as she could personally, but she wasn't going to get in a big fight with her kids over baby tees, MTV, or Waffle Crisp.

My mom was wise to pick her battles. I don't just say that because it meant I got to go to the mall a few times a year. At the turn of the millennium, consumerist pop culture *was* culture. It was everything. Trying to fight it was like trying to beat up the ocean.* And teens were its core demographic. That year, they spent more than $150 billion: on clothing, entertainment, electronics, junk food. Most youth entertainment was packaged and sold by five companies: News Corp, Disney, Viacom, Vivendi Universal, and AOL Time Warner, accounting for all major TV networks, film studios, and music labels. This consolidation was enabled by Bill Clinton's signing of the Telecommunications Act in 1996, which deregulated the industry, allowing for previously illegal mergers.

_____

* A reference, by the way, to *The Adventures of Pete & Pete*, a show targeted at people my age a few years before my period of study, delivered to you by a subsidiary of Viacom.

My generation of teenagers—the children of baby boomers, at the time called "the baby boomlet" or Gen Y and later called millennials—was the largest cohort of teenagers ever, at 32 million. Mass consumer culture began in the nineteenth century, and teens became a major marketing demographic after World War II. By the time millennials hit puberty, teen marketing had gone into hyperdrive, aided by globalization, mass media (especially the internet), and corporate consolidation.

"Teens run today's economy," television marketing executive Bob Bibb told a PBS *Frontline* crew in fall 2000.

Culture and tech critic Douglas Rushkoff described the world of teens in the Y2K Era as one "made of marketing," noting that "a typical American teenager will process over 3,000 discrete advertisements in a single day, and 10 million by the time they're 18."

"[Corporations] look at the teen market as part of this massive empire that they're colonizing," said communications professor Robert McChesney. "Teens are like Africa."

In order to do this most effectively, corporations began to perform ethnographic research on teen subcultures. Cool hunting consultancies brought research groups full of cool teens into their Manhattan offices to administer long surveys. What concepts did they associate with Sprite, with Nelly, with Abercrombie & Fitch? Did they still watch *Dawson's Creek*, or had it been supplanted by *Titans*? What kinds of kids wore Nikes, wore Pumas, shopped at Hot Topic?

Cool hunters conducted field research, visiting malls and skate parks and beaches, stopping trendsetting teens on the street to photograph their board shorts and puka-shell necklaces, their Slipknot band shirts and spiky hair, their tongue rings and cornrows.

All that data—the surveys, the photos, the interviews—was packaged up and sold to corporations at a premium. For the first time, companies had a direct line to the teenage psyche, and products could be developed and marketed accordingly. This phenomenon was widely discussed in the media at the time, from a Malcolm Gladwell article for *The New Yorker* in March 1997 to Naomi Klein's 1999 anti-consumerist manifesto *No Logo* to the Rushkoff-narrated PBS *Frontline* documentary *The Merchants of Cool* in 2001.

In 1997, MTV used cool hunting to transform itself from a has-been Gen X cable channel to must-see millennial TV. The company sent researchers across America to talk to teens in their own bedrooms about what was cool, what was uncool, their hopes and dreams. This research reversed the network's falling ratings, especially after the participatory video countdown show *Total Request Live* was launched in September 1998. *TRL*'s glass-fronted studio at 1515 Broadway became the headquarters of this totalizing system: the leviathan of teen-led consumerist pop culture at the turn of the millennium. Every weekday afternoon, the sidewalks below thronged with sign-waving fans hoping to catch a glimpse of NSYNC or Britney, Limp Bizkit or Korn, Nelly or Eminem.

Conservatives despaired at this state of affairs, though for entirely different reasons than the WTO protesters or Douglas Rushkoff or Naomi Klein or my mom. Rush Limbaugh and Matt Drudge and Pat Robertson didn't mind the economic policies of outsourcing and corporate consolidation, and they didn't mind the materialism either. They hated that we now had a borderless, cosmopolitan society that promoted race mixing, sexual promiscuity, feminism, and queerness while challenging the supremacy of white Christian American masculinity. There was too much permissiveness, too much moral relativism. We were also—in the peace that followed the end of the Cold War—becoming soft. We lived in a decadent age, conservatives claimed, and we would soon pay the price.

THE NIGHT OF September 11, 2001, I watched CNN with my dad. Fairfax County had canceled school the next day—for reasons of both safety and mourning—so the two of us were able to stay up late together watching the Towers fall again and again. The narrative that had been settled on was "AMERICA UNDER ATTACK," which ran on the chyron. My mom was putting my brother to bed when the president came on to address the nation.

"Today, our fellow citizens, our way of life, our very freedom came under attack in a series of deliberate and deadly terrorist acts," he said. "The search is underway for those who are behind these evil acts. I've directed the full resources of our intelligence and law enforcement communities to find those responsible and to bring them to justice. We will make no distinction between the terrorists who committed these acts and those who harbor them."

The day I had just experienced wasn't yet called 9/11. What had happened that morning was still just called "the attacks," and the date had not yet become synonymous with them. But there on CNN the narrative was beginning to congeal.

There is this cliché that 9/11 marked a new phase in American history, policy, and culture. In his book *The Nineties*, Chuck Klosterman argues that "the nineties collapsed with the skyscrapers." Even at the time people were saying it. Ten days after the attacks, critic Edward Rothstein wrote in the *New York Times* that the attacks marked the end of "postmodern relativism." *Vanity Fair* editor Graydon Carter declared that it was "the end of the age of irony." The September 28 issue of *Entertainment Weekly* featured nothing but an American flag on its cover, with the caption "WHAT LIES AHEAD: THE CHALLENGE FOR OUR CULTURE."

In other words, the message was that we had been living high on the postmodern hog, living decadently, focused monomaniacally on shopping and popular culture and denying the supremacy of any one set of values over another. In a post-9/11 world, everything would be different. Maybe all the conservatives screeching throughout the '90s had been right all along. It was time to bring back moral absolutism. It was time to forge ourselves in battle (though not, of course, the kind that occurred in Seattle two years earlier). It was time to grow up, Get Serious, and enter a new chapter.

Part of this was true. We did enter a new chapter (though it was part of the same book). But that chapter wasn't about getting serious, unless getting serious meant doing a different kind of shopping and consuming a different kind of media and telling ourselves a different kind of story about America's place in the world. Cosmopolitanism was out, patriotism was in. Free speech was out, censorship was in. And the new chapter was most certainly not about moral absolutism. All of a sudden, torture became a nuanced issue. Freedom required domestic surveillance. In this new chapter, everything was flipped. Or perhaps everything was a curdled version of what it had been all along.

I first noticed the changes on MTV. The day of the attacks, the network suspended normal programming. Instead, they played messages of support from Nelly, Carson Daly, and Ja Rule. The videos that remained were either uplifting or patriotic. "Drive" by Incubus and "Alive" by P.O.D. aired multiple times a day. I also remember, at least after a certain point, the video for Fabolous and Nate Dogg's "Can't Deny It" being permitted—despite its violent lyrical content—due to its fortuitous pre-9/11 use of a red, white, and blue color palette. But, for the most part, anything that felt violent or overly sexual, anything that appeared to critique the government, and anything that might inadvertently remind viewers of the attacks was off-air.

Limp Bizkit got really unlucky. The band was at the peak of their career, and the video for "Rollin' (Urban Assault Vehicle)" won MTV's Video Music Award for Best Rock Video less than a week before, on September 6. Unfortunately, that video features the band performing on top of the World Trade Center. On September 10, the Port Authority of New York (which owns the World Trade Center site) sent the band a fruit basket and a letter congratulating them for their win and thanking them for the publicity.

"Boy, did the video for 'Rollin'' backfire," said guitarist Wes Borland. "After 9/11 everyone stopped playing it. Nobody wanted to see it. Neither did we."

On the radio, there was the notorious Clear Channel Memorandum. Now known as iHeartRadio, Clear Channel was the nation's largest radio chain at a time before music could be streamed. Two days after 9/11, the company circulated an internal memo advising its stations to avoid playing songs that could be interpreted as "lyrically questionable." These included all songs that mentioned airplanes, death, violence, jumping, Tuesday, and the Middle East. "Learn to Fly" by the Foo Fighters was banned, as was "Benny and the Jets" by Elton John, "Jump" by Van Halen," "Ruby Tuesday" by the Rolling Stones, and "Walk Like an Egyptian" by the Bangles.

Also banned was the entire oeuvre of Rage Against the Machine. At the turn of the millennium, Rage Against the Machine was an anomaly: a world-touring, multi-platinum-certified rock band with videos in frequent rotation on MTV, whose lyrics explored topics like US imperialism, militant labor history, Marxism, dollar hegemony, police brutality, mass incarceration, the work of Noam Chomsky, and the Zapatista movement.

This certainly couldn't be allowed. Not after the events of 9/11. Any kind of critical or thoughtful or challenging work was seen as part of the same problem of turn-of-the-millennium decadence. It had probably gotten us into this situation in the first place. And besides, it was simply *in bad taste* at a time like this.

What was in good taste were flags, and lots of them. When we returned to school that Thursday, we all wore red, white, and blue. I remember hearing that the president told Americans to do that, though I can't find any evidence this happened. Students clamored to put patriotic emblems on their faces and arms and hands. I asked a girl in my symphonic band class to paint a small American flag on my cheek.

Flags—many made in the same Chinese, Bangladeshi, and Indonesian sweatshops as other American goods—went up on houses all the way down my street. Not just on my street, but on what felt like every street. There were flag magnets for cars and little flags to attach to your car antennae. Politicians began wearing flag pins on their lapels, a practice which has remained customary ever since. There were flags on hats and T-shirts and stickers and blankets and commemorative plates. Sometimes these flags were accompanied by images of the Twin Towers and the Pentagon, by crying bald eagles, by the words GOD BLESS AMERICA and UNITED WE STAND and NEVER FORGET.

The firefighters and police officers who responded to the attacks became The Heroes, and people clamored to honor them by purchasing FDNY and NYPD merchandise. Soon, the category of Heroes would expand to include The Troops, and there would be yellow ribbon magnets and camouflage-patterned items for sale as we invaded first Afghanistan, then Iraq. Also popular was any piece of merchandise having to do with New York City. For once, everyone in America wanted to support the Yankees. President Bush threw out the first pitch for them during game three of the World Series.

When music video production started up again, everyone seemed to have gotten the memo, and cautiously adhered to the new expectations. For example, P!nk's video for "Get This Party Started," which came out in October 2001, features the singer riding up a construction elevator conspicuously draped in an American flag. It wasn't enough to avoid talking about airplanes or Tuesdays or Marxist revolution. You now had to be actively, emphatically, unquestionably patriotic.

I begged my mom to buy us a flag so we could be like everybody else. That summer, her old Corolla finally broke down and she begrudgingly replaced it with a Saab 95 station wagon. Our family had never owned such a nice car before, but my mom said it rated highest for safety, and besides, she planned to keep it for as long as she'd kept the Corolla. Amortizing, she called it.

Whatever, I thought. What mattered to me was that, inside the Saab, I finally felt like I belonged. The seats were gray leather and the steering wheel matched. Burl-wood accents adorned the dashboard and the thick floor mats were embroidered with the word SAAB. A sunroof slid open with a soft whir. It was so quiet in that car. When I saw other late-model vehicles on the road I felt like we were part of a club together, just like I did when I went to the mall.

Now, without a flag, my family was going to stand out in a new way. Yet again, the ranks were closing in. But my mom remained skeptical of consumerism, national tragedy or no. In fact, she worried that making 9/11 into an excuse to buy stuff was disrespectful to the victims and their families, that it was an inappropriate way to mourn mass murder.* Even though the president himself told us to stick it to the terrorists by going shopping, to "get down to Disney World."†

George W. Bush had a 90 percent bipartisan approval rating in the months following 9/11. And the attacks elevated New York City Mayor Rudy Giuliani to a popular national figure. Oprah called him "America's Mayor." *Time* magazine named him Person of the Year. In this supposedly new post-9/11 era, Americans were expected to put aside partisan grievances and get behind these strong Republican leaders. After all, men like President Bush and Mayor Giuliani were here to protect "us" from "them."

In an address on September 20, the president told Congress and the American people that "either you are with us, or you are with the terrorists." The word *freedom* appeared thirteen times in this speech. We were told that "they" (the terrorists) "hate our freedoms," particularly "our freedom of religion, our freedom of speech, our freedom to vote and assemble and disagree with each other."

Of course, anyone actually trying to exercise these freedoms was at best publicly excoriated or blacklisted and at worst surveilled, kidnapped, or tortured.

When Susan Sontag wrote in *The New Yorker* that 9/11 was "an attack on the world's self-proclaimed superpower, undertaken as a consequence of specific American alliances and actions," and suggested that "a few shreds of historical awareness might help

---

* She reminded me, too, that she hated the Taliban years before most Americans had even heard of them. She despaired over what they had done to the country of her early childhood, and what they had done to women.
† A place that was out of the question for our family vacations, both because it was too expensive and because it wasn't educational enough.

us understand what has just happened, and what may continue to happen," she was practically run out of public life. She was criticized for her "sheer tastelessness," and called an "America-hater," a "moral idiot," and a "traitor."

Sontag wasn't even necessarily making a left-wing point. What she was referring to was blowback—a concept that originates from inside the CIA. She was talking about the fact that the American economic, military, and cultural order at the turn of the twenty-first century—the one described at the beginning of this essay—had many negative effects in the developing world, from increasing economic inequality to homogenizing local cultures, and this made Islamic terrorism appealing to some of its denizens.

What's more, the United States had backed the radical Islamic Mujahideen following the Soviet invasion of Afghanistan in 1979. Out of this group emerged the Taliban, whom we also supported. We even invited a Taliban contingent to the State Department headquarters in 1997, the same year Osama bin Laden took up residence in Afghanistan. Sontag was actually doing the thing that 9/11 was supposed to have led all Americans to do: taking the safety of the American people and the problem of terrorism seriously, like an adult would. Stanley Fish and Joan Didion defended her, but few other public intellectuals did.

A similar thing happened to Bill Maher. Maher, at the time, had a late-night talk show on ABC called *Politically Incorrect*. When he suggested one evening that the 9/11 terrorists had committed evil acts but were "not cowardly," there was an explosion of public outrage. His show was canceled several months later.

There was the shunning of Gilbert Gottfried, a stand-up comedian who spent decades working in an old Borscht Belt tradition: processing trauma using humor and vulgarity.

"I have to catch a flight to California," he told an audience of fellow comedians at the Friars Club in November 2001. "I can't get a direct flight, they said they have to stop at the Empire State Building first."

The joke was received with a combination of silence and boos, with one audience member yelling "Too soon!" For generations, Jewish comedians have joked about their mothers, the pogroms, and even Hitler. This tradition was honed at downtown nightclubs, Catskills resorts, and eventually in Hollywood with the work of Mel Brooks and Larry David, where it shaped American comedy as a whole. But the message after 9/11 was clear: this was the one topic comedy was not allowed to touch.

Reading the room, the Strokes changed the release date of their debut album, *Is This It*, in order to replace the track "New York City Cops" with a new song. "New York City Cops" was considered inappropriate after 9/11 due to lyrics musing that the NYPD "ain't too smart."

"The band stands by 'New York City Cops,' but feels after witnessing the valiant response of the [NYPD] during last week's tragedy, that timing was wrong to release it during these highly sensitive times," the band's publicist said in a statement.

A year and a half later, in the lead-up to the invasion of Iraq, Dixie Chicks frontwoman Natalie Maines told a London concert audience that she was "ashamed the president of the United States is from Texas." In reaction to this mild criticism, country stations stopped playing the band's music, and there were boycotts and mass burnings of their CDs, with one group of protesters in Louisiana using a 33,000-pound tractor to destroy a pile of albums. The band's career was damaged for years.

As for the alter-globalization movement, it was toast. Sure, there were still small protests at WTO conferences and G8 Summits, where groups of black-clad anarchists still fought with the cops. But the terrain had shifted since the Battle in Seattle two years before. Now that Bill Maher and the Dixie Chicks were traitors, no one wanted to hear critiques of American power from aging trade unionists or kids in bandannas. And now that patriotism amounted to consumerism, any critiques of the economic system amounted to treason. What political energy remained on the left would be channeled into the anti-war movement and the fight to protect civil liberties at home and abroad. There would be no mass movement focused on economic concerns until Occupy Wall Street in 2011.

In the president's speeches, 9/11 was a constant incantation. In October, the USA PATRIOT Act was passed 98–1 in the Senate and 357–66 in the house. The sweeping law, of course, was because of 9/11. Because of 9/11, the government would be allowed to suspend due process. Because of 9/11, the government would be allowed to do almost unlimited dragnet surveillance, listening to phone calls and monitoring the library records of private citizens. Because of 9/11, the very definition of terrorism would be expanded so broadly that it could include peacefully assembling with an environmental advocacy group or attending a service at a mosque. Freedom of assembly and religion didn't matter anymore. Because of 9/11, Guantánamo Bay detention camp would be opened early in 2002 to hold anyone the government felt like holding, indefinitely. Because of 9/11, the administration started talking about using "advanced interrogation techniques"—like waterboarding, sensory deprivation, sensory bombardment, humiliation, and "stress positions"—on the detainees there and at black sites around the world. Moral relativism didn't matter when it came to shackling naked, hooded prisoners to the door by their hands and feet, beating them, urinating on them, and blasting music at them at top volume for hours until they vomited.

The preferred music? Britney Spears, Christina Aguilera, Limp Bizkit, Eminem, and Drowning Pool: the same pop, rap, and nu metal that was playing on MTV back in the States. Rage Against the Machine's music may have been removed from Clear Channel stations, but it continued to be a hit with interrogators. Before 9/11, American pop culture was a form of soft imperialism, enticing people around the world to embrace an American-led economic system. After 9/11, the imperialism hardened, and American pop culture was exported by force.

WHAT THE DOMINANT narrative gets right is that 9/11 itself was a tragedy. But I must be very clear where I deviate from that dominant narrative. None of what happened *after* 9/11 happened *because* of 9/11: not the flags, not the commemorative plates, not the T-shirts, not the War on Terror, not the PATRIOT Act, not the silencing of dissenting voices, not the stress positions, not the surveillance, not the invasions of Afghanistan and Iraq. Those things did happen, but this way of speaking makes them seem natural, inevitable. There was a *because* there, however. All these things happened *because* of choices made by the Bush administration. Different choices would have allowed for a different—and perhaps less awful—sequence of events.

And 9/11 was not, as Chuck Klosterman and others say, the end of one era or the beginning of another. It was, rather, a midpoint. What defined the Y2K Era *as an era* was the unquestioned rule of American-led global capitalism, which began after the Cold War ended in the early '90s and the dot-com bubble inflated in the late '90s. 9/11 never challenged that story. It was merely another chapter within it. Only in this chapter, we became meaner, stupider, more violent, more conformist, more childish, more materialistic, more racist, and more vindictive than we had been before. In this chapter, America was still the hero, and shopping was still the most important part of citizenship. In this chapter, we stalked the global village in our "Never Forget" hats, waving our flags and hunting for blood.

It took nearly another decade for the story of the Y2K Era to end. On September 29, 2008, the stock market crashed, announcing the Great Recession. This time, nobody went shopping. There were no recession-themed shirts; no hair accessories, bumper stickers, or commemorative plates to buy. You couldn't watch the recession on *TRL*. Two weeks earlier, MTV announced that the show was going off the air. The last episode aired on November 16, 2008. Finally, it was the end of an era.

Get Naked

IN SEPTEMBER 2000, LUDACRIS RELEASED HIS DEBUT single, "What's Your Fantasy" (featuring Shawnna). I was in seventh grade, and my friend Hannah and I would talk on the phone for hours about whatever was on MTV. I hadn't seen the video yet, but Hannah told me it was "really nasty." I was intrigued. She recited some of it—"I wanna, li-li-li-lick you from your head to your toes, and I wanna, move from the bed down to the, down to the, to the flo, I gotta know, what-what's your fan-ta-ta-sy?"— and we giggled furtively. I pretended I knew what a fantasy was, and why Hannah thought it was "nasty." I had a vague sense, but not the specifics.

"He talks about doing it in the library *on top of books!*" she continued.

I was trying to think why anyone would want to do that. It seemed uncomfortable, but maybe that was the point. I knew what sex was. I knew that a penis got an erection and ejaculated semen into a vagina. I knew it felt good, and that some religious people thought it was wrong. I knew you had to wear a condom to keep from getting AIDS or getting pregnant. I knew what masturbation was, and that some religious people thought that was wrong, too. I masturbated thinking about doing it with Danny Rivera, this hot eighth-grade punk with gelled hair. I was ashamed of that even though I wasn't religious. Maybe if Danny and I ever did it in real life we would do it in the library on top of books.

When I finally did see the video, it was a bit of a letdown. I guess I was expecting it to be actual porn or something, based on Hannah's titillated descriptions. Instead, the video featured Ludacris driving around Atlanta in a vintage convertible. Throughout the city, there were women in short shorts and crop tops licking lollipops, walking around, or sitting on porches, and they periodically got into his car. These scenes were intercut with a fully clothed dance party in a parking lot.

The lyrics, though, were more "nasty" than I could have possibly imagined. I couldn't believe what I was hearing. Ludacris talks about doing it not only in a library, but in a public bathroom, in the back of the classroom, a sauna, a Jacuzzi, a car, a boat, a plane, on a football field, on hay in the middle of the barn, and in the garden all in the dirt. He talks about doing it with strawberries and cherries on top. He talks about rose petals, silk sheets, whips, chains, and handcuffs.

This was by far the most explicit sexual content I had ever encountered. It made concrete things about sex that were vague before. I knew that sex was full of these subtexts and details that went beyond the mechanics I already knew. If it was just the mechanics, people wouldn't get so crazy about it. And I started to wonder: Maybe I would like having sex in a Jacuzzi or with strawberries or with handcuffs. Maybe I would enjoy pretending to be a schoolteacher. Or if I didn't, maybe I was supposed to. All I wanted was to be an adult already, and maybe that's what that was all about.

Other lyrics were a puzzle that occupied me for a long time. In particular, I thought about the line "maybe your girl and my friend can trade, tag team, off the ropes." What could that possibly mean? Was it something to do with wrestling? I also wondered at length what "the dirty birds" meant. I thought it was probably some kind of really crazy sex position. In reality, it was the nickname of the Atlanta Falcons.

MTV provided me with a kind of 201-level sexual education. In "Butterfly," Crazy Town said, "I'll make your legs shake, I'll make you go crazy." For me, that line connected the concept of sex with what it could actually look and feel like. I felt like I was part of some secret club, the way I knew exactly what they were talking about. In the video, the band performs in a colorful, CGI-generated field that alludes, also, to ecstasy and LSD (made more salient by the fact that Epic Mazur, one of the band's two front men, ironically sports a D.A.R.E. T-shirt). Mazur and the other front man, Shifty Shellshock, are tattooed and pierced, and they eye the camera soulfully between shots of scantily clad hippie women cavorting in the grass as CGI butterflies alight around them.

In "Come On Over Baby (All I Want Is You)" by Christina Aguilera, there is a scene where she wears a yellow leather jumpsuit with a zipper up the front. She grinds against a backup dancer who wears a lime-green shirt and pants. At one point, she takes his hand and guides it down the front of her body as he unzips her. The camera zooms in close. Just when we think we're going to see her crotch, instead the zipper reveals a whole other scene, with Christina and the dancers in new outfits and new hairstyles, against a new background. Christina Aguilera's pussy is a portal to another dimension.

With "Peaches & Cream" I learned that you could say something as a kind of sexual code and hide it in plain speech. When 112 sang about eating peaches and cream, they were talking about eating something, but it definitely wasn't fruit. The video is intercut with shots of wet peaches splashing onto a blue surface in slow motion. "Know what I mean?" they sing. And I did know what they meant.

The song and video for "One Minute Man"—by Missy Elliott featuring Ludacris and Trina—took verbal and visual double entendre to new levels. The surreal, high-concept video is set in a by-the-hour hotel (a reference that would at first fly over my head). Ludacris and a teddy-clad woman bounce around on a vibrating bed. He calls himself "the maintenance man."

In another scene, the rapper reaches into a sudsy bathtub while a naked girl appears to moan in ecstasy. In another, set in a psychedelic nursery, he rocks two women to sleep while bragging that he makes women "so wet that their bodies start to leak and shit."

In the next verse, Trina wears fishnets and a metallic-green lingerie set. She writhes around, telling us "lil' mama ain't with that quick shit. You better break me off, stiff tongue or stiff dick."

The most profane video I saw was probably for Methods of Mayhem's 1999 song "Get Naked." I only saw it once, late at night. I think there was some kind of rule that it could only air then. Methods of Mayhem was a rap metal supergroup consisting of Tommy Lee and a rapper named TiLo. The song features Fred Durst, George Clinton, Lil' Kim, and Mix Master Mike. Everyone in the video (except, for some reason, Fred Durst) is nude, and their genitals are strategically covered with remote controls, cartoon stars, and flashes of light.

The lyrics reference Ron Jeremy, a "porno tape," a "cum stain," "jizzy-jizzum," and "blue balls." Lil' Kim rides a mechanical rooster.

"Fuck a blow job, it's a motherfucking hobby," she brags. "Under seven inches? Uhh! Sorry!"

In "Get Naked," all subtext is (forgive the pun) stripped away.

And then there was the 2001 video for "Lady Marmalade," which debuted with great fanfare (there was a whole episode of

Making the Video about it). A cover of a Patti LaBelle song from 1974 about a Creole prostitute in New Orleans, it is an all-star ensemble production featuring Missy Elliott, Mýa, P!nk, Lil' Kim, and Christina Aguilera made to promote Baz Luhrmann's *Moulin Rouge*, which was itself inspired by Puccini's opera *La Bohème*. In the video, Missy Elliott plays the MC (really, the madam), handsome in coat and tails. She introduces the four girls, and then the music begins, and each emerges as a high-end prostitute clad in extravagant lingerie and makeup. There are all the trappings of the bordello or the cabaret: satin and lace, corsets and top hats, balconette bras and fishnet stockings and rhinestones and glitter and garters.

This video (and the movie, where Nicole Kidman plays a prostitute in fin de siècle Paris) is how I learned about the existence of the world's oldest profession. *This* is what people at school or in rap songs meant when they called a girl a "ho." I didn't get it. These women all seemed smart, business-oriented, and beautiful. Like a lot of things surrounding sex, the more I learned, the more questions I had. I didn't understand why you were supposed to be a sexy woman but you weren't supposed to make money off of it—at least not directly. You had to be a sexy woman if you wanted to have a music career where your videos got played on MTV, but at least part of that money was supposed to go, I supposed, to record executives.

More than any specific information about sex acts or the sex industry, the videos on MTV taught me what it meant to become a sexy woman myself. I learned how sexy women dressed, yes, but also how they moved; how they shifted their eyes in a come-hither glance, how they bit their glossed lips, how sucking a lollipop could have a second, dirty meaning. I learned how sexy women walked by slowly shifting their hips from side to side—so different from my own rapid, shuffling gait. Before MTV, I thought sexiness was a kind of genetic quality, and that I was born without it. But MTV taught me that anyone could become a sexy woman if they tried.

IT WASN'T JUST MTV. When I started puberty, the entirety of American culture was going through its own sort of sexual awakening. Bill Clinton was leaving office after discussing, on national television, whether or not he got a blow job or put a cigar in a woman's vagina. Lil' Kim showed up to the 1999 Video Music Awards in purple sequined pasties, and to the 2000 Grammys, Jennifer Lopez wore a green Versace dress that somehow showed her cleavage, her navel, and her underwear all at the same time. This dress, in fact, prompted the creation of Google Images, when the search engine was flooded with so many queries about pictures of "the dress" that in-house engineers realized they needed to create an entirely new way for users to search the web. Viagra hit the market in 1998 and was advertised on prime-time television* by former presidential candidate Bob Dole. And now, with the internet, you could look at porn—immediately, limitlessly, and for free—from the privacy of your home computer. The technology of ever-faster home internet allowed for a dissemination of sexual imagery never before possible in human history. People made porn on cave walls and the Gutenberg press, but it took a lot longer.

Porn drove the growth of the internet, and the internet drove

* Thanks to the 1997 FDA Modernization Act, which significantly relaxed the rules for direct-to-consumer pharmaceutical advertisements.

the growth of porn. Sexual content was popular on Usenet, the precursor to the World Wide Web (erotica, mostly, due to the text-only constraints of the system, though there were some instances of pornographic ASCII art). Once the Web opened up to the public in 1991, porn sites began appearing almost immediately. It's challenging to find good statistics on exactly how many porn sites were online at any given time in the 1990s or 2000s, or exactly how many people were looking at them across the internet as a whole. In a 2000 article, CNN estimated that 37 percent of web users had visited porn sites (a number that strikes me as low). Journalist David Friend—quoting *Forbes*—claimed that, by the late '90s, there were more than 500,000 porn sites online, with 100 new ones going live each week. By 2000, the internet porn industry was making $2 billion a year.

Porn sites pioneered some of the internet's biggest marketing innovations, like banner ads and subscription content. A Seattle-area stripper named Danni Ashe founded Danni's Hard Drive in 1995, offering access to homemade pornographic photos, videos, and interviews for $15 a month. Pretty soon she was making $2.5 million a year. Her swift success earned her a write-up in the *Wall Street Journal* in 1997 (headline: "As Other Internet Ventures Fail, Sex Sites are Raking in Millions") and multiple profiles in *WIRED* (sample headline: "The Brains Behind the Boobs"). In 1999, she earned $5.9 million. The next year, in 2000, she made it to the *Guinness Book of World Records* as the most downloaded woman on the internet, with over 841 million downloads.

The creation of search engines in the mid-'90s made it much easier for internet users to find exactly what they were looking for—including porn. In 1997, a website called Eyescream leaked what it claimed was a list of Yahoo's top terms:

1. sex 1,553,420
2. chat 414,320
3. xxx 397,640
4. playboy 390,920
5. netscape software 350,320
6. nude 292,560
7. porno 257,860
8. games 217,440
9. porn 199,180
10. weather 190,900
11. penthouse 186,980
12. pamela anderson 172,760
13. pornography 172,260
14. pussy 169,840
15. persian kitty 163,620*
16. maps 163,360
17. halloween 155,680
18. music 151,780
19. adult 148,960
20. chat rooms 139,960

This is how it felt to be on the internet in the late '90s. Sixty percent of the terms are related to sexual content, with "sex" far and away the most popular, at 1,553,420 queries. Yes, the internet

---

* A site with curated porn links run by Beth Mansfield—a stay-at-home mom in Alabama—which pioneered the field of internet ad sales, making $3.5 million its first year online.

was ostensibly about chat rooms, Netscape software, and the weather report, but it was mainly about porn. And, it's worth noting, a primary function of chat rooms was facilitating sex, both cyber and IRL.

The internet made porn consumption anonymous and frictionless, especially when broadband replaced dial-up in the mid-2000s. What's more, the old legal yardstick for obscenity—the community standards rule—didn't mean much when the community was the entire planet. Porn could get niche, especially once users realized that tags and search terms allowed them to specify what kinds of people they wanted to watch having sex and which acts they wanted to see those people performing. Kinky porn and the development of hyper-specific sexual tastes were both around before the internet, but required leaving your house, going to an adult store, and flipping through the magazine titles and videotapes. And still, there was that pesky community standards rule, which placed some limits on what could be produced and sold.

Our family computer was in the rec room next to the television and my dad's home office. Perhaps this was why I didn't really watch porn in middle school. I know my male peers were consuming at least a moderate amount of it, because sometimes they'd IM me a research link for our civics assignment and it would go to whitehouse.com, where a blond woman made a face of surprise as she inhaled a very large penis. "Check this out," they would write, and it would be Goatse, a close-up photo of a man's grotesquely stretched anus. They did that, everyone said, because they were boys, and boys were pervs who loved porn and masturbation.

But what did that make me? I remember reading a story on Teen Open Diary (my friends and I all had accounts; proto Live-Journals, where we wrote about our daily lives and posted song lyrics). One day, clicking around, I hyperlinked into a diary in which the narrator—supposedly a high school girl just a few years older than I was—vividly illustrated various sexual encounters. I remember her claiming that she let a male classmate fuck her on a bench in the boys' locker room for $50. In another post, she talked about having a sleepover with a female friend with DD breasts. According to her, they slept together in lingerie. Pretty soon, they were fondling each other's breasts and going down on each other.

I began to constantly check the account for new stories, timing my computer use to make sure I only checked when the rest of my family was asleep or out of the house. Afterward, I always cleared my browser cache, even though a part of me believed I was just surfing the web, seeing where the information superhighway took me. Then, eliminating any doubt as to my true motives, I would run upstairs, lock the door to my room, sit on the floor of my closet, close that door as well, and masturbate furiously. Eventually the teen erotica account was taken down for violating terms of service. I was disappointed, but I still had plenty to think about: the rapper Nelly, various crushes from school, Billie Joe Armstrong from Green Day, Shifty Shellshock from Crazy Town, that scene in *American Pie* where Tara Reid's boyfriend goes down on her.

Porn wasn't just on the internet. If you stayed up late watching basic cable between the years 1997 and 2008 (Comedy Central in particular), you were bombarded with commercials for a new video franchise called Girls Gone Wild. Each ad began with a black screen and a sped-up legal voice-over proclaiming, "WARNING: THIS VIDEO CONTAINS ADULT CONTENT NOT SUITABLE FOR CHILDREN." This didn't stop me (or my brother, who is six years younger than me) from seeing what came next. Watching Girls Gone Wild ads with my little brother was, to put it mildly, not my favorite. I learned to change the channel as soon as that black screen appeared, before the first giggling, bikini-clad woman wiggled her breasts and doused herself with beer.

But when I was alone I would always watch the Girls Gone Wild ads. The conceit of Girls Gone Wild was that Joe Francis and his film crew would travel to spring break locations around the United States: Daytona Beach, Fort Lauderdale, New Orleans. They would find (mostly white) college-age women who were conventionally attractive and blackout drunk. Then producers would ply them with Girls Gone Wild merch and more alcohol. In exchange they would flash their breasts, make out with each other, and in some cases perform sexual acts. The ads showed censored clips of the videos, and promised that for just $9.99, you could get two videos full of "uncensored" content with "sexy coeds" (I wondered what a coed was) and "hot young girls waiting to get naked just for you." You just had to call the 1-800 number or go to girlsgonewild.com to place your order. They even offered a thirty-day money-back guarantee.

Was I supposed to be like this? These were girls—it was right there in the name!—and I was a girl, too. And it seemed like they were having so much fun: laughing and smiling and dancing and getting free plastic bead necklaces. I couldn't imagine them sad, like I often was. I wanted my breasts to hurry up and grow so that I could go down to a bar and pull up my shirt on spring break. Maybe this was why everyone liked college so much. At the same time, the ads made me feel kind of scared. It seemed that if I wanted to become like these girls, I'd have to give up some essential part of myself. I was a birder, for example, and I wasn't sure the producers of Girls Gone Wild would find my knowledge of blue jay behavior very attractive.

Years later, Joe Francis would face civil and criminal charges. Lawsuits alleged that some of the "hot young girls" and "sexy coeds" had performed those sexual acts—and signed commercial release documents—while they were too drunk to consent. Some of them, it turns out, were also under eighteen. Girls Gone Wild was forced to declare bankruptcy in 2013. Two years earlier, in 2011, Francis was charged with assault and false imprisonment in an incident involving several women in Los Angeles. In 2020, he was arrested in Mexico and charged with domestic violence there. Those charges were dropped after he completed six months of therapy.

Y2K was also the era of the celebrity sex tape, a concept that has now been fully digested by popular culture. The very first one debuted in 1996, when electrician Rand Gauthier stole a safe belonging to Tommy Lee after Lee allegedly withheld payment for Gauthier's services. Inside the safe was a homemade tape of Lee having sex with his wife, Pamela Anderson, during a vacation on Lake Mead. Gauthier made thousands of copies of the tape for distribution, then put up websites online with names like pamsex.com, pamlee.com, and pamsextape.com. The sites provided instructions for how to send a $59.95 money order to get the tape by mail. Neither Pam nor Tommy was pleased that someone was profiting off a major violation of their privacy (Anderson has said it makes her "sick"). But the tape was a hit anyway. It was the first time people could watch a real celebrity couple—perhaps the era's most famous celebrity couple—have real sex. It was also the first high-profile case of what is now called "revenge porn."

In 2004, *1 Night in Paris* was released by Rick Salomon, Paris Hilton's boyfriend at the time. The film shows the two of them having sex. It is shot, inexplicably, with night vision, a factor that brings to mind scenes from the concurrently escalating Iraq War. Semi-relatedly, the movie opens with the following dedication: "In memory of 9/11/2001 . . . We will never forget." In any case, the film became a hit, coinciding with the height of Hilton's fame.

Paris Hilton issued a statement saying she had been "out of it" at the time of the shooting and didn't consent to its release. Salomon sued her for defamation. Hilton countersued and they settled out of court. *1 Night in Paris* was mocked on late-night comedy shows, stand-up sets, a *South Park* episode, and even in a video by P!nk. Much of this was related to a widespread belief that Hilton deliberately released the sex tape to bolster her fame and fortune, as well as a secondary belief that doing so would have been wrong.

"I never received a dime from the video," she told *GQ* in 2006. She described the profits as "dirty money." In 2021, she would tell *Vanity Fair* the experience was "humiliating," and "something that will hurt me for the rest of my life."

In 2007, *Kim Kardashian, Superstar* was released by Vivid Entertainment, a major porn distributor. This sex tape featured Kim Kardashian (then a minor character in Paris Hilton's orbit) and Ray J (the younger brother of Brandy) and came out around the same time as *Keeping Up with the Kardashians*. In the show's first episode, Kim goes on *The Tyra Banks Show* to address the issue. Kim sued Vivid in 2007, stating that her tape was "being sold completely without my permission or consent." The case was later dismissed. Family friend Joe Francis has claimed that he helped Kim release and profit from the tape, but both Kim and Ray J have denied such allegations.

Despite the legal issues surrounding the Pam, Paris, and Kim tapes, the general consensus at the time seemed to be that the tapes were put out on purpose, for the sake of publicity, and that these women deserved whatever they got afterward.

The aesthetics of porn shaped many of the era's fashion trends. There was the retro porno-chic of the '70s, made popular by the 1997 Paul Thomas Anderson film *Boogie Nights*. More of-the-moment was a look consisting of low-rise jeans or a low-rise pastel terry-cloth tracksuit with a thong peeking out; high-sheen lip gloss, bleached-blond layered hair, acrylic-tip French manicures; "tramp stamp" tattoos of butterflies and tribal designs; cropped baby tees that said "99% Angel, 1% Devil" or "99% Devil, 1% Angel" or "Spoiled Brat" or even "Porn Star"; rimless pastel sunglasses with small rhinestone hearts in the corner; clothes featuring the silhouette of the Playboy Bunny. There were tube tops and ruched, skintight minidresses with cutouts everywhere except the places that would get you arrested for indecent exposure. Everything was baby pink or baby blue or black, studded with Swarovski crystals. This look achieved additional popularity from the E! reality show *The Girls Next Door*, which, starting in 2005, chronicled the lives of Hugh Heffner's live-in girlfriends at the Playboy Mansion.

I had the pink rhinestone sunglasses (Dior knockoffs that I bought at a rest stop in New Jersey). I wore the low-rise jeans, the baby tees and tube tops and spaghetti-strap tank tops. I added inches to my height with Steve Madden platform slides and I smeared on way too much lip gloss and purple eyeshadow. I made a raver-style candy necklace that said "BRAT." One day toward the end of seventh grade I cut a pair of my jeans shorts to make them even shorter and got threatened with a day suspension by one of the middle school vice principals.

I don't think I realized it at the time, but this look came from porn. For the first time, porn stars like Jenna Jameson became bona fide mainstream celebrities. She had a cameo in the 1997 Howard Stern biopic *Private Parts*, in the games *Grand Theft Auto: Vice City* and *Tony Hawk's Pro Skater 4*, and in the music video for

"Without Me" by Eminem. Her 2004 memoir *How to Make Love Like a Porn Star* spent weeks on the *New York Times* bestseller list. Similarly, Ron Jeremy became a cultural touchstone, appearing in episodes of *Chappelle's Show* and *Just Shoot Me!*, in music videos for Moby and Kid Rock, and getting name-dropped in too many songs to count. It was a kind of inside joke for anyone who watched porn. In the Y2K Era, you no longer had to pretend you didn't recognize these people from their other work. And if you didn't, well, maybe you should? Everybody else was watching porn.

Horny pubescent kids have always been like this: sexually curious, trying out a sexual persona without really understanding it. But what made my experience different was that I was growing up at a time when popular culture was as oversexed as I was. Sex wasn't a secret I discovered in a magazine hidden under a mattress or heard rumors about from older kids. Sex was something I had to contend with every time I turned on the TV or logged onto the internet or shopped at the mall or went to the movies or glanced at the grocery store magazine rack or the side of a public bus. Even in the boring *Washington Post*, I read about presidential blow jobs, the ascendent gay rights movement, and the waning AIDS epidemic in between articles on NATO, school choice, and entitlement reform.

I so badly wanted to have sex: to feel that feeling, yes, an orgasm, but not only that. I wanted to be told I was beautiful because every day at school I got told that I wasn't by the same guys who sent me unsolicited pornography. I wanted to be held. I wanted a partner, and I also wanted to have complicated feelings I couldn't explain to my partner, feelings like the ones in "Everlong" by the Foo Fighters. I thought I was ready for that. I wanted to stop being a kid and start being an adult, to have power like the sexy women with the glossed lips on MTV. I wanted it so badly I thought I might explode.

It was these terrible longings that sent me into an AOL chat room at age thirteen. I didn't lie about my age: I said I was a hot thirteen-year-old girl looking to meet hot guys. A guy claiming he was in high school IM'd me almost immediately, asking what I looked like. I told him I was five-five with B-cup breasts. When he suggested we meet I got scared. I lied and told him I lived in the nearby town of Reston, Virginia, instead of Falls Church, then logged off. I wasn't just scared that he might be a pedophile. I was also scared he would realize that I was actually five-two with A-cup breasts.

AT THE SAME time, something very different was happening with sex in America. George W. Bush came into office in 2000 riding a wave of evangelical Christian support. The president's administration put forth hundreds of millions of dollars of funding for abstinence-only education.* In school classrooms and nondenominational churches across the country, teens but especially girl teens were taught to guard their virginities, and told that if they didn't they would end up like chewed gum or cups full of spit or flowers with all the petals plucked off. Teens learned that condoms weren't reliable, that homosexuality was an affront to God, that abortion was murder, that tampons would break your hymen (thus depriving your future husband of his chance to do that). Boys, teens were taught, were more sexual than girls, so it was girls' responsibility to dress modestly and fend off male ad-

---

* Abstinence-only education actually came into popularity at the federal level in 1996 with President Clinton's Personal Responsibility and Work Opportunity Reconciliation Act (also known as welfare reform), which reserved $50 million in annual funding for five years toward programs that encouraged abstinence and did not teach contraception.

vances. There was little to no discussion of rape or sexual assault, even as major scandals would emerge decades later showing that these problems were rampant in evangelical communities.

Tens of thousands of teens poured onto the National Mall for the annual True Love Waits rally, sponsored by the Southern Baptist Convention.* At "purity balls," daughters wore white dresses and pledged their virginities to their fathers beneath crosses and American flags. Often, the high point of the evening would be the presentation of a "purity ring" for the girl to wear until marriage. One day, her husband would slide it off, replacing it with a wedding ring. This would allow him to "take" her virginity later that night: the transfer of a property deed from one holder to another. The nonprofit organization The Silver Ring Thing helped popularize purity rings as well, using federal funding to inculcate American public-school students in evangelical sexual practices. The purity movement was at its peak in the late '90s and early 2000s, with 2.5 million young people across the country pledging to save themselves for marriage.

Despite seeming to be at cross-purposes with a hypersexual popular culture, the purity movement was not at all separate from it. The two intermingled in strange ways. A teenage Britney Spears gyrated in schoolgirl outfits and red vinyl catsuits and then claimed in interviews that she had no idea why men found her performances sexual; and that she, like Jessica Simpson and seemingly every other female pop star, was saving herself for marriage.† Perhaps this was not so strange. Both porn aesthetics and purity

---

* Where a major scandal broke in 2022 showing that sexual abuse and high-level cover-ups had been going on within the organization for decades.
† Both Britney and Jessica wore purity rings, alongside slightly-after-my-time pop stars like Miley Cyrus, Selena Gomez, and the Jonas Brothers. The trend didn't really fall off until sex positivity took over in the early 2010s.

culture tell girls that there is power in their sexuality. For the former, the power comes from having sex. For the latter, power comes from refusing it. Both girls are sex objects, meant to be consumed by men, either now or later.

MAYBE IT WAS these pervasive, seemingly contradictory messages about sex that convinced my mom to sign me up, at the beginning of eighth grade, for Our Whole Lives. Described as "a comprehensive, lifespan sexuality education curricula for use in both secular settings and faith communities," Our Whole Lives (often shortened to OWL) is the standard eighth-grade curriculum for Unitarian Universalist religious education. Basically, if your family attends a Unitarian church, you will go through this class upon turning thirteen. It's like Hebrew school or confirmation but way more embarrassing.

If MTV was my sex ed 201, Our Whole Lives was my postdoc. At Our Whole Lives, each Sunday morning someone's boomer parent would explain masturbation, BDSM dungeons, dental dams, and the Kinsey scale. The class had a box where you could anonymously submit questions you were too embarrassed to ask out loud and they would be answered during the next class. I did use it once, because there was something I really wanted to know: "What is 69? What is 420?"

I got my answer the following week.

Nice.

Part of me found the class interesting: I was curious about consent and porn and golden showers and outercourse. Who wouldn't be, especially at that age? But I also thought the class was weird, and I worried it made me more of a perv than I already was. After all, no one else I knew at school was taking Our Whole Lives. I kept it a secret from friends, referring to it as a "youth group," a vague and misleading term I deliberately selected to obscure what actually went on during those Sunday mornings.

I actually started to envy kids who grew up in those religious, sexually repressed households I saw on TV: all those youth groups pledging abstinence on the National Mall, all those pop stars saving themselves for marriage. It seemed to me like sex under those circumstances had a sense of frisson, something to rebel against and transcend and discover. I got a taste of that before I started OWL, when I was piecing together sexual signs and signifiers from music videos and the internet. But in OWL it was all laid out in the open. There were books, worksheets, and PowerPoints. Before OWL, sex had seemed like an escape from school, but now it *was* school. And school, to me, was boring.

If anything, OWL achieved the aims of abstinence-only sex ed better than abstinence-only sex ed, because the last thing I wanted to do after that class was have sex. And I wouldn't, not for another four years. The funny thing is, this actually lines up with the research. Kids who do comprehensive sex ed have a later date of sexual initiation than those who do abstinence-only sex ed or no sex ed. The research says it's because comprehensive sex ed allows kids to make more informed choices. I suspect it's because comprehensive sex ed takes the fun out. After all, anything condoned by adults becomes automatically uncool.

It was pure coincidence that I reached sexual maturity at the exact moment when there was a pitched battle over sexual ethics in America. Who could have known that a technological revolution would put a nearly infinite supply of porn inside every home with a modem, which would in turn reshape the entire landscape of popular culture? Who could have guessed that they'd be allowed to say "cum stain" on MTV by the time I was old enough to wonder what that meant? It was bleeped out, but I had the internet.

The evangelicals who championed purity rings saw the short-comings in porn and the culture it created. Maybe sex was sacred and important, a private connection between two committed individuals, not something to be sold or given away freely or used to advance one's career. Maybe sex had risks, from disease and violence to heartbreak and jealousy. Maybe looking at an endless parade of strangers having increasingly specific types of sex online was affecting our ability to enjoy sex in real life. Plus, family structures had changed starting in the 1970s: there was an increase in divorce, single-parent families, and women in the workplace, a decrease in community involvement. If women just kept their legs together, gay people stayed in the closet, and everyone stopped jacking off, evangelicals reasoned, we could get back to how things were in the 1950s.

But there are two issues with this argument, besides the underlying assumption that the social norms of the 1950s are an ideal to which we can and should return. First, evangelicals were ardent supporters of a deregulated free market, which led to exactly the sort of sexual liberalism they despised. Both sex and novelty sell, and under capitalism the once outré becomes normal. Second, the effects of a deregulated free market that took hold in the '70s and accelerated during the '80s and '90s—deindustrialization, falling wages, mass incarceration—likely undermined the stability of the American family far more than seminude pop stars, gay rights, birth control, abortion, or internet porn. To me, it doesn't seem like a coincidence that purity culture arose shortly after these changes began. Purity culture was a conservative coping mechanism for a society spinning out of control. But what conservatives refused to see was that they helped set it spinning in the first place.

The Unitarians saw the evangelical project as one led by backward, intolerant yokels. I mean Unitarians both specifically and as a kind of metonym: what I experienced in OWL overlapped with the cultural norms of elite college campuses and certain online spaces. The UU church functions as a social club for liberals who like putting bumper stickers on their Subarus, the types of people who tell you they believe in *science*, who are squeamish about the fact that most religious services include prayer and discussions of God and maybe even days of fasting and atonement. Many adults who become UU grow up in other religions, experiencing faith as blunt force trauma: shame, rigid gender roles, misinformation or just outright silence about sex. A disproportionate number of UU members, at least back then, were LGBTQ: UU was one of the first religious institutions to affirm openly LGBTQ people and allow them into the ministry.

And so the UU church—and most especially OWL—operates as a kind of socially liberal reaction to the Christian right. But the organization is a closed circuit. Most Americans are not UU and never will be. In fact, most Americans have probably never even heard of UUism, except maybe from a handful of national news stories about this crazy church that teaches a sex ed class for teens. And so, any project operating within the institution's confines will have trouble making inroads outside of it. It will certainly never be able to take on a well-funded operation like conservative Christianity, though even that political bloc has fallen into disarray since its apex in the early 2000s.

While researching this book I came across a piece from a 2005 issue of *UU World* magazine, written by a physician and OWL facilitator named Cynthia Kuhn, based in the abstinence-only stronghold of North Carolina.

"UU parents should feel proud that their kids, by participating in OWL, are the smartest kids on the block about these issues," she writes. "Teaching our kids about safe, mutually respectful sexual behavior in the context of our value system, I believe, is indeed nothing less than saving the world."

Kids should learn about safe, mutually respectful sexual behavior (although I think how and when is an open question). Internet porn, hypersexual pop culture, and conflicting information on sex that varies wildly in its factual accuracy make this all the more important. But I'm skeptical that learning comprehensive sex ed will *save the world*. And thinking that it will displays a kind of smugness that might blind a person to their own impact on that world, including with their sexual partners. I believe that mutually respectful sexual behavior requires humility. How can you be humble when you're convinced you're the smartest kid on the block?

Sometimes a cigar is just a cigar. But sex is often about more than just sex. Sexual desire can feel uncontrollable, thrilling, and even frightening, causing us to act and think in ways we otherwise wouldn't—say, going into chat rooms to meet strange men or masturbating in a closet next to a hamper of dirty laundry. Most important, sex is something we do with our bodies, and we all have those. That fact makes sex appear far easier to control than large, abstract concepts like *technology* or *politics* or *the economy*. During times of technological and political and economic upheaval—like the Y2K Era—it seems that if we can only impose our preferred sexual ethic on the world, we can fix everything.

But, returning to Ludacris, that's just a fantasy.

Larry Summers Caused My Eating Disorder

IT HAS BEEN CALLED THE GREATEST FASHION EDITORIAL of all time. Photographed by Annie Leibovitz, presided over by Grace Coddington, and set up with the help of hundreds of workers at the Louis XIV folly garden outside Paris, the December 2003 *Vogue* feature stars Natalia Vodianova as Alice in Wonderland. Thirteen of the era's greatest designers make appearances as well, as various characters in the story.

It opens with the only black-and-white picture, where Olivier Theyskens plays Lewis Carroll himself, photographing Natalia as the real Alice, Carroll's prepubescent muse. She reclines in cascading Rochas ruffles, her eyes staring straight at us. From there, the rest is in color: Tom Ford as the White Rabbit, John Galliano the Queen of Hearts, Jean Paul Gaultier the Cheshire Cat. Natalia wears a dazzling array of dresses that emphasize her ice-blue eyes. She falls down the rabbit hole in a cerulean satin gown from YSL Rive Gauche. She turns to the camera, scowling with concern, having grown so large that she fills up a room, her bare legs folded close to her body, echoing the pleats in her azure Helmut Lang minidress. In a field with Karl Lagerfeld, she holds a piglet and wears powder-blue Chanel and thigh-high white leather boots.

In each photo, that look of concern, counterposed against the fine chiffon and satin and organza. It's those eyes, really, that make it, showing surprise and delight. Though the model is twenty-one, her gaze is not the confident, sexy gaze of a woman with breasts and hips, but the naughty fear and boredom and surprise of a child who has not yet developed secondary sex characteristics. And she has the face of an angel: the blue, the blond.

"Natalia had to be Alice because somehow she just was Alice," Grace Coddington would say on a *Vogue* podcast two decades later.

Natalia's Aliceness was not just her stature and her coloring but also her backstory. Four years earlier, in 1999, she was seventeen and living in her hometown of Nizhny Novgorod, Russia. She shared an apartment with an older boyfriend who worked as a model/debt collector. She sold fruit on the street to support her mother and disabled sister.

"I remember no food sometimes," she said of her upbringing. "Every day I would have to wake up and survive that particular day and I would never look into the future. I would never look into what is going to happen in a week."

When a casting call came to town, her boyfriend insisted she go. She didn't own a miniskirt, so she cut up a long skirt with a pair of scissors borrowed from her mom. In that big room amid all that pale Slavic flesh, a casting agent selected *her* to go to Paris. She went, learned English on the way, and that was that.

In the late 1990s and 2000s, there were many such stories: young girls plucked from the ash heap of the former Soviet Union and catapulted onto runways and into ads for Calvin Klein Euphoria. Natalia Vodianova was among the most successful, alongside Sasha Pivovarova and Natasha Poly, who the fashion press called "the Russian supers," "the Russian mafia," or simply "the Russians." They were young, blond, and shockingly thin, with sharp hips, gaping rib cages, and barely any muscle to pad their arm and leg bones. The look of their bodies was angular and hard, their faces hollow and gaunt. As Karl Lagerfeld said, "No one wants to see curvy women."

At the turn of the twenty-first century, these women from the former Soviet Union constituted over 50 percent of runway models in Paris and Milan. Fashion scouts traveled from the steppes to the taiga, scouring every postindustrial city and crumbling housing bloc and onion-domed agricultural town for the next girl.

"Voronezh, Karaganda, Alma Ata, Rostov, Minsk—these are the great wells of beauty, raw girl crude to be pumped and refined," wrote British-Ukranian journalist Peter Pomerantsev.

The girls were prized for their paleness, their blondeness, their thinness, their very young age.

"If you catch the girl at twelve, then you have more power or more influence to guide and direct," a model scout explained in the 2012 documentary *Girl Model*.

Most of all, post-Soviet models were prized for their desperation. Casting call after casting call, teen girls lined up by the thousands, in swimsuits and underwear and ad hoc miniskirts, hoping to be the next Natalia, hoping to wire money back to their families to cover food and rent and medical care. A few of these girls would be picked, would be flown to New York or Paris or Tokyo or Milan. Fewer still would become wealthy. Mostly they would remain anonymous, crammed into tiny model apartments, racking up debt to their agencies. Far away from home for the first time, they would sign contracts in English, a language they couldn't read, and the only thing they would know is that if they gained a centimeter in their waist, their contract would be terminated but they'd still have to pay off their debt. It was this set of conditions that made "the Russians" so pliable, so flexible, so easy for agents and casting directors and photographers and designers and creative directors to work with. It was this set of conditions that encouraged them to eat cotton balls and tissues to keep down their weight. And it was this set of conditions that made them so very desirable as models.

ON CHRISTMAS DAY 1991, the Kremlin lowered the Soviet flag for the very last time. Up went the new tricolor, overseen by President Boris Yeltsin, leader of the newly established Russian Federation. It was supposed to be a joyous occasion, a door closing on an era of censorship and gulags and secret police. The Cold War could finally end, and the ever-present fear of nuclear annihilation gripping the globe for the previous four decades could finally end, too.

After the New Year, in 1992, Yeltsin got to work. He lifted price controls, cut pensions and public programs, and oversaw a fire sale of the country's publicly held assets, creating a new class of billionaire oligarchs and kleptocrats like Vladimir Putin. Yeltsin's vice president called the plan "economic genocide," but the president was undeterred. Prices rose with hyperinflation, and tens of millions of Russians were forced into poverty as the country underwent an economic downturn that may have been worse than the Great Depression. Life expectancy plummeted as Russians drank themselves to death, overdosed on heroin, and died by suicide.

These policies were helped along by the Harvard Boys. This group of well-connected quants included Andrei Shleifer, David

---

* By 1994, consumer prices were 2,000 times what they had been in 1990.

Lipton, Jonathan Hay, and Jeffrey Sachs, head of the eponymous consulting firm. It also included, crucially, Larry Summers: Bill Clinton's deputy US Treasury secretary (later Treasury secretary), former chief economic adviser for the World Bank, and the future president of Harvard. All were affiliated with the Harvard Institute for International Development, which helped guide the creation of Russia's new economic plan. The advice from the Harvard Boys to the Russian government seemed to be: keep up the looting.* And so billions of dollars kept disappearing into the pockets of the emergent oligarch class, as more and more Russians struggled to afford food, watching their jobs and their pensions disappear.

Joseph Stiglitz was one of the few members of the Clinton administration who disagreed with Summers, on Russia and other matters.

"The people in Russia who believed in shock therapy were . . . a few people at the top that rammed it down everybody's throat," Joseph Stiglitz told *The Progressive* in 2000. "They viewed the democratic process as a real impediment to reform. The grand larceny that occurred in Russia, the corruption that resulted in nine or ten people getting enormous wealth through loans-for-shares, was condoned because it allowed the reelection of Yeltsin."

But alas, poor Joseph was swept away by the tides of history. History, in fact, was now over, as evidenced by the fall of the Soviet Union. Mikhail Gorbachev was making Pizza Hut commercials. There was no time but now and no way of living but this one. This way of living was called *neoliberalism*—though I wouldn't learn that word until much later—and it meant that in

---

* Semi-relatedly, federal prosecutors filed a lawsuit against Shleifer and Hay in 2000, accusing them of defrauding the US government for the sake of personal enrichment. According to the *New York Times*, a settlement was reached in 2005, wherein they each paid up to $2 million.

this twenty-first-century world we were all free now, free of the ghosts of the nineteenth and twentieth centuries, of their musty old wars and their tired old struggles between labor and capital, free of regulations and social programs that interfered with the market. This was, of course, the best of all possible worlds, and if you didn't succeed here it was your own fault. We lived in an eternal present. And in this world, this eternal now, the only way to be beautiful was to look like Natalia or Sasha or Natasha.

I HAVE LOVED fashion magazines for as long as I can remember, which means as far back as 1991.* My parents would never buy them, but I gazed longingly at their covers in the checkout line at Giant. And my nana had them, and when we'd visit her condo for Chinese food on Sundays I'd flip through the glossy pages, smelling the folded-over perfume samples, looking at all the pretty pictures of Linda Evangelista and Claudia Schiffer and Naomi Campbell by Herb Ritts and Ellen von Unwerth and Patrick Demarchelier; at all the pretty clothes by Dior and Gucci and Chanel by John Galliano and Tom Ford and Karl Lagerfeld.

When I first started with *Vogue* and *W*, I didn't know any of those names. Still in preschool, I couldn't even read. I just liked the rhinestones and pinstripes and color-blocked spandex, and I liked the pretty ladies, and I hoped that when I was grown up I, too, would wear lipstick and high heels, gaze longingly over my shoulder, let my breasts spill over my corset, and kick my toned legs in the air as I lay on my back. It wasn't until a decade later— middle school, high school—that I began to take a deeper interest

---

* It only recently occurred to me that my consciousness began the same year the Soviet Union collapsed.

in what I was looking at. I bought my own magazines. I learned the names of the models and the photographers, the houses and their creative directors. I learned words like *shirring* and *epaulettes* and *prêt-a-porter*. I learned to recognize Anna Wintour and Grace Coddington and everyone else who decided what—and who— would be in those magazines, who lined the front row at New York Fashion Week and penned missives about how Alber Elbaz was redefining classic silhouettes at Lanvin or whatever. And at that time, Anna and Grace had decided that, as far as models went, "the Russian supers" were in.

At the same time, I was coming into awareness of my own body. "The John Berger thing," I call it now, referring to the way the late British art critic wrote, in *Ways of Seeing*, that "a woman must continually watch herself." She must never let down her guard, she must "survey herself continually," imagining herself as a man would see her, "because how she appears to men, is of crucial importance for what is normally thought of as the success of her life. Her own sense of being in herself is supplanted by a sense of being appreciated as herself by another."

I felt this bifurcated sense of self as a wound, as a burden that arrived with my period and 9/11 and the end of childhood. As a child I thought myself no different from a boy (and I was taught as much by my second-wave-feminist mother). I played in the dirt and sat with my legs apart. I was always on the left side of the bell curve at the pediatrician's office, in part because my genes predisposed me to thinness, and in part because I rarely had much of an appetite. At one point, the doctor told my mom I was *too* thin, and so I was given whole milk and extra servings of cookie dough ice cream. But I never worried about what I ate or what I looked like, because I did not think of myself as a body. I just was.

But that didn't last. In seventh grade, an eighth grader named Kyle told me he wouldn't sit next to me on the crowded school bus because I was ugly. Amir said, "Ooh, that was cold!" and Stephanie said it was mean, but she twirled her hair and giggled while she said it, smiling back at Kyle. I didn't say anything back because it felt like a trap where anything you said would sound stupid in response.

I had been called a lot of mean things before, but "ugly" was a new one. That night I locked myself in the bathroom and stood in front of the mirror naked, trying to figure out what was wrong with my prepubescent, twelve-year-old body. It must be my stupid brown hair or my bushy eyebrows or my gross dark circles or my disgusting stomach "fat" (that was, in hindsight, mostly a result of my slouched posture pushing my abdomen forward). Maybe it was the fat, because "fat" and "ugly" were the same thing. But I wasn't fat. I was skinny with a fat stomach. I puzzled over how to categorize my flaws. In the mirror that night, I tried to see myself as Kyle had. I've never really stopped.

That experience, strangely, did not change my relationship with food (or, if it did, the change came much later). When I was fourteen and in high school and no longer bullied, I began, for the first time, to develop a real appetite. I discovered that eating could really feel good, that it could break up my boredom, that it could sooth my sorrow. I finally finished growing, hitting five-three and surpassing 110 pounds, then 115, then 120. I finally developed breasts and hips. I was not fat, of course, but I was no longer thin. I was now, according to my pediatrician, an average weight for my height.

In the winter of 2004, when I was fifteen, I decided to go on a diet. I thought it would be a fun thing to try. But I also had this sense, under the surface, that I wanted to be skinny again. When I had been skinny I had been special. I stood out on the charts that compared me to all the other kids. Average seemed okay for other people, but for me it felt like throwing away a windfall of money.

I needed all the help I could get. Everyone was starting to talk about college, which compounded the list of things I found lacking in my self-inventory. In middle school my grades had fallen from stellar to mediocre to occasionally failing, staying there despite the attempted interventions of tutors and therapists. I could never remember when anything was due, I couldn't motivate myself to start assignments, and my dyscalculia was causing me to fall severely behind in math and science. I was terrified about my future after high school.

But thinness, I recognized, was currency. It might not get me into college, but I saw that it was socially prized. All the magazines talked about how to lose weight and get toned, praising celebrities who did these things and criticizing celebrities who didn't. Adults would greet each other by saying "You look great!" then launch into the minutiae of their weight loss plans: Atkins diet, South Beach diet, Weight Watchers, personal trainer. The only women allowed on TV were thin, even if they were journalists with advanced degrees. Most of the women I babysat for were thin, too. Their college degrees didn't matter because they stayed at home in well-appointed houses with their kids. Once, one of them told me I should marry a rich man. She didn't say exactly that, but I knew what she meant. Because of all this, I had an inchoate idea that, if I could be skinny again, somewhere along the way I could exchange it for something real.

By the summer of 2004 my life ran on a tight schedule of my own making. I exercised at least six days a week, often twice a day: swim practice, cross-country conditioning or practice, DVDs of yoga and Tae Bo and Pilates. I tried to eat no more than 1,200 calories per day. I consumed dried apricots, plain almonds, bone-less, skinless chicken breasts, skim milk, Kashi cereal, Luna Bars, baby spinach, low-fat dressing, low-fat cheese, low-fat yogurt, Wasa crackers, peanut butter, bananas, apples, blueberries, rasp-berries, Arnold's whole grain bread, Splenda, Fruit$_2$O, Diet Coke. I did not consume full-fat anything, sweets of any kind, avoca-dos. Sometimes I challenged myself to go below 1,200 if I could. I would do 800, 700, maybe even 600 if I had the willpower. I'd swap my meal for a Luna Bar (200 calories) or I'd sleep through it (0 calories).

I dropped 15 pounds and got down to 110. When I really starved myself I could get down to 107. This frustrated me. I wanted to be 100, that nice round number, the same as an A+. I felt good. I mean that in the moral sense. I felt the way I felt when I heard my parents speak of the importance of budgeting, of not indulging, of investing your money, of never, ever, ever racking up credit card debt like *some* people did, buying cars and clothes they couldn't afford. I felt the way I felt on the rare occasion I got good grades. I felt clean and competitive, like maybe I could get into—if not Stanford—at least Middlebury or Amherst. I felt like maybe I could win in this terrible war of all against all that I found myself conscripted into just because I was born after the neoliberal turn.

The adult world was ruled by metrics, it seemed: weight, money, grades, statistics. To grow up was to become a manager of num-bers, to keep your grades and bank deposits and credit score and calorie expenditures high and your bank withdrawals and calorie intake and weight low. It wasn't good enough to just be thin. You had to be the thinnest, just like you had to have the highest GPA, do the most clubs, get the best SAT scores. If you did those things, maybe you could get into the best college, which meant maybe you could get the best job. Because in this new world there wasn't room for everybody to succeed. There were only a few spots reserved for the very best, and if you didn't make the cut, that was your fault.

I would compare myself to other girls at school, and to girls in the pro-ana and thinspo communities I followed on LiveJournal. I could never go without food for a full day like some of those girls seemed to be able to do. I was very thin, but I was never at a dangerous BMI like my friend Elena, who had to be hospitalized, or Katie, who was one of the best runners on my cross-country team but kept passing out during races. No, to my shame even now, I wasn't disciplined enough for that level of starvation.

Junior year I started binging. One day I came home from school, lightheaded and exhausted as always, and there in the pantry was a box of chocolate bars. They were Symphony bars; I think my mom and brother had purchased them on a Boy Scout trip to Hersheypark. I was overtaken by something and against my will, I ate. And when I ate I was nourished as I had not been in months. I ate more, satiated now, but overtaken by the shame of having eaten.

To call what I felt shame or even self-hatred feels insufficient. "A prison of the mind" more accurately describes the feeling that took over the next two years of my life. I thought only of how disgusting I was and how I might repent. I thought of my body and my calorie intake and my binges and my purges at all times, even in class when we were reading *The Great Gatsby*, even in my dreams, even when watching *Napoleon Dynamite*. The highest virtue seemed to be self-control and I seemed to have none. Or perhaps I had it, but my moments of lapse were so extreme that it all broke even.

I would come home from school and eat bread and Nutella and peanut butter until I got sick. I would eat cheesecake and fudge brownies and Phish Food ice cream. I would eat containers of guacamole and slice after slice of Monterey Jack. I would punish myself with starvation and exercise. I needed to eat the Nutella because I hurt so badly. I hurt so badly because I ate the Nutella. I hurt because I hated school, I hated how it felt to be ranked, my wholeness dissected into statistics and put in competition with my classmates' just like my body had been. I hated thinking about applying to colleges.

My mom thought it was the magazines. And it's true that media exposure can contribute to eating disorder development. A 2003 paper from the *Journal of Paediatrics and Child Health* noted that "media exposure predicted disordered eating symptomology, drive for thinness, body dissatisfaction and ineffectiveness in women." It also found that "several cross-sectional studies have reported a positive association between exposure to beauty and fashion magazines and an increased level of weight concerns or eating disorder symptoms in girls," and that during the previous two decades, the body ideal for women had become significantly thinner over time. A 2004 study from the *International Journal of Eating Disorders* also found that "body size for fashion models decreased significantly during the 1980s and 1990s," and another study from the same year and publication said that "exposure to thin-ideal magazine images increased body dissatisfaction, negative mood states, and eating disorder symptoms and decreased self-esteem." During the period from 2000 to 2018, the prevalence of eating disorders—especially among girls and women—increased significantly among adults, children, and adolescent populations in America, Europe, Asia, and Australia, according to a 2019 systematic literature review in the *American Journal of Clinical Nutrition*.

My mom also thought it was the result of my being insufficiently feminist, of the "backlash" she was always going on and on about, that I wished she'd shut up about because I'd never read Susan Faludi and didn't want to.

But it was never about media or feminism, at least not primarily. It was me looking out at the brutal world being created around me and realizing that I needed all the help I could get. I was a child coming into this world, and I was learning my lessons. If adults didn't want me to develop an eating disorder, they shouldn't have made a world where I felt it was necessary. I was just following their rules. "You're so observant," my mom would always say to me in praise.

Neoliberalism, I would later learn, is obsessed with the term *lean*. *Lean* is part of what critic John Patrick Leary calls "late capitalist body talk," alongside words like *flexible* and *nimble*.

Nimble and *flexible* mean that you bend the ways you are told to bend, jump the ways you are told to jump, pose the ways you are told to pose. When the photographer Terry Richardson cavorts naked around photo sets and waggles his dick in your face—as one model would later allege—you do what he tells you, because there is no guarantee that if you don't you will keep working, and you must take responsibility for yourself and your debts to your modeling agency, for yourself and your family back in Russia.*

Lean imagines the firm and the self as "a disciplined, practiced body": you make do with less, you maximize your effort and productivity, you do two people's jobs for the same pay. *Lean* imagines the nation this way, too, and so the policies it promotes are

---

* I wonder if it's a coincidence that one of the first people to speak up about Richardson's workplace behavior was Danish model Rie Rasmussen. If Rasmussen were to get blackballed, she could return to a country that provides universal free health care, universal unemployment compensation, free college, state-subsidized childcare, a guaranteed retirement pension from the government, and extensive labor protections, including a mandatory twenty-four weeks of paid parental leave (per parent) and five weeks of paid vacation per year. Her parents back home are entitled to these benefits as well, meaning that—unlike many Russian or even American models' families—they would not have been reliant on her modeling income to pay for food or medical care.

austerity: cutting social programs, cutting infrastructure funding, reducing deficits. Reduce, reduce, reduce. It is economic anorexia.

IN COLLEGE I took a break from reading *Vogue*, mostly because I was trying to get over my eating disorder. I was tired of living like that, and I was ready to try anything to free myself. I figured maybe the studies were right. Plus, I *was* getting into feminism, though thanks more to the internet than my mom. Instead of compulsively reading magazines to learn about fashion and pop culture, I compulsively read about fashion and pop culture on *Jezebel* and *Feministing*, along with posts about racial justice and prison abolition and the problems with capitalism.

But things were changing at *Vogue*, too. I saw it every time I picked up an issue at the airport or the nail salon. By the mid-2010s, Ashley Graham, Kim and Kanye, and Serena Williams were getting covers. Thinness still dominated the editorials, but not exclusively, and there were Black models and Asian models and Indigenous models and trans models and nonbinary models. In 2021, Yumi Nu and Ariel Nicholson were the cover girls—the first plus-size Asian American and the first trans model, respectively. Inside, too, there was an attempted reticence to glorify thinness, white-ness, or any other -ness you could think of. There was contrition about the barriers the fashion world itself had erected to keep out anyone other than thin, white, young, blond women. There were post–MeToo apologies for the sexual harassment and assault en-abled by the fashion industry. In 2017, Condé Nast International announced they would no longer hire Terry Richardson (his most recent shoot for American *Vogue* was in 2010).

The Y2K Era—1997 through 2008—was defined by the convic-tion that politics were no longer relevant. When the 2008 financial crisis brought on the Great Recession, it felt like a dam bursting. The consensus of the post–Cold War neoliberal order was underwater, and politics now suffused every aspect of culture. This isn't to say that a new consensus surfaced, or that good things happened. Quite the contrary. That era consisted of a series of escalating and intersecting crises that show no signs of abating. But the unanimous belief that politics were over and humanity had reached its apex in a brutal form of American-led capitalism was quite obviously disproven.

There was an openness toward new ideas and new aesthetics, and in came internet feminism, the body positivity movement, trans rights activism, disability rights activism, Indigenous rights activism, Occupy Wall Street, Black Lives Matter, and, later, internet socialism. In 2021, artist Precious Okoyomon coined the term "anorexic white supremacy" to describe the most prized body type of the Y2K Era. With three words, Okoyomon encapsulated everything I've spent the past twenty years trying to make sense of. Social justice movements and tendencies primed the reading public to be less receptive to anorexic white supremacy, and magazines like *Vogue* were forced to respond. The tides of history were turning, at least at the level of marketing. Or perhaps it's just that fashion thrives on novelty. Consumers were simply bored of looking at gaunt blond women.

That hyper-political post-2008 era feels like it ended in 2020: first with the pandemic, then with the end of the Bernie campaign, and finally, with the end of the anti-police-violence protests that summer. Those protests were the largest, by attendance, in American history. And yet the only lasting results seemed to be the conviction of Derek Chauvin, some murals, some historical markers, and some press photos of Nancy Pelosi kneeling while wearing kente cloth.

A similar thing happened with MeToo. A lot of allegations were made, a lot of truths came to light, and Harvey Weinstein will probably spend the rest of his life in prison. There were some firings, some critical reevaluations of art and oeuvres, and a lot of discourse on social media. But were there any lasting structural changes to protect people from sexual violence? After MeToo, Brett Kavanaugh was still confirmed as a Supreme Court justice.

I sense a weariness about politics in others, and in myself. There is a perception that, despite these movements' moral righteousness, they largely failed. This feeling coincides, roughly, with the twenty-year anniversary of the Y2K Era, which means it's time for the nostalgia marketing cycle to kick in. But it also feels like this time, that cycle aligns perfectly with the moment's political mood. Politics are out again, just like they were when I was coming of age.

And now there are indications of the return of anorexic white supremacy as well. As Rachel Rabbit White has written, 2022 heralded the end of the (highly racialized) Brazilian butt lift. Kim Kardashian's butt shrank overnight,* and she gushed to the media about crash dieting to fit into her Met Gala dress. Around the same time, Miu Miu debuted a Y2K-inspired collection of low-rise pleated khaki miniskirts and cropped cable-knit sweaters, interspersed with a sound installation in which two white-coded women mock the BBL in a voiceover. The models cast in the show are a gaunt throwback, and the cut of the clothes emphasizes their small, flat waists and visible hip bones and femurs.

"The return of low-rise provokes an emotional response in those who lived through the early aughts heyday of normalized eating

---

* There has been much public speculation that Kim had the procedure, a claim Kim denies.

disorders and a pop culture that chastised women for their appearance," wrote Rachel Rabbit White. "Perhaps the updated part of the Y2K trend isn't the silhouette or the styling as much as the ways that these views can be hinted at."

Indeed, looking at these images makes me feel like a teenager again, forced back into that cycle of punishment and self-monitoring and comparison, forced back into that prison and that fear in a world of no alternatives, a world where I'm all on my own and everything is my fault.

On the post-left podcast *Red Scare*, hosts Dasha and Anna—both first-generation immigrants from post-Soviet states—endorse anorexia with a wink, because thinness, more or less, is simply a higher way of being, a way of raising oneself above the fray. The Annas and Dashas of the world—like the late Karl Lagerfeld—would have you believe that accepting other types of bodies is a lowering of standards, a lie. After all, beauty and glamour are, by nature, exclusionary. John Berger said so himself.

These days I'm more or less at peace with my body. There are times when I think it's because of internet feminism, because of the broader cultural move away from anorexic white supremacy and toward body positivity. But maybe I'm also just aging. My body does not have the same market value it did when I was younger. Spending so much time on its maintenance does not feel worth the return on investment.

Sometimes I look back and I feel angry about how many hours I spent obsessing over my body as a teenager. I find myself consumed with fury at Anna Wintour and Grace Coddington and all the photographers and art directors and casting agents and designers who created what I understood beauty to be as a teenager. *They* put me in that prison of the mind, I think. Fashion and the media *gave me* my eating disorder.

This strikes me as myopic. Sure, everyone from Anna Wintour and Grace Coddington on down to designers, photographers, casting directors, model scouts, and more played a role in promoting extreme thinness and whiteness as the only kind of beauty allowed in fashion, and in hiring photographers like Terry Richardson. But no one at *Vogue* was at the controls, not in the ways that mattered most. That was happening in conference rooms where no one had heard of Olivier Theyskens. In those rooms, new markets were opened up. Interest rates were raised. Labor protections were lifted. Public services were privatized and welfare programs slashed. It was these decisions that gave us this world of all against all, which in turn gave us models like Natalia. The people who made that world were people like Larry Summers.* All Grace and Anna did was find the beauty in it.

I like to think that under a different economic system—a more equal one, a fairer one, a safer one—there would be different kinds of beauty, the pursuit of which would not create such extreme psychological and bodily suffering. Or perhaps there would be the same kinds of beauty, the same psychological and bodily suffering, but the stakes would be lower.

But then I wonder if the high stakes and the suffering are part of the allure. Perhaps when I look at Natalia, what I see is not beauty at all, but what conservative philosopher Edmund Burke called "the sublime": a mixture of fear and awe brought on by that which has the power to destroy.

If you're on the wrong end of the capitalist world system—which is most of us, whether or not we're in the post-Soviet states—you can become an ultrathin supermodel or die on the streets selling fruit. That's lovely, in a way, the terror of it all.

---

* Though even he was, perhaps, only a man for his time.

They Misunderestimated Me

H EY, LISTEN TO THIS," MY DAD CALLED, LOOKING UP from his computer.

My mom padded over and my dad read aloud:

"'You know there's a problem when there's a Bush, a Dick, and a Colin in the White House!'"

They both had a good laugh about that one.

The early 2000s were a difficult time for good suburban liberals like my parents. The US had recently invaded Iraq under false pretenses, an act which would contribute significantly to the 4.5 million killed in the Global War on Terror. When the government of France sided with the United Nations against the 2003 invasion, french fries in three congressional cafeterias were rebranded as "freedom fries," a change that remained through 2006. Tom Ridge—secretary of the brand-new Department of Homeland Security—appeared on television with a color-coded chart indicating the likelihood of impending terrorist attacks. The levels were as follows:

Green—LOW—Low risk of terrorist attacks

Blue—GUARDED—General risk of terrorist attacks

Yellow—ELEVATED—Significant risk of terrorist attacks

Orange—HIGH—High risk of terrorist attacks

Red—SEVERE—Severe risk of terrorist attacks

It was unclear exactly how the likelihood of terrorist attacks was determined, or how, say, "high risk" differed from "severe risk," but terror predictions became as routine as the weather forecast.

Meanwhile, well-funded evangelical groups made inroads bringing their theory of "intelligent design" to public-school science curricula across the country. Intelligent design claimed, among other things, that evolution was impossible and that the earth was six thousand years old. And in 2004, Democratic presidential candidate John Kerry put on camouflage and awkwardly traipsed around a goose blind in a desperate attempt to convince voters that he was a red-blooded American man—not, as his well-funded Republican opponents claimed, an effete draft dodger. Yes, this was all very silly. But if you weren't with the Republicans in the early 2000s, it felt like you were at best a loser and at worst a traitor.

One of my parents' favorite copes was to forward each other anti-Bush emails. I think this one came from my dad's younger sister, a tenured professor of social sciences living in Canada who never missed an opportunity to mock him for continuing to reside in what she saw as a doomed, reactionary, and idiotic nation, a nation for which George W. Bush was the consummate leader.

If you didn't live through the Y2K Era, it may be hard to believe that people routinely read these types of emails, let alone forwarded them to their contacts. But forwarded messages were quite popular in the early days of the internet. Most had nothing to do with politics. There were webcomics, dancing hamsters, dancing babies. There were Bible verses and jokes, cute puppies and song lyrics, prayers and entreaties to ~*~FORWARD THIS MESSAGE FOR GOOD LUCK~*~. Among my middle school cohort, surveys were especially popular: you'd answer a list of questions about everything from your favorite song and the most recent thing you ate to your earliest memory and the last thing that made you cry.

But as the Bush administration stumbled on, a lot of the forwarded content turned political. The current Twitter account "G.W. Bush-era Leftism" (@DubyaEraLeft) compiles such digital ephemera. There are jerky flash cartoons of the aforementioned Bush, Dick, and Colin, alongside Donald Rumsfeld, John Ashcroft, Tom Ridge, and Condoleezza Rice. There are proto-memes made with Photoshop. In one, a photo of the president is captioned "INSTANT ASSHOLE: JUST ADD OIL." In another, from bushspeaks.com, the president shreds the US Constitution on the Resolute desk.

This content was forwarded in emails, and it also got passed around on the nascent liberal blogosphere. This collection of blogs—Talking Points Memo, Daily Kos, Wonkette, Crooked Timber, Firedoglake, and Pandagon, among others—created an outlet for fellow frustrated liberals. It also spawned a generation of media figures including Josh Marshall, Ezra Klein, Markos Moulitsas, Ana Marie Cox, Matt Yglesias, and Amanda Marcotte. Most of these people were younger than my parents—Gen X, or even older millennials—but their posts influenced the political climate online and off. The inaugural Netroots Nation* conference was held in Las Vegas in 2006 so that liberals and progressives from the blogosphere could connect in person.

And then there were the bumper stickers. They decorated the cars in the parking lot of our Unitarian Universalist church. They said things like *War Is Not the Answer*; *Bush Lied, Soldiers Died*; and *Somewhere in Texas a Village Is Missing Its Idiot*. One popular sticker counted down to Bush's last day in office, reading *1/20/09: The End of an Error*. Another I remember—I think because my parents thought it was funny—is an inversion of a popular Bush-reelection sticker from 2004 that originally said *W: The President*. The liberal version said *M: The Moron*.

I found the tone of this stuff really embarrassing. I still do, twenty years later, despite the fact that hindsight has proved the George W. Bush administration to be at least as evil as its critics knew it was at the time. Anti-Bush products—both digital and physical—paved the way a decade later for a much larger industry of anti-Trump books, T-shirts, pussy hats, bumper stickers, and yard signs, most notably the IN THIS HOUSE WE BELIEVE signs that have become hallmarks of yards and windows in cosmopolitan cities, liberal suburbs, and college towns.

So, what is it about this stuff that people like my parents love, and what does it say about how they believe the world works?

I have a working theory. The Civil Rights Movement, Watergate, and the Vietnam War created a template in the minds of certain (usually white, usually professional-class or upper-class) liberal boomers of how change was made. Let's call it "The Template for How Change Works," or, for short, "The Template." First, the

---

* Then called Yearly Kos, before rebranding in 2007.

government does something wrong, like waging a twenty-year proxy war in Vietnam. The press bravely covers it, broadcasting images of self-evident injustice into living rooms across America. Americans of conscience realize they need to exercise their First Amendment rights and take to the streets in protest. They make signs with clever slogans. The government realizes they need to change whatever is making the citizenry so upset. A law gets passed or an executive order gets signed and—ta-da!—social change. When boomers looked back at the political struggles of their youth, they imagined that if they only copied and pasted those same strategies into the present moment, they would get the same results. Progress, after all, was a one-way street; things just kept getting better and better. They had seen it in their lifetimes!

The Template for the war in Iraq starts with the presumption that the primary function of the Fourth Estate in American society is to operate as a check on the government and corporations, speaking truth to power and serving the public interest. From a historical perspective, this is simply untrue: there was widespread yellow journalism during the late-nineteenth and early twentieth centuries. Most infamously, Americans supported an 1898 war with Spain over control of the Philippines, Puerto Rico, Cuba, and Guam because a popular newspaper made up a fake story about Spain bombing an American ship. It is true that during the Progressive Era "muckrakers" helped shift public opinion on things like workers' rights and food regulation. But an even more decisive factor for progressive legislation were the massive strikes and social unrest disrupting normal business operations. Progressivism was a movement that saved business from itself.

The Vietnam War was, in fact, defined by adversarial journalism. It was this experience that cemented the idea, for boomers, that the press would always expose the truth, would always stand on the right side of history. You had influential photographs like Nick Ut's "The Terror of War" (also known as "Napalm Girl"), Eddie Adams's "Saigon Execution," Larry Burrows's "Reaching Out," and John Filo's famous photo of the shootings at Kent State. Every evening Walter Cronkite provided commentary on the war to an audience of 29 million.

"We've been too often disappointed by the optimism of the American leaders," he said following the Tet Offensive. "It seems now more certain than ever, that the bloody experience of Vietnam is to end in a stalemate."

In contrast, Wolf Blitzer covered the Iraq War like he was covering the Olympics, oohing and ahhing over all the cool missiles that would soon be destroying Iraqi power stations and hospitals. And the *New York Times* wasn't publishing the new Pentagon Papers. Instead, they ran misinformation from government spokespeople, putting out articles about the existence of weapons of mass destruction in Iraq that turned out to be completely false.* Thomas Friedman—the paper's most popular columnist—told Charlie Rose that Iraqis "needed to see American boys and girls going house to house—from Basra to Baghdad—and basically saying: Suck on this."

The next step in The Template is protest. Leading up to the March 2003 invasion of Iraq, millions of people around the world attended thousands of protests to beg and plead the US not to do it. In the US, many of the protesters were the same kinds of liberals as my parents and the members of my Unitarian church. They

---

* In May 2004 (over a year after the initial invasion), the paper issued a mea culpa, stating that "we have found a number of instances of coverage that was not as rigorous as it should have been. In some cases, information that was controversial then, and seems questionable now, was insufficiently qualified or allowed to stand unchallenged." Oops.

believed that if we could just get that Bush, Dick, and Colin out of the White House, the country's problems would be immediately fixed. There was no analysis of American history and institutions that might reveal the problems to be more deeply rooted, perhaps even inherent to America itself.

Many other protesters were leftists of some stripe: young anarchist punks in black clothes, disheveled old Trotskyists, Catholic and Quaker antinuclear activists. Many of these people had previously participated in the alter-globalization movement. Unlike many liberals, they often had a deeper structural and historical understanding of the problems at hand. But the left, as is commonly acknowledged by those on the left, was at its weakest in those years. It was countercultural and often backward-looking, skeptical of its ability to do anything more than dissent from the margins. It skewed anarchist, meaning no one was cranking out white papers offering policy alternatives. There was no *Jacobin* magazine or Bernie campaign or Chapo Trap House. Most normal people didn't want anything to do with it.

A small minority of protesters believed in conspiracy theories like "9/11 truth," which held that the attacks were an "inside job." This belief was a kind of anti-politics most common among those who sensed the structural problems but lacked the actual facts. It was a belief system based on vibes and a sense of powerlessness, an incipient form of today's big tent conspiracy theories like QAnon.

Around the world, the anti–Iraq War protests were among the largest ever recorded. Marchers clogged the streets of New York and DC, London and Paris, Madrid and Rome and Beijing and Damascus and Melbourne. They held signs that said DON'T ATTACK IRAQ and NO WAR FOR OIL, signs with images of Bush riding a missile in a cowboy hat, of Bush on a wanted poster with Tony Blair. Protesters stood at intersections imploring drivers to honk for peace. They made puppets. They brought out the radical cheerleaders.

But the invasion went on as planned, protests or not. There was a lot of money to be made there. At least $138 billion in tax-payer money was handed to different contractors during the first decade of the war. Anyone driving through McMansion-filled DC suburbs like Great Falls, Virginia, or Potomac, Maryland, over the past twenty years can see for themselves just how profitable the War on Terror has been.

The final check on injustice in The Template is the legal system: the laws, the courts, the US Constitution. In this imagining, justice is meted out by a beautiful blindfolded lady. But laws are written and interpreted and enforced by people with agendas. After all, it was the courts that handed Bush the 2000 election. If you're the one holding power, you can not only write the laws, but you can say any existing law means whatever you want it to mean.

When the Supreme Court was doing all those progressive rulings in the mid-twentieth century, it was headed by back-to-back progressive chief justices: Earl Warren in 1953, then Warren Burger in 1969. When William Rehnquist took over in 1986 under Reagan, the Supreme Court took a hard right turn, helped along by the appointment of justices like Antonin Scalia and Clarence Thomas. But it was a U-turn, not a new direction. During the court's Lochner Era, which lasted from 1897 to 1937, it adjudicated aggressively in favor of corporations and against workers. Before that, in 1857, the Dred Scott decision ruled that Congress did not have the power to ban slavery in the US or its territories, and that Black people were not—and could never be—United States citizens.

During the George W. Bush administration liberals really, re-ally, really loved to talk about the Constitution, claiming it was they who truly valued it, not Republicans. In 2001, they attempted to respond to the growing influence of the Federalist Society and its constitutional originalism by founding their own club, which they called the American Constitution Society. "Oh heavens," they proclaimed. "Bush is shredding the Constitution on the Resolute desk!"

But maybe that wouldn't be such a bad thing. Law professors Ryan D. Doerfler and Samuel Moyn describe America's founding document as "famously undemocratic," noting that the Electoral College and the Senate are "impediments to redistributive change."

"It's difficult to find a constitutional basis for abortion or labor unions in a document written by largely affluent men more than two centuries ago," they wrote in the *New York Times* in 2022. "By leaving democracy hostage to constraints that are harder to change than the rest of the legal order, constitutionalism of any sort demands extraordinary consensus for meaningful progress."

Speaking of the law, the Civil Rights Movement is another touch point for the worldview of affluent white boomers. In the '90s and the 2000s they talked like the Civil Rights Movement fixed racism. We banned Jim Crow laws, we let nonwhite people vote, and we made sure that landlords and realtors could no longer explicitly discriminate against people based on race (just implicitly). What more do you people want?

Never mind that the Civil Rights Movement lost momentum not because it accomplished all its goals, but because its biggest leaders were assassinated. Martin Luther King was arguing, at the time of his death, that the next frontier of the Civil Rights Movement must be a universal jobs program and the end of American wars abroad.

And racist laws continued in a color-blind way. Reagan's War on Drugs set about devastating Black and brown communities—

already hurting from deindustrialization—through mass incarceration and over-policing. Bill Clinton continued the damage with his 1994 crime bill—which led to a 43 percent rise in the building of adult correctional facilities—and his 1996 welfare reform law, which in a decade increased the number of children in deep poverty by almost a million.

White liberal boomers love to quote Martin Luther King saying "The arc of the moral universe bends toward justice." This is very convenient and very comforting. The arc is going to bend either way! The idea of revanchism or reaction never occurs. Nor does the idea that for some people the unjust system is working really great, and any bending of the moral arc toward justice would constitute a significant loss.

THE TRUMP ADMINISTRATION saw anxious liberals returning again to The Template. There was the inability to process the fact that Trump could even be elected in the first place. That damn arc was supposed to be bending toward justice! What the hell was this?! Then came the plaintive and increasingly hysterical appeals to all the institutions to save us: the press, the people, the courts, the Constitution, the scientists, FBI Director Robert Mueller,* the generals, the "good Republicans."

Liberals fixated on Trump's shortcomings as if these weren't what his supporters liked about him: he was mendacious, hypocritical, stupid, racist, misogynistic. He was a sexual abuser and a bully. But two of these qualities most vexed liberals about Trump,

---

* Never mind the fact that the FBI spied on the anti-war and civil rights movements throughout the '60s, going as far as attempting to blackmail Martin Luther King into killing himself.

and these were identical to what bothered them about George W. Bush: his blatant lies and hypocrisy, and his lack of intelligence as evidenced by his speech patterns.

Bush lied, soldiers died, read the bumper sticker. The lies to which this slogan referred were that Saddam Hussein was illegally hiding weapons of mass destruction in Iraq, and that he was somehow connected to 9/11. Both points formed the basis of the US case for invading Iraq, even though they had been disproven again and again: first by UN weapons inspector Hans Blix, who tried in vain to tell the administration that he looked all over Iraq and there were no weapons to be found, and later by investigative journalists. But it didn't matter. What is objectively true or untrue is less important than the fact that the Bush administration understood how power works.

Nonetheless, fact-checking Bush's speeches became a boon for liberal outlets. In 2007, the *Washington Post* started their eponymous Fact Checker, which provides context for politicians' statements, analyzes them, and awards "Pinocchios" based on veracity. The service became huge during the 2016 presidential campaign and then during the Trump administration. Just about every media outlet got in on fact-checking the president. It was easy and reliable content.

The way Trump talked and the way Bush talked were different, but the way liberals reacted was similar. Trump's tendency was toward pompous and inscrutable bloviating that required a kind of dementia decoder ring to decipher. His speech was littered with superlative adjectives and half-finished anecdotes and misunderstandings and unpredictable digressions about his wealth or his popularity or his feud with Graydon Carter.

"I never understood wind," Trump characteristically told attendees at a Turning Point USA rally in 2019. "You know, I know windmills very much. I've studied it better than anybody I know."

Everyone learned the president's speech tics—"tremendous," "beautiful," "terrible," "more than anybody," "and I, by the way," "CHIY-nuh," "bye-bye"—and took turns impersonating him at parties. My imitation got a laugh every single time.

This is similar to the way that Bush's speech patterns were received during the previous decade. While Trump's oration made W look like Abraham Lincoln, the forty-third president did have a habit of misspeaking. For instance:

"Rarely is the question asked: Is our children learning?"

"I know how hard it is for you to put food on your family."

"I know the human being and fish can coexist peacefully."

"It'll take time to restore chaos."

"There's an old saying in Tennessee—I know it's in Texas, probably in Tennessee—that says, fool me once, shame on—shame on you. Fool me—you can't get fooled again."

"They misunderestimated me."

Bush also struggled to pronounce the word "nuclear," which was unfortunate because it came up a lot during his presidency. He pronounced it "nucular."

Liberals made hay of all this. So many of those Bush-era liberal bumper stickers referenced Bush's supposed stupidity.

And this all makes sense, because liberals pride themselves on valuing "intelligence," which to them means projecting a certain kind of highly credentialed affect. Despite both presidents having attended Ivy League schools, their unusual speech patterns endlessly bothered liberals because they lacked conventional grammar or word usage or a logical flow of ideas. But many of the people who liked George W. Bush and Donald Trump liked them precisely because they talked funny.

Of course, the biggest George W. Bush and Donald Trump supporters of all are rich people and very rich people and very, very rich people who want tax cuts. Most of these voters don't care about Bushisms or Pinocchios or hypocrisy or even the culture war. They would vote for a potato if they thought it would lower their taxes. Some of them have told me as much.

During the Trump administration I kind of dreaded going to independent bookshops, an activity I normally enjoyed. Inevitably, every single one would have a centrally located display of anti-Trump "resistance" merchandise. There would be book after book purporting to "expose" the president, as if he didn't do that to himself every single day. There were guides to understanding the Constitution and hardbound copies of *The Mueller Report*. There were T-shirts, mugs, stickers, baseball caps, and enamel pins that said *resist* and *nasty woman* and *feminist* and *everyone is welcome here* and *Black Lives Matter* and *grab them by the ballot*. There were puzzles commemorating the Women's March and prayer candles featuring Ruth Bader Ginsburg. The only positive thing was that otherwise-overlooked books of history or policy or theory or poetry that could somehow be promoted as being tangentially anti-Trump ended up on those tables as well.

Comedic children's books for adults became a booming sub-industry of the anti-Trump book racket. There was *Goodnight Trump*, a parody of *Goodnight Moon*; *A Child's First Book of Trump* by comedian Michael Ian Black; *Donald Trump and the Wig of Evil*; *A Is for Autocrat: A Trumpian Alphabet, Illustrated*; *F#@K Trump: An Anti Trump Coloring Book Featuring Satirical Trump Drawings*.

But perhaps the most glaring example was a book called *How the People Trumped Ronald Plump*, a children's book for adults by the Krassenstein brothers, a pair of twins in their thirties who parlayed replying to the president on Twitter into a short-lived media career. In their book, there is a talking squirrel who lives in Ronald Plump's hair named Weave Bannon, and a character named Loudimir Tootin who farts rockets. The most notable thing about *Ronald Plump* is that it features as its hero an alarmingly buff and shirtless Robert Mueller, who wears an American flag necktie and extremely tight black pants.

The precedent for *Ronald Plump* and other "funny" children's books about Trump is arguably *Good Night Bush: A Parody*. Published in early 2008 by two former Donald Rumsfeld staffers who met while working at a dot-com company, the book is the original political rewrite of the children's bedtime classic. The bunny protagonist is replaced by George W. Bush in a flight suit, and the "little old lady whispering hush" is Dick Cheney holding a shotgun (a reference to the time the vice president accidentally shot an acquaintance in the face on a 2006 hunting trip). The mouse is recast as Osama bin Laden, escaping capture throughout the book. "Three little bears sitting on chairs" become "three war profiteers giving cheers." You get the idea. By the end of the book a scale balancing "church and state" is tipped toward "church" and the Constitution is covered in crayon.

Good Night Bush found shelf space alongside plenty of other anti-Bush books that came out between the president's inauguration in January 2001 and his departure from office in January 2009. These books promised to expose or criticize or make fun of the president, or presented an expert opinion on his supposedly unique psychology (*Bush on the Couch*), or proposed slightly less harsh Democratic alternatives to Republican-led policies like the Iraq War and the PATRIOT Act and indefinite detention at Guantánamo Bay. In a preview of the Trump Era, the fact that there were so many fake children's books here was supposed to be a kind of commentary on the childishness of Republicans and the fact that Democrats are "the adults in the room." But instead it hints at something developmentally stunted and Freudian—perhaps the desire for a mommy to read you a bedtime story and tuck you in and tell you everything will be okay, because the arc of the universe bends toward justice. Or for a strapping, shirtless daddy in a superhero cape to rescue you from the big, bad orange man. So much of liberal politics amounts to yelling "Mooooom! Daaaaaad! He's cheating!" But even as a child myself, I could see that no one was coming to save us.

IN THE LATE spring of 2004, my mom was driving me to swim practice. On NPR, they talked about the Abu Ghraib torture scandal, which recently broke on CBS News. The host soberly described various types of "advanced interrogation techniques" performed on detainees at the American prison in Iraq: the beatings, the electrocutions, the stress positions, the dog attacks, the sexual abuse. Since the beginning of the War on Terror there had been allegations of torture, but the photos out of Abu Ghraib confirmed it.

I changed the station to 92Q. J-Kwon was playing.

> Now errbody in the club gettin' tipsy!
> Errbody in the club gettin' tipsy!

"Hey!" my mom said. "Change it back. This is history, Colette."

Back on NPR they spoke as calmly as always. They said that there were investigations and maybe there would be trials. They described the procedures and how these would be followed. An expert came on to talk about human rights law. You were supposed to be very mad about this if you were a person like my mom.

But mad for what? When in my life had I seen paying attention to the news or getting mad or protesting or going to court do anything to stop what seemed like the inevitable rule of bad over good? I had seen the election stolen and I had seen us go into Iraq on falsified evidence despite millions of people showing up to protest. I had seen the government surveil its citizens and detain them indefinitely at Guantánamo Bay. I had never in my life seen justice occur. Why would this time be any different?

I switched the station back to J-Kwon.

As in Vietnam, there was a famous photo that defined the Abu Ghraib torture scandal and, by extension, the Iraq War. It was taken, like all the Abu Ghraib photos, not by journalists but by the soldiers themselves. In the photo, Ali Shallal al-Qaisi wears a black robe and black hood. His arms are outstretched like Christ's, and there are electrical wires attached to his fingers.

That day in the car at age fifteen, part of me kindled a secret hope that the al-Qaisi photo would become like "Napalm Girl," that it would itself bring an end to the war and the torture, that its very existence would set us on the proper path. Or, at the very least, I hoped that it would serve as a reminder for generations of Americans of what we had done.

According to a 2015 article from the *L.A. Times*, "few have faced consequences for Abu Ghraib." Some soldiers did jail time, most notably Lynndie England, who became the face of the scandal when some of the photos showed her grinning and giving the thumbs-up in front of groups of of naked prisoners forced into stress positions. But US-led torture continued around the world—including openly at Guantánamo Bay—with the blessing of Attorney Generals John Ashcroft and Alberto Gonzales, and Deputy Assistant Attorney General John Yoo, who had claimed that actually, the Constitution allowed it.

Recently, a professor I know who teaches history told me he showed that photo to his students. None of them knew what it was.

(Remix)

IN 1999, THE VIDEO FOR "BLING BLING" BY B.G., FEATURING the Big Tymers and the Hot Boys, first aired. In the video, the rappers appear with a range of luxury vehicles: a stretch Hummer limo, a regular Hummer, two Jaguars, a Lexus SUV, a Range Rover, a Corvette, two Honda motorbikes, a private helicopter. They lounge on a boat on Lake Pontchartrain with bikinied women. Other bikinied women gyrate outside a mansion. The rappers gesticulate at the camera to show off their watches, bracelets, pinkie rings, diamond studs, and diamond-encrusted platinum chains, their platinum teeth glinting. Cash is everywhere. There are briefcases full of it. They hold up banded stacks of it. They sit at a table set with ornate candelabras and silver bowls of the stuff, and they pick it up and they toss it, and they fan themselves with it, and they let it fall down as if it were nothing, littering the grass.

It's unclear which of these New Orleans–based rappers originally coined "bling bling," an onomatopoeic phrase to describe the visual effect of glittering diamonds. Maybe it was B.G., maybe it was Birdman, maybe it was Lil Wayne when he was still a teen and his voice had barely dropped. But "bling bling" became first the chorus and then the title of the breakout song off Cash Money Records, then quickly spread through popular culture* until old white people were using the word. In 2003, the *Oxford English Dictionary* added "bling bling" as a verb, noun, and adjective, by which point no respectable rapper was using it anymore. It went to the same linguistic graveyard as "phat," "bad," "bae," and other Black coinages killed by mass culture.

But "bling bling" lived on because it lent its name to a specific era of hip-hop spanning roughly ten years, from 1997 to 2008. During the Bling Era, hip-hop aesthetics ascended to a new level of excess (embodied by the "Bling Bling" video): iced-out chains, spinning rims, stacks of cash, Escalades. The Houston-based graphic design firm Pen & Pixel helped craft the look of the Bling Era, especially in the South. During this time, the gravitational center of rap reoriented from New York and Los Angeles to Atlanta, with satellites in New Orleans, Houston, Miami, Memphis, Virginia Beach, and St. Louis. Pen & Pixel's album covers were unabashedly maximalist, including as many of the following elements as possible in a single design: gold/platinum/jewel-encrusted lettering, stacks of cash, cigars, champagne, pit bulls (the cover of C.M.P.'s 1998 album *Da' Game* features three suit-wearing pit bulls stacking cash, smoking cigars, and drinking champagne), girls in bikinis, luxury vehicles, iced-out Rolexes, mansions, guns/ammo (in B.G.'s 1996 *Chopper City*, the rapper stands on a suburban street amid a literal rain of bullets). The rappers are often shot in a fish-eye lens (a technique also favored by Hype Williams, one of the era's top video directors). There is an element of self-conscious humor—at times verging on surrealism—to the Pen & Pixel look. Sometimes the album

---

* It was even carved onto the side of the Lakers' 2000 NBA championship rings.

covers would take place in space (Three 6 Mafia's 1996 *The End*) or in a fire (Juvenile's 1998 *400 Degreez*). Lil' Flip's *The Leprechaun* (2000) features the rapper as the titular character on a fake Lucky Charms box with a cereal bowl full of jewels and coins. *Let 'Em Burn* by the Hot Boys (2003) features the four members getting fried in electric chairs.

The Bling Era was defined not just by new aesthetics and shifting geography, but by the total merging of hip-hop with popular culture. Rap broke into the mainstream in 1979 with "Rapper's Delight," but remained mostly a pop culture niche through the '80s and early '90s; a genre marketed toward Black consumers that many white critics assumed was a passing fad. In 1986, Run-D.M.C.'s *Raising Hell* became the first-ever rap album to be certified platinum. From 1988 through 1995, rap videos on MTV were mostly relegated to the show *Yo! MTV Raps*. The Grammys didn't even have a category for Best Rap Album until 1996.

By the late '90s, things had changed. Rock music* had been the primary engine of mainstream youth rebellion for forty years, and the genre was in a rut after the death of Kurt Cobain brought an abrupt end to the grunge era. Kids who would have listened to rock were shifting their attention toward rap, whose videos were airing as part of the normal rotation on MTV. The Tupac-Biggie feud was front-page news, along with its tragic conclusion. Rap albums routinely went platinum. Guests like Nelly, Ja Rule, 50 Cent, P. Diddy, and OutKast regularly appeared on *Total Request Live*. Rap, rather than rock, began to guide the aesthetics of pop music. In the Bling Era, hip-hop was still a Black art form, but it had firmly become a part of the white mainstream.

---

* Which, of course, began as a Black art form but went through a process of whitewashing.

The way people talked about race in the Y2K Era was different from the way it's talked about now. There was no Black Lives Matter, no national discourse about critical race theory or police violence or the prison industrial complex. No one in the mainstream media was writing about microaggressions or cultural appropriation or housing discrimination. Instead, there was a narrative of triumphalism, even as the prison population and the racial wealth gap grew to historic levels. Racism, went the narrative, was a problem that had been solved sometime in the mid-twentieth century, just like all the other problems at the End of History.

In school what I learned was this: In the bad old days, there was slavery. Then there was the Civil War, which ended it. I filled out Scantron bubbles: Bacon's Rebellion, the Slave Codes, the Three-Fifths Compromise, Appomattox, the Radical Republicans. I grew up below the Mason-Dixon line: first in Virginia, then later in Maryland. Most of what we talked about in history class had happened nearby. We took field trips to Mount Vernon, where I admired the silk brocades of George Washington's dining room. I stood on the battlefields at Bull Run, in Jefferson's study at Monticello. On Colonial Day I danced the Virginia reel with a Black classmate. On Civil War Day, I met a white teenage reenactor. He wore Confederate regalia, but I forgave him for it because he was cute, and because it had all been so long ago.

I first learned about Martin Luther King Jr. in kindergarten. In January we colored in outlines of his face that said I HAVE A DREAM. Just thirty years before, that same building had been a white school. But, we learned, in the past people were silly. They didn't know it was wrong to have separate schools and separate water fountains and separate lunch counters, to make Black people sit at the back of the bus.

Now, of course, we knew better. We lived in a meritocracy. MLK's dream has been fulfilled, and now there was a whole holiday in his honor, plus Kwanzaa in December and Black History Month in February, where I learned about all the other important Black people like Booker T. Washington and Jackie Robinson and Madam C. J. Walker.

In all sectors of American society there was starting to be more diversity. Michael Jordan was the most famous athlete in the world, leading the Bulls to six championships. In the white-dominated sport of tennis, teenage sisters Venus and Serena Williams lobbed their way into victory after Grand Slam victory, swinging their beaded braids. In another white-dominated sport, Tiger Woods won the PGA, the Masters, and the U.S. Open, year after year after year. In 1997, after his first Masters win, I watched Tiger chat with Oprah about his racial identity, explaining that he was "Cablinasian" (Caucasian, Black, Native American, and Asian). Oprah, too, was on what seemed like an unending ascent as a media mogul, and in 2003 she became a billionaire. That same year, A-list actress Halle Berry made the cover of *People*'s "Most Beautiful" issue. Meanwhile, President George W. Bush's administration was the most diverse ever. His two secretaries of state—Colin Powell and Condoleezza Rice—were both Black. Attorney General Alberto Gonzales was of Mexican descent, and legal adviser John Yoo was Korean American. All across the country the president appointed judges who reflected the multiculturalism of a twenty-first-century America.

And it was in this iteration of America that the Bling Era took place. Rappers were not, of course, representative of Black life as a whole. And yet they served as emissaries of Black life to an American public that seemed intent on burying the traumas of Jim Crow and slavery, as well as the rising problems of police violence and mass incarceration. Hip-hop was one of the only places in mainstream American life where you could find honest depictions of what was actually happening in America at the time. It talked about places most Americans otherwise preferred to ignore: the deindustrialized streets, the prison cells. Sure, it was over the top. Often it was materialistic, violent, misogynistic, and homophobic. But so was America as a whole. Bling Era rap was able to slice through the layers of repression and denial that characterized the Y2K Era and show America as it really was.

But this proved psychologically intolerable. And so the rapper as a figure became a kind of scapegoat onto which all America's ills could be placed. *He* was the one causing America to be materialistic, violent, misogynistic, and homophobic. Many white listeners took pains to emphasize how different we were. This allowed us to confront uncomfortable truths about our country and then turn away, without having dealt with them at all.

TO SPEAK OF the Bling Era is to speak of the neoliberal turn. To my knowledge, that phrase never made it into any rap songs, but most Bling Era rap is about it. The songs are often about violence: the violence of the drug trade, the violence of the criminal legal system, the violence of the postindustrial, segregated urban streets. The market for crack, in particular, grew as American factories closed in the 1970s. Drug dealing offered remunerative employment in neighborhoods where options consisted of, at best, minimum-wage service work or, at worst, joblessness. The policy response to this situation was not—as in the previous few decades—an increase in public spending on welfare programs. Instead, federal and local governments cut those very programs meant to provide security to people during economic downturns. Taxpayer money was channeled toward a new project: prisons.

"The prison," writes sociologist Loïc Wacquant, "check[ed] the rising tide of dispossessed families, street derelicts, and jobless and
alienated youth." It "soak[ed] up the desperation and violence boil-
ing in the segregated enclaves of the metropolis as the protections
afforded by the welfare state receded."

Gangsta rap had been popular since the late 1980s, but during
the Bling Era a new archetype emerged: the rapper as criminal,
artist, and CEO all at the same time. The star of this picaresque was
the upwardly mobile crack dealer—typified by Jay-Z—who got
startup capital for his rap career from the black-market economy
and would, by 2019, become hip-hop's first billionaire. He wasn't
content to just go from drug dealer to artist. He would become
a CEO, and he was going to be good at it because it required the
same skill set as cooking crack and pushing H.* The criminal/CEO
rapper was as comfortable in a tailored suit as he was in sagging
jeans and a durag, as comfortable in the Hamptons as he was in
his old neighborhood. And this archetype was, without exception,
a he. Women were, at best, decorations for his album covers and
videos; at worst, nuisances obstructing his pursuit of profit.

POLITICAL SCIENTIST LESTER Spence has made hip-hop and its
politics a primary focus of his academic work. He grew up near
Detroit, where his parents and grandparents worked in the city's
unionized auto factories. Spence has emphasized in interviews
that he was able to become a tenured professor at Johns Hopkins
because of the financial stability the United Auto Workers
union gave his family. And this experience informs his interest

---

* Jay-Z even has a 1997 song called "Rap Game/Crack Game" in which he
compares the two markets, finding few significant differences.

in neoliberalism, in the decline of organized labor's influence on Black politics and popular culture.

In 2011, he published *Stare in the Darkness: The Limits of Hip-hop and Black Politics*. For the book, Spence created a coded database of rap lyrics from the years 1989 to 2004, using it to conduct quantitative and qualitative studies about lyrical content. He found that "approximately 44 percent of songs in the descriptive realist genre"—a term he borrows from African American studies professor Imani Perry—"that refer to drugs deal with drug selling in the first person." He also found that these songs were full of messages that mirror American life in that era more broadly.

"Neoliberalism promotes the idea that individual freedom and liberty are best attained by reducing the role of government in ameliorating social suffering and relying instead on the market," Spence writes. "The consequences of the neoliberal turn are several—increased inequality and insecurity, decreased transparency and accountability, decreased use of government to ameliorate suffering, and increased incarceration of undesirable populations. The neoliberal subject, the *homo economicus*, is the entrepreneur, the enterprise-corporation of one, the hustler."

The story of the *homo economicus* is told in several Bling Era songs. The second song off Jay-Z's 2001 album *The Blueprint* is called "Takeover." A "takeover" is another word for a hostile merger, and in 1999 CNNMoney reported that "this year has seen the six largest hostile merger bids ever launched, in terms of dollar value." That article makes downsizing and takeovers sound as bloodless and boring as a manila folder. And yet, what CNNMoney is really saying is that all those downsized people that year were marked for death. They couldn't buy food or pay rent. Their health insurance was taken from them. "Get zipped up in plastic, when it happens, that it." Jay Z never challenged capitalism, but at least he was honest about how it actually functions.

Meanwhile, all those corporate takeovers made it hard for Beanie Siegel to find comfortable employment outside the black market. He explained:

> With no union, and no benefits, no dental plans
> I can't eat off no hundred grand

So, his story goes, he turned to a life of crime. The cover of his 2005 album *The B. Coming* shows us the consequences: he's slouched glumly in a cell dressed in prison khakis, a series of tally marks charting time served. Perhaps if he had been born in the mid-twentieth century, the Philadelphia native would have found a unionized factory job and settled down in a tidy row house to raise his family.

Meanwhile, Clipse promoted crack dealing as the ultimate self-help solution, sounding indistinguishable from Bill Clinton.

> Throw it on the scale feed your goddamn self
> Get it how you live, we don't ask for help

In 1996, the president signed the Personal Responsibility and Work Opportunity Act, which "end[ed] welfare as we know it." He told the audience that getting rid of welfare would promote "the dignity, the power, and the ethic of work."

Standing next to the president as he signed was Lillie Harden, a Black single mother and onetime welfare recipient from Little Rock, Arkansas.

"Going to work gave me independence to take good care of my children," she told the audience.

But her job at a grocery store was not enough to keep her out of poverty. In 2002, she had a stroke, and was unable to get on Medicaid. She couldn't afford the $450 a month bill for her prescription drugs. In 2014 she died at age fifty-nine.

50 Cent's 9x Platinum 2003 album was called *Get Rich or Die Tryin'*. The lyrical content—like that of Jay-Z's early albums—chronicles the ins and outs of 50's experience as a crack and heroin dealer in Queens, where he was shot nine times, a fact that played a significant role in his public image. But part of what made the album so popular was that its message could apply to just about anyone in America in the year 2003. Stable employment was gone and the economy was increasingly winner-take-all. Everyone was hustling to get into a good college and get a job with health insurance, to stay in business and stay in the black, to literally stay alive. Your only choice was to destroy your competitors and come out on top. Kill or be killed.

I am skeptical that any of these songs made our country more violent, greedier, or more materialistic than it already was. Research on this topic is, at best, inconclusive. A 2006 article from the *Journal of Studies on Alcohol and Drugs* found that "young people's substance use and aggressive behaviors may be related to their frequent exposure to music containing references to substance use and violence," but also noted the possibility that "substance use, aggression, and music preference may be independent constructs but share common 'third factors.'" A 2019 study at the University of Wisconsin found that violence at rap concerts is no more likely than violence at country concerts or karaoke bars. A 2014 study from the *Journal of International Consumer Marketing* found that hip-hop fans were more likely to value materialism and conspicuous consumption, but did not establish that the music itself was the causal factor.

Bling Era rap also provided a convenient throughput for misogyny. The Y2K Era arrived after several decades of second-wave-feminist gains. Since the 1970s, women had entered the workforce in unprecedented numbers. There were federal protections for abortion and against sexual harassment. But the Y2K Era was also a very sexist time; a time, to use the term favored by feminist writer Susan Faludi, of "backlash." At school, boys talked about who was a slut, who was a smokeshow, who was a butterface ("she's hot, but her face"). Rape jokes were common in movies and standup routines, and if you pointed that out you would be told to *shut up, feminist*, told to go shave your hairy legs or your hairy pussy. The tabloids dissected the appearance of any woman in the public eye, from celebrities to politicians. And yet—as with the narrative around racial progress—there was this widespread belief that we were somehow in a postfeminist age.

Bling Era rap was depicted by its critics as uniquely misogynistic, perhaps even causing whatever remained of sexism in society at large. Much of rap at this time certainly was sexist. Women were called bitches, hos, and chickenheads. "Let go off in a ho's mouth, I ain't picky," said Nelly. "Slob on my knob like corn on the cob," Juicy J demanded. "Find a bag to hide the ho face." Meanwhile, the Ying Yang Twins told a theoretical stripper to "make that pussy fart for the Ying Yang Twins." "What it is, ho, what's up," asked Trillville. "Can a n-- get in them guts?" At least they were asking for consent. In rap videos, dozens of video vixens writhed around in bikinis while rappers threw cash at them (or, in the case of Nelly, swiped a credit card between their ass crack). I suspect one reason for rap's popularity was that it gave you, the listener, license to ogle these women, to say those words if you happened to rap along. It was the rappers who were objectifying and degrading women—not you.

A 2007 study in the *Journal of Applied Social Psychology* found that exposure to rap music with misogynistic lyrics did, in fact, prompt sexist beliefs in listeners. But, said one of the researchers, "sexism is imbedded in the culture we live in, and hearing rap music can spontaneously activate pre-existing awareness of sexist beliefs. We feel it's unlikely that hearing lyrics in a song creates attitudes that did not previously exist."

A similar dynamic played out around LGBTQ rights. On the one hand, there was growing public acceptance of same-sex relationships. There were shows like *Queer as Folk* and *The L Word* on cable and *Will and Grace* on network TV. The "triple cocktail" treatment for AIDS became available in 1996, transforming the disease from a death sentence to a manageable condition (at least for those who could afford treatment). In 2000, Vermont became the first US state to allow same-sex couples to gain legal recognition in civil unions, a precursor to gay marriage.

At the same time, hate crimes were rampant. In 1998, Matthew Shepard, a twenty-one-year-old gay man, was beaten, tied to a fence, and left to die in Laramie, Wisconsin. In 2004, George W. Bush was reelected on a promise to stop gay marriage. Gay and trans jokes were standard in movies and TV, from *Dude, Where's My Car?* to *South Park* to *I Now Pronounce You Chuck and Larry*. In a skit at the 2003 MTV Movie Awards, Gollum from *Lord of the Rings* called Dobby from *Harry Potter* "a fag." That word peppered teenage speech, along with "gay" as a synonym for "stupid" or "uncool."

And Bling Era rap was full of homophobia. "Last I heard, y'all n––s was havin' sex with the same sex," DMX announced. "I show no love to homo thugs . . . how you gonna explain fucking a man?" Lil Wayne cast aspersions at "homo n––s getting AIDS in the ass." Eminem kept it short and simple: "Hate fags? The answer's yes." On the outro of his 2002 song "Welcome to New York City," Cam'ron clarified his sexual preferences: "Get the fuck off our dick, no homo." That interjection—*no homo*—quickly spread throughout hip-hop and beyond. "With me, 'no homo' is basically installed in my vocabulary, man," Cam'ron explained in an interview on New York's Hot 99.7. "So it's like, even if I'm in a meeting, I'll be with my lawyer, and might say something and be like 'no homo,' and my lawyer will look up and I'll be like, 'I know you have no idea what I'm talking about but I need to say that because I said something real homo—no homo.'" In other words, the prohibition against homosexuality in hip-hop at this moment was so strong that a popular rapper felt the need to interrupt business meetings to assure people he wasn't gay.

As with misogyny, critics of hip-hop often used the genre's homophobia as a gotcha, but it wasn't all that different from what was happening in other parts of American life. And it conveniently allowed listeners to say the f-slur while attributing it to someone else.

Bling Era rap wasn't just useful for processing race, class, and gender dynamics at home. It could also make sense of foreign policy. This era of hip-hop took place during the War on Terror. The US was permitting torture at its prisons and black sites. Random Afghan farmers were getting picked up by US interrogators on bad tips because the previous random farmers wanted to snitch on a rival or just give any name they could think of to get out of custody (this was, of course, not so different from what was happening in American cities under the War on Drugs). Iraq had become a charnel house. The Bush administration had forbidden the media from showing the coffins of American service members.

As Martin Luther King noted in his 1967 "Beyond Vietnam" speech, American war-making abroad and the abandonment of Black neighborhoods at home are directly related.

"A few years ago there was a shining moment in that struggle," King said. "It seemed as if there was a real promise of hope for the poor—both black and white—through the poverty program. There were experiments, hopes, new beginnings. Then came the buildup in Vietnam, and I watched this program broken and eviscerated, as if it were some idle political plaything of a society gone mad on war, and I knew that America would never invest the necessary funds or energies in rehabilitation of its poor so long as adventures like Vietnam continued to draw men and skills and money like some demonic destructive suction tube. So, I was increasingly compelled to see the war as an enemy of the poor and to attack it as such."[*]

In the Y2K Era, military imagery featured prominently in hip-hop. Rappers bragged about their use of military-grade weapons like AK-47s, wore bulletproof vests, and called themselves soldiers. The prevalence of this motif coincides with and reflects the War on Terror, but also predates it, drawing influence from the War on Drugs (both locally and globally) and older foreign policy events like the Gulf War.

"N–– I'm the colonel of the motherfuckin' tank!" announced Master P on his 1997 single "Make 'Em Say Uhh." The tank, of course, was the logo of No Limit Records, the influential New Orleans hip-hop label he founded in the early '90s. In the video for "Make 'Em Say Uhh," a gold-plated No Limit tank bursts onto a basketball court and shoots down the opposing team's backboard with a missile.

In one promotional photo, Master P wears head-to-toe camo streetwear: baggy pants, a matching jacket, a flat-brim cap, and black Air Jordans. In the world of streetwear, camo adorned garments from crop tops to sneakers to durags. You could find the

---

[*] For some reason, I never learned that one in school like "I Have a Dream."

pattern not just in standard-issue army and navy colorways, but in red, yellow, orange, pink, and purple. Later, BAPE, the Japanese streetwear brand founded by Nigo—close friend of Pharrell's—became popular for their stylized, psychedelic updates on the traditional camo pattern.

B.G. had a 1999 song called "Cash Money Is an Army" ("Cash Money is a army n––, a navy n––, so if you ever try to harm me n––, it ain't gravy n––"). B.G.'s group the Hot Boys had an album that came out the same year called *Guerrilla Warfare*. "This is the army n––, whoa wodie keep it cool," says Lil Wayne over a military drumbeat on the song "Boys at War." "N––s be shell shocked, knockin' heads off of shoulders," says Turk. "Many MAC-10's, grenades blowin' shit up." On "Takeover," Jay-Z bragged, of his record label, "Roc-a-Fella is the army, better yet the Navy." Destiny's Child released a single called "Soldier" featuring T.I. and Lil Wayne. In the video, T.I. wears a baggy shirt adorned with fake service ribbons and five-star insignia. "See Cash Money is a army, I'm walkin' with purple hearts on me, you talkin' to the sergeant," says Lil Wayne, wearing a camo-print shirt, ice, and sagging jeans. "I blend in with the hood, I'm camouflage, bandanna tied so mami join my troop, now every time she hear my name she salute."

These lyrics conflate the violent neighborhoods where drugs are dealt with war zones. Atlanta's Bankhead and New Orleans's 3rd Ward become the battlefields of Fallujah and Helmand. And war is tied, explicitly, to moneymaking. "I'm in a battlefield tryna get my mills," says B.G. on "Cash Money Is an Army." Similarly, the rappers Capone-N-Noreaga had a 1997 album called *The War Report*, and its cover features the duo dressed in full-camo combat uniforms, presiding over an army of Photoshop-duplicated versions of themselves, the apartment towers of Lefrak City, Queens (which they call "Iraq") looming in the background.

Rappers played the other side, too. Noreaga named himself after Manuel Noriega, the drug-trafficking Panamanian dictator the US first supported and then deposed in 1989. The duo regularly collaborated with the rapper Tragedy Khadafi, who took as his namesake the authoritarian ruler of Libya. Crime Mob compared themselves to Saddam Hussein and Osama bin Laden. Three 6 Mafia talked about smoking "Bin Laden weed."

"That shit some straight killer," Juicy J said.

On "Rubber Band Man"—one of T.I.'s first singles—the Atlanta rapper introduced himself.

"Hey, who I'm is? Rubber band man, wild as the Taliban, nine in my right, forty-five in my other hand."

Again, Bling Era hip-hop became a way for many white Americans to engage with uncomfortable truths about their country without really reckoning with them. They could keep on projecting: it was these scary Black men in sagging camouflage pants who were violent, not the entire structure of American global power.

IN THE HALLWAY of my suburban Baltimore high school in 2005, two white peers of mine—Will and Hunter—talked about the new Three 6 Mafia album, *Most Known Unknown*.

"It's fuckin' dope," said Will.

"'Puff, puff, pass, n—— roll that blunt, let's get high, n——, smoke us one,'" said Hunter, quoting "Stay Fly."

They laughed, they talked about their other favorite tracks. Then they switched back, talking white again. They bumped fists and parted ways.

The interaction struck me as odd. They were white, and their friends were almost all white, members of the lacrosse and golf teams. They wore Vineyard Vines. I overheard some of them refer to nonwhite Baltimore neighborhoods as "sketchy." Some of them were in the Young Republicans. Republicans, I knew, thought anyone caught selling drugs should go to jail. How could they love Three 6 Mafia when they believed these things?

Later in the year, Hunter and Will formed a comedy rap group called Northside Thugz with their friend Andrew. Northside Thugz dropped original MP3 tracks on their website, rapping over beats for Jay-Z's "Money, Cash, Hoes" and Afrikaa Bambaataa's "Planet Rock." Their lyrics joked about smoking crack and raping white women and committing murder. At the end-of-year school talent show, the group appeared on stage alongside seven other white guys in their friend group to perform "My Humps." They all dressed alike, in sagging jeans and wifebeaters and fake ice. They performed a dance routine and the whole auditorium laughed. It was funny, because we were affluent and white, not poor and Black, and it felt good not to know what that was like.

We weren't the only comfortable white people laughing. Across LiveJournal and Myspace, it was common practice to pose for digi-cam photos making fake gang signs with your friends against the backdrop of a custom kitchen or a college dorm. "Thug life" was a common college party theme, alongside toga party, ugly sweater party, and ABC ("anything but clothes"). A popular series of hip-hop dance parties called "Kill Whitey" were held in the burgeoning hipster mecca and historically Puerto Rican neighborhood of Williamsburg, Brooklyn. They were hosted by a white DJ calling himself Tha Pumpsta, and the mostly white crowd dressed for the theme, showing up in everything from tall tees to blackface. 2005's "Lazy Sunday"—one of the first viral videos on YouTube—consists of white *SNL* comedians Chris Parnell and Andy Samberg rapping about eating expensive cupcakes and going to a matinee screening of *The Chronicles of Narnia* over an aggressive beat. In a 2006 episode of *SNL*, the demure, Harvard-educated Natalie Portman joined Parnell and Samberg for a profanity-laced comedy rap. Georgetown-educated comedian Mike Birbiglia has a 2006 joke where he discusses the differences between himself and Busta Rhymes. This same premise would find its way, years later, into Notorious RBG merch.* The whole joke of Notorious RBG is that Ruth Bader Ginsburg is an Ivy League–educated Supreme Court justice. She's nothing like the high school dropout/former crack dealer Biggie Smalls!†

"Blackface minstrels were the first self-consciously *white* entertainers in the world," wrote David Roediger in his 1991 book *Wages of Whiteness*. "The simple physical disguise—and elaborate cultural disguise—of blacking up served to emphasize that those on stage were really white and that whiteness really mattered. One minstrel pioneer won fame by being able to change from black to white and back in seconds. Playbills continually featured paired pictures of the performers in blackface and without make up—rough and respectable, black and white . . . All whites could easily participate in minstrelsy's central joke, the point of which remained a common, respectable and increasingly smug whiteness under the makeup."

The jokes, the impressions, the quick-change act. For Hunter and Will and the rest of the Northside Thugz, it seemed to be a way of letting go, of openly embracing materialism and greed, violence and misogyny and drug use, while projecting all of these things back *onto* rappers. And rappers, at least in the context of my high school, were almost a stand-in for Black people in gen-

---

* Which, shockingly, started as late as 2013, five years after the Y2K Era ended (but also before the Black Lives Matter movement rose to national prominence).
† Who, it's worth noting, loved the novels of Charles Dickens.

eral, as if they were the real materialistic, violent, misogynistic drug users and criminals in this country, which is of course why they deserved to be in our prisons, and Hunter and Will and the Northside Thugz deserved to walk free.

In 1885, a fifteen-year-old boy named Howard Cooper was lynched at the old Baltimore County Jail, less than a mile from my high school. He was accused of assaulting and raping a white woman whom the press described as "a lady of refinement and intelligence." Pursued by a mob, Howard fled to a neighboring property and hid in a barn, where he was found by police and arrested. At the county courthouse, he was put on trial and found guilty, sentenced to death by an all-white jury in less than a minute.

His mother, Henrietta, tried to delay the sentence, working with local activists to appeal the conviction. But as the case was wending its way through the circuit court a mob broke into the jail. They dragged Howard from his cell and hanged him from a sycamore tree. His mother buried him in an unmarked grave in the neighborhood where I lived between the ages of fourteen and eighteen.

I didn't know this history in 2006, and I am going to assume the members of the Northside Thugz didn't know it either. Regardless, when I think about it now, their talent show performance starts to feel less like a celebration of Black culture and more like a touchdown dance on the grave of a dead teenager.

BY 2021—WHEN THE Maryland Lynching Memorial Project put up a marker commemorating the murder of Howard Cooper—it was no longer considered socially acceptable for white people to impersonate rappers as a joke. Racial politics in the post–Y2K Era were shaped by the Black Lives Matter movement, which led large-scale protests in reaction to police violence (which could now be recorded and disseminated via smartphones and social media). Accompanying this were public discussions about white supremacy, structural racism, the prison industrial complex, Confederate statues, the drug war, environmental racism, and redlining. It is difficult for me to imagine the Northside Thugz performance taking place now. When I look back at it, I cringe. How could I have laughed? I attempt to reassure myself: it was just how things were back then.

But even in the Y2K Era, not all white kids listening to rap were laughing about it.

In his 2005 book *Why White Kids Love Hip Hop*, former editor in chief of *The Source* Bakari Kitwana argues that for most white fans, their love of the genre has nothing to do with psychological distancing or ironic posturing or a revival of the minstrel tradition. The love, he writes, is at times complicated but usually genuine, often stemming from an "intensifying sense of alienation" and "the same sense of disenfranchisement as other dispossessed Americans, Black and otherwise" in an era when "the government has increasingly abandoned the interests of working-class people and is aligned almost exclusively with the interests of the rich and superrich." Plus, the music just *goes*.

In 2000, Eminem became one of the era's biggest rappers with his album *The Marshall Mathers LP*, which sold more than 25 million copies. His face was on all the magazine covers, from *The Source* and *XXL* to *Rolling Stone* and *Spin* to the *New York Times Magazine*. Much of Eminem's image centered around his biography: growing up with an abusive single mom in a Detroit trailer; dropping out of high school; his tumultuous relationship with Kim, the mother of his daughter, Hailie.

"Eminem comes from a socioeconomic background not vastly different from that of many Black rappers," writes Kitwana. "Like his Black counterparts, he's a victim of America's education and economic policies of the 1980s and 1990s—from inadequate schooling and education budget cuts to NAFTA."

Eminem had prison-style tattoos and he mean-mugged the camera and he sagged his pants. He "talked Black"—all the time, not just as some kind of joke or affect. As a famous story goes, when Dr. Dre first heard his 1996 album *Infinite*, he thought Em *was* Black. And yet, Kitwana says, "Eminem is not seeking to become Black and abandon whiteness." In another context Eminem might have been called a redneck or white trash. Instead, he was called a "wigger." A wigger is a white person who comes to hip-hop culture from a place of solidarity and fellow feeling. Not—like Northside Thugz—from a place of projection, mockery, or contempt.

There was a similar dynamic at my majority-nonwhite middle school in suburban Virginia. There, in one of the most ethnically diverse zip codes in America, Korean, Vietnamese, Salvadorian, Ethiopian, and Egyptian kids wore sagging pants and Rocawear and figaro chains, talked about Cash Money Records versus No Limit, about Jay's new album versus Cam'ron's, about whether Ja Rule was a good rapper or just overhyped. This dynamic would be illustrated later in Eddie Huang's sitcom *Fresh Off the Boat*. "If you were an outsider, hip hop was your anthem," he says in a voiceover during the show's first episode.

For downwardly mobile whites, for immigrants, and for anyone else who was ready to see America as it was—hip-hop provided a template for how to survive, even thrive. Black people in this country invented hustling because they had to. Rappers in the Bling Era just reinvented it.

They're Just
Like Us!

O N AUGUST 31, 1997, PRINCESS DIANA'S CAR CRASHED
into the wall of the Pont de l'Alma tunnel in Paris. Diana,
her boyfriend, Dodi Al Fayed, and their driver, Henri
Paul, were all killed. It happened just before I started fourth grade,
and it was the first celebrity death I remember: in part because it
was so violent and so shocking, and in part because I adored the
former princess of Wales, with her skirt suits and bike shorts and
anti-land-mine advocacy and post-divorce blond pixie cut. While
brushing my teeth that night, I pressed my mom for answers. How
could this have happened?

"She was being chased by the paparazzi," my mom said.

"What's the paparazzi?" I asked.

"They're people who try to take pictures of famous people in
private and sell them to the press for money," she explained.

"Even going to the bathroom?" I asked, imagining the most
private thing I could think of.

"Probably," she said.

I wondered how much photos of Princess Diana on the toilet

would go for. People would be shocked to learn that the princess peed and maybe even pooped. I announced to my mom that I would never become famous. I already had enough hang-ups about myself and my own bodily functions; the last thing I needed was a mob of angry people with cameras broadcasting these things to a global audience. I imagined the photographers peeping through the crack of a public bathroom stall. I pictured the A1 story in the *Washington Post*.

In the weeks and months following Diana's death, a public dialogue developed around the role of the paparazzi, the media, and fame in society. Perhaps, it was suggested, it should be illegal for photographers to chase celebrities going about their private lives. Perhaps publications should stop running photographs obtained in this way. Perhaps consumers should stop buying and watching media that featured this stuff. Perhaps the entire celebrity-media economy was dehumanizing to everyone involved, and we all just needed to pump the brakes.

That moment of introspection didn't last long. The business was simply too lucrative. In the late '90s and early 2000s, paparazzi photos started at around $10,000 a piece, but could go for far more than that. An exclusive 2000 photo of Brad Pitt and Jennifer Aniston on the beach went for $500,000. A 1997 photo of Princess Diana and Dodi Al Fayed cuddling on a yacht sold for $6 million. The photo was taken a month before they both died.

The nascent internet was creating a bigger, faster market for celebrity gossip than even the twenty-four-hour cable news cycle could, especially once blogging took off in the early 2000s. The new genre of reality television would provide what appeared to be behind-the-scenes content about existing celebrities, while also creating fresh celebrities who would then end up in tabloids and on blogs: an ouroboros of fame. And, in January 1998—after months of gossip about the events surrounding Princess Diana's death—a new scandal emerged on the other side of the Atlantic. President Bill Clinton, it was revealed, had carried on an affair with a young intern named Monica Lewinsky. The Clintons, their friends, their political rivals, and *especially* Monica immediately became not only front-page news but gossip staples, appearing on magazine covers and blogs years after the president's subsequent impeachment trial concluded in February 1999. From then on, political figures and their retinue were celebrities, too. The death of Princess Diana was not—as some speculated—an end point, but rather the opening salvo to a cruel, celebrity-crazed era of media and pop culture that would last for a decade.

IN 2004, A paunchy, twenty-six-year-old Cuban American gay man with hot-pink hair named Mario Lavandeira Jr. launched a celebrity gossip blog called *PageSixSixSix*. Lavandeira was a struggling actor whose biggest role was as a nameless box office clerk in a 2001 episode of *The Sopranos*. On his blog, Lavandeira found the attention denied to him by Hollywood's indifferent gate-keepers. He built an audience, and the *New York Post* took legal action, claiming he was ripping off the name of its gossip blog. Mario renamed his site *Perez Hilton*. Perez Hilton the person was indistinguishable from *Perez Hilton* the blog. His site screamed at you in hot pink (the same color as his hair), and the layout kind of hurt your eyes. But you would overlook that, because you needed to see what Perez had to say. With television you'd have to wait a few hours or a few days to get your gossip. With magazines, a week. With Perez, the hit you'd get was instant. It was a forerun-ner to the endless scroll of social media, to the dopamine-based attention economy. By 2007, the *New York Times* reported the site was "among the top 10 entertainment news sites," with 2.6 million unique views per month.

Perez was unique not only for the frequency of his posts, but for his lewd editorializing. Photos of celebrities were embellished with a white pen in Microsoft Paint. Cum dribbled out of mouths, dicks were scrawled on foreheads, middle school–level insults like "ho" were added to photos. Everyone had a nickname: Britney was Brit Brit, Kate Moss was CoKate, Misha Barton was Mushy Fartone. He fixated, for some reason, on Bai Ling. He made up cruel insults and then wouldn't lay off, like when he kept calling Bruce Willis and Demi Moore's teenage daughter Rumer "potato head." He made fun of people's (mostly women's) bodies, faces, mental health issues, alleged promiscuity, substance abuse problems, and legal troubles. He was obsessed with outing celebrities he believed to be closeted. In doing all this, he became a celebrity himself, even appearing in a cameo in the 2011 Rihanna video for "S&M."

The archetype of Perez Hilton is familiar to anyone who has attended an American middle school. He is the kid who is bullied— for being gay, for being fat, maybe even for being Cuban—who figures out that he can deflect the abuse by becoming a bully himself. He enters the cafeteria shrieking about who cheated on whom, whose clothes are busted, who is a fat ho and an ugly bitch. The popular girls sit all around him, even though they find him a little annoying, and they say as much when he gets up to leave. Sometimes, a brave soul tells him he's being too mean. He looks wounded, because don't they know what he has to deal with every day? And besides, he's just saying what everyone is already thinking.

THE WHOLE TIME I was there. Not in the boutiques or nightclubs, not in the beach resorts or on the red carpets, but in my bedroom and my rec room, at school, in strip mall nail salons, on the tread-mill at the Y. I was flipping through *In Touch* and *Us Weekly* and watching MTV's *Cribs* and VH1's *The Fabulous Life of . . .* and, most of all, going online to scroll through Perez Hilton. I wasn't doing my homework but I was learning plenty: about every shop-ping spree, fashion don't, shocking weight gain, shocking weight loss, rehab stint, baby bump, post-baby body, diet, divorce, work-out routine, feud, fairy tale wedding, and mega-home purchase. Everyone knew that the best part of *Us* was "Stars—They're Just Like Us!" The section showed paparazzi candids of celebrities going about their daily lives, similar to the ones for which the press hounded Princess Diana until her death.

I got into celebrity gossip the same way and for the same reason I got into drinking Diet Coke: gradually, and because it was everywhere and also felt like a little treat. But it became a part of my daily life. By 2007, I was checking Perez Hilton every couple hours on my white MacBook. At the time I was taking community college classes and trying to get my GPA up high enough to transfer somewhere better. I was also trying to get over an eating disorder and having daily panic attacks back be-fore everyone talked about their panic attacks publicly. I wasn't particularly happy with my life or myself, and Perez was a useful distraction.

As *Us* said, the stars were just like me. But they weren't, not really, and that was the point. I watched them in pap shots the same way I went to a theater to watch their movies or turned on the TV to watch their shows or pressed play on my iPod to listen to their songs. There was no confusion about our roles. I was here and they were there and that was that. Or so it seemed. Under these conditions, star watching was pure leisure.

PEREZ HILTON'S NAMESAKE, Paris Hilton, was born in New York in 1981. The great-granddaughter of Hilton Hotels founder Conrad, Paris grew up between New York and Los Angeles. She began appearing in the tabloids in the late '90s while she was still in high school, when she'd go clubbing underage with the likes of Leonardo DiCaprio at places like Moomba. "Paris the heiress," the press called her.

"Of all the girls in gossip land, people gossip the most about the Hilton sisters," wrote Nancy Jo Sales in a September 2000 *Vanity Fair* profile of Paris and her sister, Nicky, just before Paris would become arguably the most famous person in America. The profile positions its subjects as representatives of a new type of celebrity, centered not around one's accomplishments as a Hollywood actor or a commercially successful musician or a professional athlete or even as a member of, say, the British royal family, but around attending all the right parties and wearing all the right outfits and getting photographed in all the right tabloids. This new type of celebrity was—according to a common gripe in the ensuing years—"famous for being famous."

The profile—titled "Hip-Hop Debs"*—was paired with portraits by David LaChapelle. In one photo, a nineteen-year-old Paris stands in her grandmother's well-appointed Holmby Hills living room. She's wearing a hot-pink micro miniskirt, hot-pink fingerless gloves, black platform sandals, and a black fishnet tank top with no bra. She's wearing aviator sunglasses and her straight

---

* A very 2000s title. It is predicated on the assumption that hip-hop was causing debutantes to focus on parties and shopping, and not that this is the way debutantes have behaved for as long as there have been debutantes, or that an expanding media landscape that made money covering the salacious details of debutantes' lives made this behavior more widely known.

blond hair is in tousled, slightly-'80s layers with bangs. Her fuchsia lipstick matches her skirt and gloves. She's biting her lip and giving the camera the middle finger.

"People think I'm just this party girl," she says in the superimposed pull quote. "Well, I'm not like that."

After the *Vanity Fair* profile, Paris's star continued to rise. In 2002, she had a series of A-list twenty-first birthday parties in Las Vegas, New York, Paris, London, Tokyo, and Los Angeles. Her friend DJ AM spun the songs. She wore a procession of outfits, including a backless minidress by Heatherette made of Swarovski crystals. Now, if you google "Paris Hilton fashion" you will get ads for knockoffs of this dress. "I think every girl should wear that dress on their 21st birthday, it's so epic," she told *V* magazine recently.

In 2003, she leveraged the medium of reality television to launch her star beyond the stratosphere with *The Simple Life*, which she appeared in alongside her childhood friend Nicole Richie (daughter of Lionel). The premise of *The Simple Life* was: Paris and Nicole were rich, famous, beautiful, and spoiled. They would leave behind their cell phones, credit cards, and BMWs, and move in with a series of "regular" American families in places like Altus, Arkansas. They would work "regular" American jobs at farms, fast-food restaurants, and sausage factories. They would pretend not to know what a Walmart was.

The Simple Life was predicated on Paris being famous, but it made her famous, too. She invented the now innately understood formula of taking fame and money, using it as the premise for a reality television show, and thus growing that fame and money into a diversified and lucrative celebrity empire with product sponsorships, cameos, albums, etc., which itself brought even more fame and even more opportunities to make money. Jessica Simpson would do this with *Newlyweds* (MTV, 2003). Hulk Hogan's daughter Brooke would try to do it with *Hogan Knows Best* (VH1, 2005). Most successfully, Kim Kardashian would do it with *Keeping Up with the Kardashians* (E!, 2007), bringing her whole family along with her. Before Kim's fame and net worth eclipsed Paris's, she was a minor celestial body in the Paris universe, appearing on episodes of *The Simple Life* as her friend who ran a closet organizing business.

During the 2000s, Paris's name became a metonym for vacuity, excess, entitlement, and celebrity culture itself. My mom railed against "that Paris Hilton crap," by which she meant a kind of pink, bedazzled maximalism that dared you to hate it. Paris was very, very tan, with long, straight blond hair and gleaming white teeth. She punctuated her deadpan statements with the phrase "that's hot," which she later trademarked. At events she wore micro mini-skirts and crop tops that showcased her hip bones and her long, flat torso. Everything she wore was pink and lavender and baby blue and turquoise, made of ripped chiffon and ruched jersey, adorned with rhinestones and strings and straps and revealing cutouts. Off duty she schlepped around Los Angeles in Juicy Velour tracksuits, trucker hats, Ugg boots, and oversized Dior sunglasses, exiting luxury vehicles while gripping Starbucks cups or shopping bags. She claims to have never been photographed in the same outfit twice. She had a coterie of Chihuahuas and Pomeranians with names like Dolce, Sebastian, Peter Pan, and Tinkerbell that she carried around in designer purses, like the now-discontinued Takashi Murakami "multicolor" line for Louis Vuitton, which featured the brand's iconic logo in a rainbow of pastel colors on a white background. In 2009, Paris announced that she bought her dogs their own "doggy mansion" for $325,000, featuring pink walls, Philippe Starck furniture, and air-conditioning.

The Consumer Aesthetics Research Institute cites Paris as a major touch point in the McBling aesthetic, which was popular from approximately 2000 to 2008. McBling, they write, marked "a hard shift away from the minimalist futurism of the Y2K Aesthetic era towards maximalist remixes of mainly 1970s and early 1980s trends & motifs." The era celebrated "aspirational luxury in all its forms," encompassing everything from "tattoo motifs, oversized designer glasses, celebutantes, designer ripped jeans, pink hummers, overly-flourishy vector art, grunge effects applied to 'gothic' fonts, reality tv shows, Dubai, bling, spinning rims, [and] spray tans." Paris never wore a shirt that said "STOP BEING POOR," but it says a lot about what she and her aesthetic represented that people still pass around that altered photo of her thinking it's real.

Even though I thought there was a difference between myself and the celebrities I watched, I found myself dabbling in the McBling aesthetic by the end of high school. I saved my babysitting money to buy a pair of black Versace bug-eye sunglasses with the gold Medusa on the side, to buy Ugg boots. I amassed a tiny collection of Coach handbags and accessories: a brown canvas saddlebag covered in logos, another saddlebag in black pebbled leather, and a lavender keychain wallet with a small logo print. I had a couple discounted Juicy pieces I found at Loehmann's: a green terry-cloth halter dress and a pair of pink and brown terry-cloth shorts with a hibiscus pattern. At home, I bleached my teeth with Crest Whitestrips (introduced in 2001) and slathered myself in Clarins self-tanning gel (when I wasn't frying my pale skin outside in a bikini). I abused my wavy hair daily with a straightening iron. In fall 2006, I bought a cashmere Burberry scarf in signature beige plaid.

This aesthetic was a kind of emotional armor. I almost wanted people to think I was obnoxious. Because, if they thought this, that meant they envied me. And if they envied me, they would feel the way I often felt about others. I have never been particularly comfortable in my own skin. I think, had I been born at another time, these feelings would have been filtered through whatever its prevailing feminine aesthetic was. Because it was the mid-2000s, I imagined myself in pap shots.

PARTICIPANTS IN A 2006 survey published by *Forbes* voted Paris Hilton the "most overexposed celebrity" during that very celebrity-focused year. Others who made the list included Lindsay Lohan, the Olsen twins, and Britney Spears. By that point Lindsay, like Paris, was on a first-name basis with the American media. Born in 1986—two years before I was—she had been a child star, appearing in television commercials and on soap operas since she could talk. Her big breakout as a preteen was in Disney's critically acclaimed 1998 remake of *The Parent Trap*. She then starred in a series of teen comedies: *Freaky Friday, Confessions of a Teenage Drama Queen, Mean Girls*. She appeared on the cover of the July 2003 issue of *Vanity Fair* (caption: "IT'S TOTALLY RAINING TEENS!") with fellow young A-listers including Mandy Moore, Amanda Bynes, Raven-Symoné, and the Olsen twins. Then she branched out into music. Her first album, 2004's *Speak*, went platinum. Its first single, "Rumors," is a dance song that tells the story of her relationship with the media.

"I've gotta say respectfully, I would like it if you take the cameras off of me," she sings. "Cause I just want a little room to breathe, can you please respect my privacy?"

"She's become the face of teen culture," announced the nameless British man who narrated VH1's *The Fabulous Life of . . .* At nineteen, he reported, Lindsay had a net worth of $17 million and had already done branding campaigns with Barbie and Dooney & Bourke.

Grown men commented on her newly developed body. "She's hot, she's rich, and she's living like no other teenager on the planet," that strange man on *The Fabulous Life of...* told me. In May 2004, Lohan became one of the youngest-ever hosts of *Saturday Night Live,* at age seventeen. During the episode, she starred in a Harry Potter–themed sketch called "Hermione's Growth Spurt" in which the entire adult cast spends over five minutes ogling her breasts.* The fact that she had once been a child and was becoming a woman—but was still underage—was depicted as particularly titillating. Following her eighteenth birthday, an August 2004 *Rolling Stone* cover featuring Lohan declared that she was "Hot, Ready, and Legal!"

She went on "legendary shopping binges." *The Fabulous Life of...* described her $5 million Beverly Hills estate, $10,000 custom cell phone, $20,000-a-day spa sessions at New York's Cornelia Day Resort, and $70,000 designer handbag collection. She spent wild nights at pre-recession clubs like NYC's Cain, Suede, and Bungalow 8. She suddenly got very skinny. There were rumors of drug use and unreliable behavior on set. In 2007, she went to rehab, then left rehab, then lost control of her Mercedes convertible in Beverly Hills and was arrested for driving under the influence and possession of cocaine. She went to rehab again. She wore an alcohol-monitoring ankle bracelet. She got arrested again for driving under the influence and possession of cocaine, this time in Santa Monica with a suspended license. She went back to rehab. She went to jail for eighty-four minutes. Her name became a synonym for substance abuse problems, for spoiled bitches deserving of punishment. She became a punch line on late-night television back when people still watched it.

---

* That was it. That was the joke.

In 2008, she started dating DJ and socialite Samantha Ronson (sister of Mark). The press reacted to this relationship with what could most charitably be described as confusion. How could the ostensibly straight Lohan be suddenly dating a woman? It must be a cry for help. This homophobic concern trolling around the relationship of two adult women was notable, given another narrative in celebrity media at the time.

In 2006, Mary Kate and Ashley Olsen shared two distinctions with Lohan: they were fellow alumni of the "IT'S TOTALLY RAINING TEENS!" cover, and they were fellow contenders for that year's distinction of "most overexposed celebrity." Like Lindsay, the Olsen twins had been child stars, first as toddlers alternating the same role on *Full House* and then in a series of extremely popular home videos where they played preteens who solved crimes, traveled the world, and wore matching, on-trend outfits. Unlike most child stars, the Olsen family managed their daughters' finances well, and by the time they were staring down their shared eighteenth birthday in June 2004, they were looking to gain legal control of a $300 million personal fortune.

"Hollywood's little girls are all grown up," announced *The Fabulous Life of . . .* , calling them "the richest self-made teenagers in the world."

But there was another reason the countdown to their eighteenth birthday became a major cultural phenomenon. At sixteen, they appeared on a September 2003 cover of *Rolling Stone* under the headline "America's Favorite Fantasy." Howard Stern made frequent jailbait jokes. Now-defunct websites ran countdown clocks to the Olsens' eighteenth birthday. The media—parts of it, at least—put forth a collective underage-lesbian incest fantasy. As a teen girl myself, I felt weird about this, to say the least.

"Lock up the boyfriend," the *New York Post* article announced on the twins' birthday. "The Olsen twins are legal—and they're loaded."

"It was a private milestone for two young women, and a disturbing rite of passage for a nation of creepy men," wrote Peter Hartlaub at the *San Francisco Chronicle*, one of the only people in the press to call the insanity what it was.*

As with Paris and Lindsay, what made the Olsens so interesting was the way they embodied so many contradictions. They had been child stars, but now they were smoking cigarettes. I remember one pap photo of Mary Kate filling her cart with wine at an LA Whole Foods. They drove matching $75,000 Range Rovers, sat front row at Fashion Week, spent $2.5 million a year on a private Gulfstream jet, and bought a $3.5 million riverfront condo in the West Village where they lived as NYU freshmen.

And they were so, so thin, especially Mary Kate, who in 2004 checked into rehab for anorexia after months of rumors. On the pro-ana LiveJournal communities I frequented, Mary Kate was one of the most commonly posted "thinspos" (inspirations to lose weight). Everyone wanted to look like a "lollipop"—huge head, tiny body. Tabloids would describe Mary Kate as "scary skinny." But "scary skinny" still felt aspirational. Why else would the press call every celeb with a normal BMI "curvy," and heap praise upon them if they "slimmed down"? I remember one magazine where a registered dietitian assessed the bodies of celebrities (mostly women). She said Nicole Richie—who was probably a size 6 at the time, like

---

* Is it any wonder that once the Olsens got to their twenties the style they adopted was sexless and the opposite of body conscious, consisting of shapeless, floor-length frocks with high necks and long sleeves, dresses that seem intended for a seventy-year-old attending a Victorian funeral? They went on to found luxury brand The Row, which specializes in minimalist handbags and simple, loose-fitting garments with exceptional tailoring.

I had been before I developed an eating disorder—needed to lose 5 to 10 pounds. Later, she would slim down, becoming as skeletal as Mary Kate. On the red carpet at the MTV Movie Awards in 2005, Nicole traded compliments with Lindsay.

"You look really skinny!"

"No, you look really skinny!"

Though it was never my preferred clothing look, "Olsen style" was a kind of religious faith among many teenage girls I knew. Mary Kate, in particular, was regarded as a fashion icon. She pioneered the boho look, which consisted of peasant skirts, band tees, scarves, chunky necklaces, long Edie Sedgwick earrings, and gladiator sandals, finished with huge designer sunglasses and an "it" bag like the Balenciaga Moto. Everything was a little mismatched, and the idea was to look like you bought it all at Goodwill, even if you paid luxury prices. Much to my chagrin, boho remained a popular trend, shaping the inventory at Nordstrom, Neiman Marcus, Urban Outfitters, and H&M.

In the midst of this overheated, celebrity-filled moment, the biggest story yet was developing. Britney Spears (yet another "most overexposed celebrity" contender) had been *the* pop star for my entire generation, stepping onto the public stage in 1998 in a schoolgirl skirt and knee socks and marabou-accented blond pigtails, her white button-down tied above her belly button to show off her abs. She was "the Princess of Pop," beloved by one type of teenager and hated by another for being fake, plastic, inauthentic, a "teenybopper." She was a sex symbol but she was also, famously, preserving her virginity until marriage. In April 1999, David LaChapelle photographed her in her underwear for the cover of *Rolling Stone*. She's on her back on pink satin sheets, chatting on the phone and cradling a stuffed Teletubby. The caption promises to take readers "inside the heart, mind & bedroom of a teen dream." In the magazine, another photo shows her looking over her shoulder while pushing a pink children's bicycle, and the butt of her short white shorts says *BABY* in rhinestones. She became the blueprint for the turn-of-the-millennium pop star: the straight blond hair, the crop tops, the abs, the breathy vocals, the hypersexual virginity.

For years the resentment had been accumulating. It was ready in 2004, when she began to be photographed walking around LA barefoot, staying out late at nightclubs, smoking cigarettes, and wearing T-shirts with slogans like *I am the American Dream*. That was the year she married her hometown friend Jason Alexander at a Las Vegas twenty-four-hour chapel and then got the marriage annulled fifty-five hours later. "It's getting nasty!" said the cover of *Us Weekly*. "The groom says he's fine. Friends say he's furious. She's in seclusion. Worry sets in as Britney's bad behavior creates heartache & career chaos." It might as well have said, "You thought you were so special, bitch? Well, now what?"

That September, Britney married Kevin Federline. Here was "the Princess of Pop," and she had married this white trash gold-digging loser, a backup dancer who, before he met her, had shared an apartment with six roommates?! "Britney the Bridezilla!" *Us* reported. "Inside the fights, deceit and drama of Britney's fall wedding." The cover showed Britney in her veil and wedding gown, her mouth agape mid-speech, appearing disoriented. Britney and K-Fed had a son. She drove with him on her lap instead of buckled into a car seat. She almost dropped him while leaving a Manhattan hotel. She did a *Dateline* interview with Matt Lauer. Pregnant again, in a frayed denim miniskirt and heavy makeup, she loudly smacked her gum, assuring him that her marriage was "awesome."

Then, in November 2006, Britney and Kevin filed for divorce. That's when things really got started. She was at the clubs again, smoking and drinking and dancing without underwear. On November 29, 2006, she took part in a meeting whose importance rivals the Yalta Conference: she partied with Paris *and* Lindsay at the same time. "BIMBO SUMMIT," read the front page of the *New York Post*, showing the three of them squished into the front of a vehicle. There were custody hearings and rumors: of rehab, psych hospitals, and child protective services. It was clear her behavior was a response to the stress of being hounded by the paparazzi every time she left the house (not to mention being famous and sexualized from a young age, going through a difficult divorce in the public eye, and being postpartum). But, like Diana, her reactions to the press just made them hound her more.

And then, in February 2007, it happened. She walked into a Tarzana, California, barbershop, grabbed a set of clippers, and shaved her own head. This moment was the most definitive of turning points. Britney's perfect blond hair had been her trademark, and to get rid of it was to publicly reject everything she had been forced to be thus far in her life. A few days later, the now-bald Britney attacked a group of photographers with an umbrella. "TIME BOMB," announced *Us Weekly*, promising "new details on that night," including "aunt: 'she needs to be on suicide watch.'" "BRITNEY'S MELTDOWN," blared *OK!*, telling readers that they spent "a heartbreaking day with the star and witness[ed] firsthand an emotional cry for help that will leave you shocked & sad." *People* promised a feature "INSIDE BRITNEY'S BREAKDOWN: wild partying, sobbing in public, shaving her head. With the family fearing for the star and her children, she enters rehab." "MOMMY'S CRYING," announced an *Us* cover featuring her son looking confused, as if Mommy had abandoned him somewhere. Later that year, another *Us* cover would read, "SICK! BRIT SLAMMED BY PARENTING COACH."

I'll never forget her performance at the VMAs that September. She wore a sparkly black and silver bra and matching underwear and knee-high boots, with limp extensions sewn into what remained of her natural hair. Her face had a blank expression as she gave the debut performance of "Gimme More." She missed steps in her choreography and her lip syncing didn't line up with the vocal track. She gave a half-hearted shimmy amid the backup dancers. Though she was still slim by most standards, she no longer had the visible abs that made her famous. She looked soft, damp, and despondent.

As soon as the performance ended, Perez Hilton responded in a characteristic post.

"Dear Britney," he wrote, "Fuck you! FUCK YOU!!!!!!! We are insulted, offended, and disgusted by your 'performance' at the VMAs. Are you fucking serious??? You didn't even try!!!!! You should have just cancelled, bitch."

For what felt like months afterward, he would repost photos of her from that performance taken at the least flattering moments, when she appeared, in mid-motion, to have a gut or a double chin. The pictures would be decorated with his signature scrawl: "mess," "I miss rehab," "unfit mother."

It had been exactly a decade since the car crash at Pont de l'Alma. Unlike Princess Diana, the tabloids didn't hound Britney to death. But at that moment it seemed like they could. Every time I checked Perez Hilton, there was a sense of frisson. Maybe this would be the Princess Diana moment, when I'd come across the post announcing her drug overdose or suicide or fatal car accident. I was among the millions who drove Perez's traffic during the Britney breakdown.*

One of the most perceptive critiques of the media's role in Britney's rise and fall came, surprisingly, from *South Park*. In an episode from March 2008 called "Britney's New Look," the show depicted Britney making a botched suicide attempt to escape the constant tabloid scrutiny. Though she blows off the top two-thirds of her head, she is still, somehow, alive. Her management pushes her to keep performing anyway. As the episode progresses, it becomes evident that we are in a retelling of the Shirley Jackson story "The Lottery." In that story, a small southern town has an annual ritual where they randomly select one citizen for a collective execution by stoning.

BRITNEY'S MELTDOWN ENDED anticlimactically, with a February 2008 court case. As the subprime mortgage crisis roiled and the housing bubble was about to burst, the State of California put Britney and her estate under a conservatorship run by her father, Jamie. She was not permitted to manage her own finances or set her own work schedule or see her own children without prior authorization from the state. She would later allege in court filings that she was forced to have an IUD inserted to ensure she would not get pregnant (though her father's attorney contested this claim). Britney was, in effect, returned to where she was at age sixteen, property of her father, but with the added humiliation of being herself an adult woman in her twenties and then in her thirties. She would remain in this situation until 2021, when years

---

* When Heath Ledger died of a drug overdose in January 2008, Perez sold shirts with a photo of the late actor's face and the words "Why Couldn't It Be Britney?"

of her own effort alongside activism by the Free Britney movement would come to fruition, terminating the conservatorship.

It felt like a kind of generational justice. And the press responded not with contempt but with celebration. "Freedom after 13 years!" announced the cover of *Us Weekly* on November 29, 2021. "What's next for Britney?" By the mid-2010s, the press—even the tabloid press—had begun to reassess its treatment of Spears during the previous decade. Or at least they quietly reframed their coverage of Spears and kept it moving. In 2021, the *New York Times* released a buzzy documentary called *Framing Britney Spears*, which sympathetically covered the singer's yearslong legal fight to end the conservatorship. It also turned a critical eye toward the press, arguing that their coverage of Spears in the 2000s led to the conservatorship. In 2023, Britney released her memoir, *The Woman in Me*, which immediately became the second-bestselling book of the year. Spears tells the story of her career and her conservatorship her way.

"Thirteen years went by with me feeling like a shadow of myself," she writes. "I think back now on my father and his associates having control over my body and my money for that long and it makes me feel sick."

Britney wasn't the only celebrity the media allowed to reclaim her narrative. In Paris Hilton's 2020 documentary *This Is Paris*, and in her 2022 memoir, the once-hated star revealed that she created her dumb rich girl persona to cope with an extensive history of trauma, from being raped as a teenager to being sent to an abusive reform school, where she was starved, beaten, deprived of sleep, sexually abused, and kept in solitary confinement. In her 2020 memoir *Open Book*, Jessica Simpson revealed that she, too, experienced sexual abuse, and her mental health and body image strained under cruel scrutiny from the 2000s tabloids. Lena Dunham and Alissa Bennett's podcast *The C-Word* did a two-part episode on Lindsay Lohan in which Lohan is cast as a victim of the era's relentless sexism, female objectification, and contempt toward people with substance abuse disorders. As millennials have settled into adulthood, this entire cottage industry of books, podcasts, documentaries, and essays has developed, reevaluating the treatment of female celebrities by the media during that peak era of gossip. Now celebrities routinely open up about their mental health struggles, which the press covers sympathetically.

It feels different now. Paris, Lindsay, Britney, the Olsen twins: All of these young women had their celebrity inflated like the housing bubble. When they were so puffed up that they couldn't contain all the contradictions of fame and wealth and femininity in America anymore, they collapsed in public. Then the collapse itself became the entertainment.

And then the actual housing bubble popped and the entire global economy collapsed. Suddenly, with 10 percent unemployment and 3.8 million foreclosures, the public lost its taste for Chihuahua mansions and *The Fabulous Life of...* As one YouTube commenter on an old *Fabulous Life* episode put it, "it's weird that people were so fascinated by these shows in the 2000s. Just seems like people don't want celebrities rubbing their wealth and excess in their faces anymore." I know I got sick of it. I found my attention drifting, instead, toward politics. Instead of checking Perez, I read *Jezebel*, which explicitly challenged awful, sexist narratives like his. I started to follow the financial crisis, first by watching *Rachel Maddow* and then by reading publications like *Jacobin*, which was founded by fellow millennials in 2010.

I WISH I could say it ended there: that we all learned our lesson and banished those nasty tabloids for good. But it wasn't just the recession that killed the Y2K-Era fame ecosystem. It wasn't just feminist blogs or generational moral outrage over the media's treatment of Britney. The changes were really technological (which was of course to say they were economic). And the Y2K-Era fame ecosystem wasn't killed, not exactly. One of its heads was cut off and several more grew back.

In 1997 when Princess Diana died, getting on the internet required making sure no one was on the phone, going to your home computer, and using a dial-up modem to log on (a very noisy process that alone took thirty seconds). There was no spontaneity. The dial-up modem provided a barrier between the self and the internet. This was Web 1.0, where you could read the news, search for a fan site, send an email, visit a chatroom, or talk to your friends on AOL Instant Messenger.

By the early 2000s, the shift was underway to the interactive, user-generated Web 2.0. This was the internet that gave us blogs and social media, that made Perez Hilton possible and then obsolete. A series of new websites revolutionized what the internet meant for users. Myspace started in 2003, Facebook in 2004 (open to the general public in 2006), YouTube in 2005, Twitter in 2006. In 2005, wireless internet overtook dial-up. This change made internet use spontaneous, ingrained in daily life. In 2007, Apple released the iPhone, allowing users to be connected to the internet everywhere at all times. Finally, in 2010 Instagram debuted.

As Natasha Stagg and others have written, social media in general and Instagram in particular meant that celebrities no longer needed the media to distribute their images. If I want to see what a celebrity is up to, I'm more likely to visit their Instagram page than read about them from a third party. Social media killed fame as it existed between 1997 and 2008, but it didn't kill fame itself. It changed some of fame's aesthetics, some of its calculations, some of how it was created and consumed and reproduced. But mostly it expanded fame, giving rise to the influencer, a person who, like people griped about Paris, is "famous for being famous." Some influencers are now A-list celebrities, and better people than me have written about this at length.

Now, we have all been conscripted into influencer-dom, which is to say fame. We are all micro celebrities. We are all our own publicists and stylists, selecting our clothes and makeup with an eye toward how we will be perceived on social media. I follow my peers the way I once followed Britney and Lindsay and the Olsen twins. Who are they wearing? What furniture are they putting in their homes? Who are they dating? Where are they vacationing? Are they getting married or getting divorced or going to rehab? Are they having a kid or having a mental breakdown in public?

And in the world of micro celebrity, who even are my peers? Strangers have come up to me at parties and asked if I'm Colette Shade from Twitter. On social media I've met people whose music I used to buy, who I used to watch on TV, who directed movies I enjoyed. The barriers are permeable now. Then there are the people I know in real life who parlayed social media into a career in TV or movies or whatever. Sometimes I think I should do that, though I know what the odds are. Maybe I'll delete all my accounts and move somewhere rural and throw my phone in the ocean.

I don't, though, and nobody I know does either. We're all stuck in a relationship with social media similar to the one Britney had with the paparazzi, raging against them with an umbrella while needing them for our own careers. I meant it when I was nine and I told my mom I didn't want to be famous. I still don't. But, like the celebs I used to follow, I find myself in the position of not wanting to be famous but needing to be famous. We're all Britney now.

Maybe she can show us the way, umbrella in hand.

Stupid Ugly Vehicles

T HERE IT WAS: 6,400 POUNDS OF STEEL, RUBBER, PLAS-
tic, and aluminum. More than 6 feet high and 15 feet long.
Painted gleaming cadmium yellow. I had heard rumors of
its size, of its menacing military design, and most of all of its fuel
inefficiency, its 32-gallon gas tank that burned through just 11
miles per gallon. But now I stood face-to-face with it, the 2004
Hummer H2, in the driveway of the house next to a family I babysat for. I felt something I couldn't yet name, something cold in
my stomach like when I went to the dentist. Terror, I would call it
now. And then despair.

My whole life I heard from my parents about the environment,
and how we were destroying it, how we had to save it or the consequences would be dire. My parents taught my brother and me
to reuse and recycle, to put on a sweater instead of turning up
the heat, to switch the lights off when we left a room. They taught
us the names of the birds and the trees. I could identify pin oaks
and cardinals and poplars and chickadees before I could read. My
dad was a vegetarian, and if there was a turtle in the road he'd pull
over and move it to the side. If there was an SUV on the road he'd
tell us it was a "gas guzzler." He'd tell us that the people driving

it must not know or understand the science on global warming, which told intelligent people like him that SUVs were raising the global temperature by pumping carbon into the atmosphere. He'd announce—as if we hadn't heard this a million times already—that, *actually*, he called SUVs "Stupid Ugly Vehicles."

It wasn't just my parents. Throughout the '90s, there was a general cultural feeling that "we" needed to "save the environment." Baby boomers like my parents were the ones who held the first Earth Day, in 1970. My mom had an original Earth Day button she got at the march she attended in Palo Alto. "Gasp!" it says, inside a cloud of pollution. Brands like Aveda and The Body Shop promoted their ecological bona fides. Media mogul Ted Turner—at the height of his fame—regularly spoke out about environmentalism. He produced *Captain Planet and the Planeteers*—an ecologically themed children's superhero cartoon—which I watched every day after school. In second grade I joined a club at school called Project H.O.P.E. (Help Our Planet Earth). We ran stream cleanups, made posters promoting environmental best practices, and sold T-shirts with animals on them to support the rainforest.

In the 1990s, environmentalism was preoccupied with the preservation of the Amazon rainforest. There was a popular candy called Rainforest Crunch, a Brazil nut and cashew brittle whose proceeds, supposedly, went to saving the Amazon. The company teamed up with Ben & Jerry's to do a special-edition ice cream flavor, which lasted from 1989 to 1999. In 1992 I requested a rainforest-themed fourth-birthday party. My mom cut tropical leaves out of green construction paper and the goodie bags contained little plastic tree frogs. In fifth grade we had a unit on the JASON Project, which culminated in a visit to the National Geographic Society in downtown DC, where a biologist explained his fieldwork in Brazil.

The Rainforest Cafe, which began in Minnesota in 1994, was a

chain of rainforest-themed restaurants in malls around the world.
The concept allowed shoppers to feel like they were connecting
with nature in between stops at Abercrombie and Sharper Image.
The walls and ceiling were covered with fake vines. Fake mangrove
trees sprouted from the floor. You could order an "Amazon Flat-
bread pizza" or an "African Wind Salad" or a "Spotted Chocolate
Monkey milkshake." There were large plexiglass statues of tree
frogs. There was a soundtrack with birds and screeching monkeys.
At intervals, the sounds of a thunderstorm would interrupt. The
lights would flash and fog would pump from the ceiling. The whole
place smelled vaguely like a swimming pool.

Despite all this—the recycling and the rainforest stuff and *Captain Planet* and the fact that people were, as I wrote in 1999 for
a school assignment, "start[ing] to realize that we are destroying
our environment"—SUV sales rose steeply through the '90s. In
1990, 7 percent of cars sold in the United States were SUVs. By
1999, that number was 19 percent. There were just over 243,000
SUVs sold in 1980. Over 3 million SUVs were sold in 1999.

And SUV buyers weren't just conservatives (though I think the
family with the H2 was). Another family we knew drove a Chevrolet
Suburban (despite the father being an environmental attorney) because, well, it was hard to get three sons to basketball practice and
Outer Banks vacations otherwise. And of course, you almost had to
buy an SUV if you cared about your family's safety. SUVs had great
safety ratings, performing well in crashes due to their size, even as
they made other, smaller cars and the families inside them less safe.
The Suburban, in other words, was perfectly named for its target
demographic: professional-class families in car-dependent suburbs
who wanted to cocoon their children in safety, even at the expense
of other children's safety, and, in a future sense, at the expense of
their children's and their children's children's safety.

ON JUNE 23, 1988—four days before and just a few miles away from where I was delivered in an ambulance by a Fairfax County EMT—a NASA scientist named James Hansen gave a testimony before Congress.

"Number one, the earth is warmer in 1988 than at any time in the history of instrumental measurements," he said. "Number two, the global warming is already large enough that we can ascribe with a high degree of confidence a cause-and-effect relationship to the greenhouse effect. And number three, our computer climate simulations indicate that the greenhouse effect is large enough to begin to affect the probability of extreme events such as summer heat waves. . . . It is changing our climate now."

James Hansen's testimony marked the first time climate change was brought up in the halls of Congress, but it was a story some scientists had been telling for a long time. In the 1860s, when coal was the primary fossil fuel, physicist John Tyndall discovered what is now called the greenhouse effect: that carbon dioxide can absorb and hold heat. In 1912—when oil was just beginning to eclipse coal, before commercial flight, before cars became the dominant mode of transportation—there was a small article in a New Zealand paper.

"Coal consumption affecting climate," read the headline. "The furnaces of the world are now burning about 2,000,000,000 tons of coal a year. When this is burned, uniting with oxygen, it adds about 7,000,000,000 tons of carbon dioxide to the atmosphere yearly. This tends to make the air a more effective blanket for the earth and to raise its temperature. The effect may be considerable in a few centuries."

As early as the 1970s, Exxon knew that fossil fuels were causing climate change. In 1977, a scientist working for the company told executives internally that "there is general scientific agreement that the most likely manner in which mankind is influencing the global climate is through carbon dioxide release from the burning of fossil fuels." According to a subsequent internal memo from 1978, "present thinking holds that man has a time window of five to ten years before the need for hard decisions regarding changes in energy strategies might become critical."

In the late '70s, Exxon assembled a world-class research team to study these findings more deeply. This team of scientists predicted the next decades' timeline of carbon concentration, temperature shift, and climate breakdown with astounding accuracy. But the company kept the information secret. If it had been public, we could have started decarbonizing decades earlier. Instead, by the late '80s, the oil industry was pouring millions into spreading misinformation, funding research that claimed the exact opposite of the internal reports. Actually, these other scientists claimed, an increase in atmospheric carbon concentration *wasn't* causing climate change. Recent increases in global temperature, these scientists said, were just the Little Ice Age ending, which just so happened to line up with the exact moment in history when humans started burning a lot of fossil fuels.

The timing for Hansen's testimony couldn't have been worse. 1988 was right in the middle of the neoliberal turn: a political moment when there was a widespread belief that the only role of government was to prop up the private sector. What governments needed to do, Hansen would argue, was work together to regulate—then abolish—the fossil fuel industry. But in the story told by neoliberalism, this kind of intervention is impossible. In the neoliberal story, humans are rational actors living at the culmination of a technological, scientific, and economic revolution that began with the Enlightenment in the seventeenth century.

In 1620, Francis Bacon invented the scientific method, a rigorous process of hypothesizing, experimentation, measurement, and deduction still in use to this day. In fact, it's the same process that allowed Hansen and other researchers to measure the effects of climate change. Francis Bacon argued, in 1623, that science would allow humans "to hound nature in her wanderings, to lead and drive her." We shouldn't, he argued "make scruple of entering and penetrating into those holes and corners when the inquisition of truth is [the scientist's] whole object." The planet's resources, he asserted, were theoretically infinite, and endless growth was possible if we got good enough at science. By the neoliberal era, challenging this belief was seen as irrational and anti-progress.

Many environmentalists in this era made their claims without disputing the neoliberal story. Climate change, they argued, was caused by *humans*—not by corporations, not by billionaires, and certainly not by capitalism. This narrative was helped along by the fossil fuel industry. In 2004, BP released the first-ever carbon footprint calculator, which helped people track how much CO_2 they put into the atmosphere from eating food, commuting to work, having children, and taking the occasional vacation. Not mentioned is the fact that one's individual carbon footprint is insignificant next to the carbon footprint of a company like BP. Or the fact that human civilization had been around for twelve thousand years, but carbon emissions didn't go up significantly until industrial capitalism was introduced in the nineteenth century. To put that another way, human civilization has only caused climate change for about 1.6 percent of its existence. But no one talked like that in the Y2K Era.

IN CHILDHOOD, I envisioned the new millennium as a boundless, glittering future. But Hansen's prophesy cast a lone shadow. I remember December 1998. That summer in the mid-Atlantic there had been a heat wave and a drought, but by October things finally cooled down. November was mild but still felt like it was supposed to. It rained a bit. I wore a jacket or a coat most days. And then, on the last day of the month, as people were putting up their Christmas lights, it suddenly felt like spring. It was 64 degrees, said Bob Ryan. He told us to get outside and enjoy the day if we could. I wore a T-shirt and biked around the neighborhood after school. I wasn't enjoying it.

It was an Indian summer, everybody said. It was El Niño. It was just typical, crazy mid-Atlantic weather. Every day I waited for the cold front to come and make it feel like December again, but it stayed warm and then a few days later got even warmer, up to the seventies. It culminated in a record-breaking 79-degree day in December. I put on a Fair Isle sweater, as if this could will the weather back to normal. Sweating as I walked around outside, I relented and put on a tank top. The next day the temperature made news in the *Washington Post,* which ran photos of women sunbathing in the unseasonable weather.

A year later, in 1999, it was the middle of the night. I couldn't sleep. I did what I always did when that happened and went downstairs to the rec room to watch music videos on VH1. "Meet Virginia" by Train was playing. I hated that song because it was whiny and the tempo was weird and the video was boring, so I switched to the Weather Channel, hoping they'd have news of a cold front. It had been another warm winter, and outside it was overcast and almost sticky. Again, there was a dissonance to everyone's Christmas decorations being up when it felt like May. But the warm front would remain in the East. In the Midwest there would be storms. As the smooth jazz* played, I watched the pixelated green clouds pass over

---

* In 2007, the Weather Channel released a compilation album of this music called *The Weather Channel Presents: The Best of Smooth Jazz,* which went to

Oklahoma, Kansas, and Nebraska. I thought about all the people living there that I had never met, and wondered if they were sad about the weather like I was. I switched back to "Meet Virginia."

The weather didn't seem to bother adults. They all commented on how "glorious" or "beautiful" it was, instead of being concerned that they were wearing short sleeves in December. My parents told me to quit worrying because I couldn't control the weather. I was an anxious kid, prone to worst-case-scenario thinking. I thought every headache was brain cancer and, at one point, believed a street gang would confront me on the walk home from school and force me to try drugs.

But, like my therapist told me, I had no evidence for those worries. Meanwhile, I knew every tree in my neighborhood like the back of my hand, and I could tell things weren't right. The dogwoods weren't supposed to be blooming in March. And the first frost was supposed to come in early October. The mid-Atlantic never got that much snowfall—white Christmases were a rarity— but in winter 1998, for the first time in my life, we got none. In March 1999 there was a snowstorm, and the following winter of 1999 to 2000 it snowed a bit, but not as much as it had all the other years of my childhood.

I recognized the difference between weather and climate, and knew that some years would always be outliers. I knew about El Niño, about Indian summer in November, about the way March and even late February could go from wintry to mild and back again. In fact, I was obsessed with the Farmers' Almanac, memorizing statistics about historical highs and lows, averages, and storms. But I knew that what I was seeing with my own eyes was different. Climate change—at that time called "global warming"—

---

number one on Billboard's Contemporary Jazz Albums chart.

was still being talked about as a problem of the future, a problem for "our grandkids," or maybe even "our grandkids' grandkids." But this was happening *now*. Couldn't anybody else see?

There is a famous chart from 2020 measuring average global temperature from two thousand years ago to present. Each year is a thin vertical stripe, color coded from dark blue (coldest) to dark red (hottest). It looks kind of like one of those striped Paul Smith shirts so popular in the Y2K Era. From the years 0 to 1300, the stripes are a mixture of blue and white, with some light red mixed in. After 1300, the stripes are a mixture of darker and lighter blues, indicating the Little Ice Age. And then, just after 1900—about a century after industrial capitalism first began large-scale burning of fossil fuels—the stripes turn a mixture of white and light red, with only a little blue. This is redder than any part of the map so far. By the end of the twentieth century, there is a thick stripe of bright red, and then, at the very end, indicating the 2000s to the present, a new color: a stripe of deep red the color of clotted blood.

IN THE RAINFOREST Cafe '90s, there was a tacit acknowledgment that a future shaped by climate change should be rejected, even if many Americans' actions—namely the purchase of fuel-inefficient SUVs, the growth of McMansions and exurbs, and eating at places like the Rainforest Cafe—were guaranteeing that future. But there was at least some sense that you ought to feel shame or conflict over your consumption habits. With the Bush administration and the War on Terror, that changed. The president was a Texas oil guy whose administration told Americans to be patriotic after 9/11 by going shopping. Bush promised to keep gas prices down even if we had to illegally invade Iraq to do it. The H2 hit the market in 2002—one year before the US invasion of Baghdad—and was sold until 2009, when spiking gas prices and the 2008 recession decimated its market base (Hummer's parent company, GM, also filed for bankruptcy). Its top-selling years were 2003, 2004, and 2005, when it moved more than 34,000, 28,000, and 23,000 units, respectively.

The H2 summed up an entire way of thinking about the Earth and Americans' place on it, about the future and Americans' duty to it. The Hummer was an SUV without apology, without the fig leaves of safety ratings and seating capacity occasionally proffered by its more respectable peers: the Suburban, the Ford Expedition, the Chevrolet Tahoe, the Jeep Liberty, the Toyota Highlander. The Hummer's design and colorways were a flashy celebration of profligacy and violence. People who drove Hummers did so because they knew all about climate change, and they didn't give a fuck.

The American way of life, we were told in the 2000s, was all about rejecting the idea that there were any kind of limits on the Earth's capacities. It was about taking what we wanted no matter who it hurt. In fact, it was about celebrating the hurt that our lifestyles caused. Anyone who tried to live otherwise—let alone get in our way—was a pussy and gay and un-American, and they deserved whatever was coming to them.

South Park devoted several episodes to skewering anyone who deigned to care about the present and future habitability of the planet. In a 2002 episode, Stan becomes a vegetarian. He develops sores on his face, which turn out to be vaginas. Because, get it? Tofu and carrots are for pussies, not real Americans. The show's tenth season featured a 2006 episode in which Kyle's dad buys a Prius, which emits a substance called "smug" that itself causes climate change. Because, get it? The real existential problem the world was facing that year was people being annoying.

In 2005, my dad bought his own Prius—the anti-SUV—and, like Kyle's dad in South Park, couldn't stop talking about it. In 2006, Al Gore put out a soporific documentary called *An Inconvenient Truth*. The ninety-four-minute movie is centered around the former vice president (and 2000 election loser) standing onstage delivering a PowerPoint. He talks about polar bears and statistics and ice caps and LED lightbulbs. At an early screening of the film, several studio executives fell asleep.

Nonetheless, *An Inconvenient Truth* became a genuine cultural phenomenon. It received standing ovations at Sundance and broke box office records for a documentary (despite executives' early reservations that "we do not believe that anyone will pay to have a babysitter come so that they can go see this movie"). After its release, there was a sharp increase in Google searches for "climate change."

"You owe it to yourself to see this film," wrote Roger Ebert. "If you do not, and you have grandchildren, you should explain to them why you decided not to." *An Inconvenient Truth*, he said elsewhere, has "the potential, I believe, to actually change public policy and begin a process which could save the Earth."

The film turned Al Gore into a conservative bête noire. *South Park* mocked his climate crusade with a 2006 episode that depicts Gore as hysterical and climate change as a myth. Oklahoma senator James Inhofe compared the film to *Mein Kampf*. When George W. Bush was asked if he would see *An Inconvenient Truth*, he responded, simply, "Doubt it."

For all the Prius owners, *An Inconvenient Truth* was a message to pat themselves on the back. They were the rational ones. They believed the science.

But it was never about science, not really. The fault lines were more psychoanalytic. Liberals, as usual, played the superego, saying, "No! No! Don't be naughty! Drive a Prius." Mainstream environmentalism at this time didn't really have a positive vision. It was all about "don'ts": don't drive a gas guzzler, don't use plastic bags, don't use incandescent lightbulbs, don't live in a McMansion, don't eat meat, don't go shopping. Its psychic pleasures were about self-control and self-deprivation.

Conservatives, as usual, played the id, saying, "Give in! Kill as many people as possible with your vehicle AND its emissions!" The id, of course, contains the libido. And burning carbon is not just violent; it is also erotic.

"The aesthetics of fossil fuels—most particularly oil—are ripe for recoding as expressions of sexualised power and orgasmic satisfaction," writes political scientist Cara Daggett, noting that environmental destruction is often described as raping the Earth. Since at least Francis Bacon, the Earth has been depicted, in the West, as female. Its existence, like that of women and their wombs, allows for the continued reproduction of human life, and later, the accumulation of profit. But in both cases, sexual desire and violence intermix. The Earth, like a woman, must be dominated and tamed, shaped to the rational will of man whether she likes it or not. Fossil fuels don't just appear. They have to be taken, by penetrating the Earth until she gives you what you want. Daggett calls this framework "petro-masculinity."

The academic Stephanie LeMenager notes that in Upton Sinclair's book *Oil!* (which later became the much-quoted 2007 film *There Will Be Blood*), there is a scene where, "for a thirteen-year-old male narrator, industrial-scale pollution and waste translate into arousal and premature ejaculation." The spurt of an oil well is compared to a female orgasm. LeMenager talks about "oil's primal associations with earth's body, therefore with the permeability, excess, and multiplicity of all bodies." In other words, it doesn't take a psychoanalyst to understand that, when Sarah Palin said

"Drill, baby, drill" on the 2008 campaign trail, she meant it in more ways than one.

"Burning fossil fuels in an age of global warming can offer a compensatory practice of violence," says Daggett. "Fossil fuel systems provide a domain for explosive letting go, and all the pleasures that come with it—drilling, digging, fracking, mountaintop removal, diesel trucks."

In other words, as Freud observed, hurting people feels good. It feels especially good if you live in a country where you've been getting hurt your whole life. You've been watching your living standard decline for decades. You can't get a good job anymore. The air you breathe and the food you eat is making you sick. Your slipped disc is acting up. You don't have health insurance or if you do, you can't afford the surgery that will make you better. You barely have time off to go on vacation, not that you could afford it. You're working your ass off and not getting anywhere.

Or maybe that's not exactly the story. Maybe you're working your ass off and you have a lot to show for it. You have a Mc-Mansion and a four-car garage. You're the boss of the company. You're living the American dream. But still, you work hard, long hours, high stress. You make sacrifices to provide for your wife and your kids.

Either way, now some asshole is coming in to tell you what to eat and what car to drive. They're trying to take away the things that make you feel good. They're telling you to feel bad for having a cock, for using it as men always have. But—goddamn it!—you're a man, so you're up for a fight. And they're fucking hypocrites, too! Al Gore flies around the world in a private jet. Does he really think some lightbulb or a gay-looking car is going to stop the end of the world?

THE END OF the world would arrive unevenly, is arriving unevenly. In violin class in 1993, we five-year-olds kept 4/4 time with *Mis-sis-sip-pi Mis-sis-sip-pi Mis-sis-sip-pi Mis-sis-sip-pi*—"Like the river that's flooding now, maybe you've seen it on the news"— our bows creaked in tempo as the teacher said this. Or in 1995, when someone like Robert Siegel said something on *All Things Considered* like "Over seven hundred people have died following a historic heat wave in Chicago," and I had a feeling that I had no words to describe, except to say it felt like falling, and that it still feels that way even now, or maybe especially now. These events were reported as points without a graph, disparate pieces of information not yet shot through with the line of master narrative, even as Hansen's warning loomed in the background.

Hurricane Katrina made landfall on the Gulf Coast on August 29, 2005: a decade after the Chicago heat wave, seven years after the hot December, and three years after the Hummer H2 went on sale. I watched the hurricane on TV like I watched *My Super Sweet 16*. On the eve of the storm's arrival, long lines of cars backed up the elevated highways around New Orleans. Other people—maybe 150,000 or 200,000—stayed behind in the city, nailing boards to their windows and telling reporters they weren't *going anywhere.*

The storm arrived as a Category 4. Its rain and its storm surge collapsed the levees and flood walls, leaving 80 percent of the city underwater. Hit worst was the mostly Black Lower Ninth Ward. I saw people rescued from their attics and their rooftops by the National Guard. I saw people waving down helicopters with their hands or American flags. In white spray paint they had written HELP and SOS INSIDE and THE WATER IS RISING PLEAS. There were aerial shots of the Superdome with parts of its cladding ripped off. There were interior shots, the camera panning out and out to show the 25,000 people crowded onto the floor and the seats in that "shelter of last resort," which, reporters told us, had no power and no air-conditioning as temperatures rose into the nineties. There was no plumbing, reporters told us, and people were relieving themselves in the sinks and the trash cans.

Elsewhere, images of looting were shown. Fires burned before the floods had even receded. On the Danziger Bridge, New Orleans police officers shot six unarmed civilians, killing two of them. Inside the Orleans Parish Prison, inmates were locked in their cells as waters rose neck-high. A few days later, corrections officers came back to get them, ordering them out onto buses bound for other jails. Later, Human Rights Watch found that 517 prisoners simply vanished, unaccounted for. Humanity, citizenship, even life: all of these things were conditional now.

The events of Hurricane Katrina were interpreted as an undeveloped relic of America's past, rather than a preview of America's future. Though the hurricane is now viewed—at least in some circles—as the moment when climate change stopped being "our children's children's" problem, it wasn't covered that way at the time. And the problem, too, is the word "our." I guarantee that most of the people waving down helicopters on their roofs were not the people buying Hummer H2s, even though the people buying Hummer H2s were the ones making the floodwaters rise.

We talked about the hurricane in AP US Government. The teacher set aside time at the beginning of class for us to process the tragedy together. There was this kid Ryan who sat on the other side of the room from me. He was in the Young Republicans and his wealthy father was later implicated in a white-collar crime scheme. After a few people talked about their anger with the Bush administration's handling of the crisis—especially the president's appointment of bumbling FEMA director Michael Brown—Ryan raised his hand to share his thoughts.

"Maybe, if those people in New Orleans didn't want their kids to drown, they shouldn't have gotten addicted to crack," he said.

This, too, was a preview of the future. Ryan was not—as some might think—speaking the hateful language of an unenlightened past. Rather, his blithe dismissal of racialized mass death was the way people would need to speak in the future, at least in any future where SUVs would still exist.

CLIMATE CHANGE ISN'T like other crises. For around twelve thousand years, human civilization—agriculture, cities, trade, the arts—has developed under relatively stable conditions. But climate change has pushed the Earth beyond these planetary boundaries. According to one climate scientist, "We don't know that we can thrive under major, dramatic alterations." A 2023 *New York Times* article discussed how, starting around the year 2000, climate change and groundwater depletion began to alter the tilt of the Earth's axis. A recent study found that planetary conditions are now in "uncharted territory," that "we are entering a situation no one has ever witnessed firsthand in the history of humanity." One of the biggest risks comes from feedback loops. For instance, climate change is causing more wildfires. Smoke releases more carbon into the atmosphere, which then worsens climate change, causing even more wildfires. There are also climate tipping points: irreversible changes that quickly accelerate the climate change process.

For decades, carbon emissions have been rising. Once emitted, carbon stays in the atmosphere for 300 to 1,000 years. As long as the current system of carbon throughput is in place, time passing equals climate change getting worse. Which means that the younger you are, the more severe the crisis will be during your lifetime. And, because climate change effects the entire Earth, there's nowhere to escape.

In 2021, *The Lancet* published a study on feelings of climate grief and climate anxiety among 10,000 people age 16 to 25 in ten different countries.

"Respondents across all countries were worried about climate change (59% were very or extremely worried and 84% were at least moderately worried)," the study found. "More than 50% reported each of the following emotions: sad, anxious, angry, powerless, helpless, and guilty. More than 45% said their feelings about climate change negatively affected their daily life and functioning, and many reported a high number of negative thoughts about climate change. . . . Respondents rated the governmental response to climate change negatively and reported greater feelings of betrayal than of reassurance. Climate anxiety and distress were correlated with perceived inadequate government response and associated feelings of betrayal."

Young people seem to suffer the most when their government—a kind of parental figure, basically—doesn't appear to give a shit about their futures. I don't think it's an accident that, in recent years, the Goya painting of Saturn devouring his son has become a popular meme online.

Years before Greta Thunberg started her school strike, I wondered what the point of doing homework was when the end of the world was being hastened by Hummers and other SUVs. I wondered why the government wasn't protecting me. As I got older, the climate crisis worsened. Each year the wildfire season did more damage, not just in California, but in places typically not prone to severe wildfires, like England, Greece, Sweden, and northern Canada. So-called "once in a generation" storms devastated New York

City, Houston, Puerto Rico, Japan, and Pakistan. Eighty-degree days in November and February became a regular occurrence. All the flowers bloomed at once. Heat waves scorched the trees, and one year in August I was driving through rural Maryland and I noticed something new. The normally green canopy was marred by patches of brown, dead leaves, like the whole forest was rotting.

At one point, between 2016 and 2019, my fixation on climate change got so bad that I could barely focus on anything else. Why was I making oatmeal and going to work when the world was ending? Why was I getting out of bed? What was the point of having a career when there wouldn't be a society? Why save for a house if it would only burn down in a fire or get washed away in a hurricane? What was the point of writing if no one would be alive to read my thoughts in the future? (That *Lancet* study found, by the way, that 55 percent of respondents believe "humanity is doomed.")

I started to have obsessive thoughts about ending my own life. These thoughts have crossed my mind periodically since middle school. But they would always be fleeting, and I could always talk myself down by reminding myself of the things I loved: a crisp fall day, a juicy pear, the song of a bright red cardinal. I took comfort in the fact that cardinals were indifferent to whatever heartbreak or petty yearning was upsetting me at the time. Fall would come every year regardless of whether I killed myself or not, so shouldn't I stick around for another one?

But climate change would kill all the cardinals. With increasing heat waves, the pears would bake on the trees. Climate change would shatter the wheel of the year that had turned so reliably for millennia; there would be no more fall, no more winter, or spring, or summer. If all of that was gone, and no one was doing anything about it, why should I keep going? Friends and family told me I was being irrational, that they were worried about me and I needed help. I knew they were right; I was going crazy. But wasn't our society going even crazier?

AT THE BEGINNING of the twenty-first century, my parents said that we could save the environment with backyard composting and seitan burgers and hybrid cars and reusable tote bags. That we just had to believe the scientists and cite our sources and watch documentaries. But none of these individual actions challenged the true cause of climate change: a completely irrational economic system that values short-term profit making over a livable future, that values domination over survival.

Climate change continued to get worse. The aperture of the future narrowed. And then, a few years ago, a new type of movement offered a story different from the one my parents told. Forget about your carbon footprint, the climate movement said. Forget the Priuses. The people causing this crisis have names and addresses. It's capitalism versus the climate, they said. What we need is a Green New Deal: a chance to fix our seriously screwed up, totally irrational society. This proposition is different from the environmentalism I grew up with, which emphasized the smug satisfaction of personal sacrifice (a tough sell for people who already feel squeezed by decades of neoliberalism). The contemporary climate movement promises, instead, actual pleasure: the pleasure of leisure, of public amenities, of publicly funded health care and childcare. Pleasure, the climate movement argues, needn't mean driving a giant car that kills people. This new movement came to prominence in the late 2010s: a time when I most needed hope.

Here is what still worries me, though. The fossil fuel industry is among the most lucrative and powerful the world has ever known. In the Y2K Era—at the exact moment that climate change's direr effects were starting to become visible—the institutions required to rein in fossil fuels were becoming increasingly dysfunctional. Laws were passed to reclassify nonviolent environmental protests as "ecoterrorism." And police got ever more funding and ever-better weapons, allowing them to handily defeat seemingly any mass movement. Border patrol kept on caging and deporting immigrants, many of whom were effectively climate refugees. The stakes are now higher than they've ever been, and so are the risks. It's hard for me to believe only in a movement.

The twenty-first century was supposed to belong to the Enlightenment. It was supposed to signify a boundless future powered by science and technology, where we could take what we wanted without asking, just as we had for the previous four hundred years. And all this was supposed to be good; to be rational.

Then things flipped. Enlightenment logic still ruled the twenty-first century. But it had created instead the conditions for futurelessness, for crisis, for total irrationality. Yes, the enlightenment gave us the tools to measure climate change. But it also gave us the Hummer H2.

The Enlightenment was also a process of storytelling. Old stories were tossed out: from religion, from psychoanalysis. They were replaced with stories of logic and science and human triumph over nature. By the time I was a kid, that process was just about finished. I laughed at the idea that people actually, literally believed that thunderstorms were caused by Zeus getting mad, or that the whole world survived a flood because Noah—a six-hundred-year-old man—put two of every animal on his boat. Why had people in the past been so backward, so superstitious? Couldn't they see they were being irrational?

These sentiments hardened as I entered my teenage years. I became a fan of the New Atheist movement, which was at its

cultural high-water mark in the mid-to-late 2000s. The New Athe-
ists consisted of commentators, scientists, and comedians like
Richard Dawkins, Christopher Hitchens, Bill Maher, Sam Harris,
and Penn Jillette. They wrote books and hosted TV shows and
starred in stand-up specials and put out documentaries explaining
why, empirically, God wasn't real and religious rituals were silly.
They argued that society's biggest problems—from war to climate
change to sexual repression—were caused by stragglers stuck in
an unenlightened past. If we could all get really, really literal and
really, really scientific, we might have a shot at a nice planet together. I held on to that worldview through college. I would corner
you at parties to explain why atheism was objectively true, or why
we shouldn't study Freud, since he had been debunked by the
behaviorists. I became less annoying about it later, but that's still
basically what I believed.

It wasn't until those years of climate despair that I began to question my commitments. It occurred to me that the stories I once
dismissed—from religion, from psychoanalysis—could teach me
things about climate change that science couldn't. These weren't
things that could be measured, like how old the Earth is (it's obviously 4.5 billion years old, a fact accepted by the pope since 1950).
These things were outside the scope of Bacon's scientific inquiry:
power, morality, desire, evil. For example: What might possess a
person to destroy everything for their own perceived short-term
gain? How might we set things right? Who will we fight with?
And how might we keep going when the odds seem so stacked
against us?

Then, for the first time, I prayed.

It's Definitely About Coffee, but It's About a Lot More Than Coffee

MY FIRST TRIP TO STARBUCKS WAS IN THE SUMMER of 2000. I had just turned twelve years old, and we were in Ottawa visiting my dad's side of the family. We had spent the afternoon walking around Chapters bookstore downtown, my cousin Louise explaining to me which Francesca Lia Block novels she liked the best. Louise was a raver, with short pink hair and JNCO jeans. She bragged to me that she had read *Lolita*.

"I bet you don't even know what *Lolita* is about," she said.

"I know what *Lolita* is about," I replied.

And I did know, though I hadn't read it yet.

As we passed the in-store Starbucks counter, she announced, "I want a Frappuccino."

"Me too," I said, hoping to impress her.

My mom was hesitant. She didn't want me getting addicted to coffee, she thought the drink had way too much sugar, and she felt it was an overpriced milkshake I had been tricked into desiring by corporate advertising. But Louise was allowed to have Frappuccinos. She was just a year older than I was, and her mom hated sugar and multinational corporations at least as much as my mom did.

So I followed Louise to the register. Like her, I ordered a tall mocha Frappuccino, paying with a handful of loonies and toonies.

When I picked up my order from the end of the counter I paused for a few moments to take it all in. There was so much to love: the clear, domed cup, the way the green straw contrasted with the white whipped cream drizzled with dark chocolate syrup, the light brown slush of the drink itself. It was rich and refreshing at the same time. I felt like an adult.

Frappuccinos became a treat I could have two or three times a year if we happened to be at an airport or a mall. But once I was in high school—especially after I could drive—I would get them once or even twice a week. I branched out into caramel macchiatos, peppermint mochas, and iced vanilla lattes. I would walk in late to my first-period AP Government class, aloof, clutching a clear cup with a green straw, just like celebrities did in *Us* magazine. I started hanging out at Starbucks on weekends and after school, doing my homework there instead of at the dining room table. Everything in the store was the color of different types of coffee and chocolate, shot through with green. My mom continued to tell me I was wasting my babysitting money and getting tricked by advertisers. My dad told me Starbucks coffee was low quality and I should instead try the artisanal fair-trade coffee he ordered from Minneapolis off a website.

In college, in the very late 2000s, I would come to agree with my dad. I lived in Burlington, Vermont, then, and I got my beans at City Market, an organic co-op downtown. In the bulk section I would choose among varieties from specific farms in Kenya and Indonesia and the Dominican Republic. Each morning, I'd make black coffee in my Bodum French press, a practice I still keep to this day. I didn't go to Starbucks often during those years. There was only one location in town, and there were about a dozen better coffee shops, shops that made peppermint mochas, too, but with single-origin beans and local milk and artisanal chocolate (Vermont, I often tell people, transformed me into a food snob). But I didn't give up my habit entirely. A few times a year I'll still go in for a pumpkin spice latte or an iced vanilla latte or even a peppermint mocha.

I don't even really enjoy them. I do it because Starbucks, quite frankly, fascinates me, the way it fully embodies its historical moment. When we speak about Starbucks, we speak not only of the company itself, but what it means: the pop culture references, the political discourse (or lack thereof). What people are saying about Starbucks at any given time can tell us a lot about where we've been and where we're going, economically, politically, and culturally. And to truly understand Starbucks, I think, requires looking at the moment of its steepest ascent: the Y2K Era.

STARBUCKS WAS FOUNDED in Seattle in 1971 by history teacher Zev Siegl, writer Gordon Bowker, and former English teacher Gerald Baldwin. These three friends from the University of San Francisco wanted to sell gourmet dark-roast coffee from Sumatra, Ethiopia, and Costa Rica at a time when most Americans were likely to be drinking pre-ground Maxwell House from provenances unknown. The founders were inspired by a proliferation of coffeehouses in the 1950s and '60s, which served as countercultural hubs for folk music, beat poetry, and antiwar organizing. Siegl, Bowker, and Baldwin were a classic type of mid-twentieth-century white man: the bearded, bohemian, often West Coast boomer who, in his later years, follows his passion to a big payout in the once-hated corporate world.[*]

Siegl, Bowker, and Baldwin met with artist Terry Heckler to develop the store's brand. According to Starbucks, the founders "wanted the company's name to suggest a sense of adventure, a connection to the Northwest and a link to the seafaring tradition of the early coffee traders." Bowker wanted to call the company Pequod after the whaling ship in *Moby Dick*. The *Pequod*, it's worth noting, traverses the world in search of the novel's titular whale, captained by the ambition-mad Ahab, who enlists his employees in a kind of world domination, no matter the stakes. By the story's end, the novel's titular whale smashes the *Pequod* to bits, killing everyone on board but the narrator. Heckler voted down the name Pequod because he was skeptical that people would want to patronize a coffee shop whose name contained the word "pee." The company settled on the name Starbucks, after the *Pequod*'s first mate.

For the logo, Heckler and the founders stuck with the nautical theme. While poring through old books, they came across a sixteenth-century Norse print of a Siren: a two-tailed mermaid with bare breasts and a crown atop her wavy hair. Heckler drew her inside a brown circle, surrounded by text that said STARBUCKS COFFEE, TEA, AND SPICE. The logo has changed a few times over the years—most notably in 1987, when the Siren's color was swapped from brown to green and her breasts were hidden by her hair—but she has remained a staple of the brand's identity since the beginning.

---

* You could call it the Jerry Rubin hippie-to-yuppie pipeline. Other famous examples include Steve Jobs, Ben Cohen and Jerry Greenfield of Ben & Jerry's, and Tony and Maureen Wheeler, the husband-and-wife founders of Lonely Planet.

"I hope when people see the siren on their cup, of course it's going to stand for what they're going to get from Starbucks," creative director Steve Murray said in 2016. "If the siren is on that cup of coffee, it's going to be awesome. It's definitely about coffee but it's about a lot more than coffee. It's about . . . being good to people, being good to the world."

Siegl, Bowker, and Baldwin each invested $1,350 of their own money and took out an additional $5,000 bank loan, then set up shop at 2000 Western Avenue near Pike Place Market, where they offered customers thirty varieties of gourmet whole-bean coffee in an industrial space with hand-built fixtures. The company experienced local success, expanding from one store to five.

Howard Schultz entered the picture in 1982 as the director of retail operations and marketing. Schultz was another type of classic mid-to-late-twentieth-century white guy: the upwardly mobile working-class ethnic. The Jewish Shultz grew up in the housing projects of Canarsie, Brooklyn. His father was a truck driver (among other things), and Howard was the first person in the family to graduate from college, earning a bachelor's degree in communications from Northern Michigan University, which he attended on a football scholarship.

As he describes in his 1997 business memoir *Pour Your Heart Into It: How Starbucks Built a Company One Cup at a Time* (his first book of four), he fell in love with Seattle on his first visit, with its "air so clean it almost hurt my lungs" and "snow-capped mountain ranges," and Pike Place Market, which he describes as "so handcrafted, so authentic, so Old World" with its bakers and buskers and salmon hawkers. At the Starbucks flagship, the barista at the counter fixed him a cup of pour-over coffee with freshly ground Sumatran beans.

"Although the task took only a few minutes, he approached the work almost reverently, like an artisan," Schultz wrote. "Even from a single sip, I could tell it was stronger than any coffee I had ever tasted."

As the story goes, Schultz was hooked. He begged Baldwin to hire him, taking a pay cut and relocating with his wife from New York to Seattle in pursuit of entrepreneurial adventure. In the 1980s, while attending a conference in Milan, Schultz had another revelation. He visited an espresso bar, where he tried "a handcrafted cappuccino, topped with a head of perfect white foam." As he walked around the city, he saw espresso bars on block after block, each one filled with regulars. He had an epiphany: not only should Starbucks sell gourmet coffee *beans*, but it should sell the *experience* of consuming elaborately prepared, Italian-style gourmet coffee drinks in an appealing social space—a "third space" that is neither work nor home.

In 1987, Baldwin and Bowker decided to sell Starbucks' stores, roasting plant, and name. They cashed out for $3.8 million to a group of investors led by Schultz. After his purchase, Schultz embarked on a total brand redesign, which included switching the company's signature color from brown to green and covering up the Siren's breasts. The privately held corporation of 17 stores grew its number to 116 stores by 1991, expanding throughout the Pacific Northwest and testing the waters of the Chicago market.

"I saw Starbucks not for what it was, but for what it could be," Schultz wrote. "It had immediately captivated me with its combination of passion and authenticity. If it could expand nationwide, romancing the Italian artistry of espresso-making as well as offering fresh-roasted coffee beans, I gradually realized, it could reinvent an age-old commodity and appeal to millions of people as strongly as it appealed to me."

Starbucks had its initial public offering on June 26, 1992, debuting on the NASDAQ under the ticker name SBUX at $17 a share. The price jumped to $21 just after the opening bell, and was the second most active stock that day. The IPO raised $29 million, and in a single day its market capitalization was $273 million. The share price rose, going as high as $33 a share in just three months. It was one of 1992's most successful IPOs, and on Wall Street "the next Starbucks" become synonymous with the next hot stock. Schultz was featured on the cover of *Fortune*. The stock rose steadily through the '90s.

Starbucks continued to expand throughout the West, then went east in 1993, first in Washington, DC, and then New York and Boston. In 1994 they opened stores in Minneapolis, Atlanta, Dallas, Fort Worth, and Houston. In 1995 they opened stores in Las Vegas, Austin, San Antonio, Philadelphia, Pittsburgh, and Baltimore, and they introduced the Frappuccino, which originated as a specialty drink at Coffee Connection, a Boston-area chain acquired by Starbucks in 1994. By 1996, Starbucks had 1,015 stores, including their first forays outside North America, in Japan and Singapore. By 2000, when I had that first Frappuccino, Starbucks had 3,501 stores across America and the world, including in Australia, New Zealand, Taiwan, Thailand, China, the UK, South Korea, Kuwait, Lebanon, Bahrain, Qatar, Hong Kong, Malaysia, Saudi Arabia, and the United Arab Emirates.

All of a sudden, Starbucks was everywhere. And it had its own language: employees were *baristas*, small was *tall*, medium was *grande*, large was *venti*. You could order drinks called *cappuccino* or *caffè latte* or *mocha*, with Italian names as frothy and adorned as the milk foam and whipped cream and sugar syrups that topped them. Everything could be customized, and customers would rattle off their orders as espresso machines clanked and steamed in the background atop a soundtrack of world music, which you could buy a CD of for $19.99 from a display by the register.

"Is it impossible to get a cup of coffee-flavored coffee anymore in this country?" asked Dennis Leary in a 1997 stand-up special. "You can get every other flavor. They got mocacchino, chocacchino, cappuccino, frappaccino, rappacino, Al Pacino. What the fuck? WWW dot what the fuck dot com?" He then jokes about coping with his frustration by doing a mass shooting inside a Starbucks franchise.

"The whole purpose of places like Starbucks is for people with no decision-making ability whatsoever to make six decisions just to buy one cup of coffee," Tom Hanks tells Meg Ryan in the 1998 Nora Ephron rom-com *You've Got Mail*, which did a product placement deal with the company.* "Short, tall, light, dark, caf, decaf, low-fat, non-fat, et cetera. So people who don't know what the hell they're doing or who the hell they are can, for only $2.95, get not just a cup of coffee but an absolutely defining sense of self."

Other jokes focused less on the drinks themselves and more on the company's staggering growth in both market share and store numbers. In the 1998 *Simpsons* episode "Simpson Tide," Bart visits the Springfield Mall and walks past two separate Starbucks on the way to an ear-piercing studio.

---

* This fact did not go unnoticed by critics. "The protagonists of Nora Ephron's new romantic comedy spend so much time either logged on to their e-mail accounts or ordering designer coffee that the film feels like an extended commercial for AOL and Starbucks," wrote Michael O'Sullivan at the *Washington Post*. Even the normally agreeable *TV Guide* pointed it out. "In a film about the ruthless corporate destruction of small businesses, it's hard not to flinch at the prominent placement accorded IBM, Starbucks and AOL logos." A November 1998 article in *WIRED* noted that the deal between AOL and Warner Brothers, who produced the film, was likely "the biggest film product-placement arrangement in history." There is no evidence of this, but I also wonder if the deal was meant to bolster both companies' images ahead of their historic and ultimately disastrous 2000 merger.

"Can I help you?" asks the proprietor.

"I'd like to get my ear pierced," says Bart.

"Well, better make it quick, kiddo, in five minutes this place is becoming a Starbucks."

The scene cuts to show Bart walking out of the former studio with his new earring, sipping a latte. It pans out to reveal row after row of Starbucks on two floors: an entire mall made of Starbucks.

In the 1999 film *Austin Powers: The Spy Who Shagged Me*, Dr. Evil and his henchmen have set up their new headquarters in Seattle's Space Needle, which has been converted into a Starbucks.

"Several years ago we invested in a small, Seattle-based coffee company," says one of the henchmen. "Today, Starbucks offers premium-quality coffee at affordable prices. . . . If we shift our resources away from evil empires and toward Starbucks, we can increase our profits fivefold."

This exchange is followed by a prolonged scene where Dr. Evil gets cappuccino foam on his nose (because of course there has to be a joke about how silly cappuccinos are).

Director David Fincher has claimed that in his 1999 movie *Fight Club*, there is a Starbucks cup in every shot. This is intended as a commentary on the ubiquity of branding and the problem of corporate monopoly in '90s capitalism. Starbucks, of course, was the perfect metonym. The company permitted Fincher to do this, though they drew the line at using their brand in a scene where a character "trash[es] a franchise coffee bar" by throwing "a piece of corporate art" through the plateglass window.

But in November that same year, people smashed Starbucks windows in real life. During the 1999 World Trade Organization conference in Seattle, stores in the company's hometown were targeted for looting and vandalism because they represented the same thing as the conference itself: multinational corporations, branding, and globalization trammeling every inch of the planet, all under the auspices of a cleaned-up West Coast counterculture. Images of smashed plateglass bearing the green Siren's face were broadcast around the world, inspiring ex–Soul Coughing front man Mike Doughty to write a 2002 song called "Busting Up a Starbucks."

In the '90s, much anxiety about *how we live now* was steamed with milk and poured into a disposable cup with a proprietary green Siren on it. Starbucks had taken the countercultural institution of the coffee shop and commodified it—the ultimate boomer move. Starbucks represented the selling out of the aging baby boomer generation, the frivolity of an ever-increasing consumer culture where yuppies spent $5 a day on customized coffee, the thrill of the booming stock market, the crisis of American masculinity, the death of small businesses, the consolidation of capital around multinational corporations, the homogenization of the American and global landscape, and the exploitation of the Global South by the Global North under a new banner of free trade. There were endless jokes about how complicated people's Starbucks orders were getting.

In this proto-culture war, what didn't come up much was the topic of labor. This wasn't surprising, as the absence of the labor question defined the Y2K Era psychic landscape, particularly in the United States. Unions existed, but membership had been on a downward slide since its peak in the 1950s, when around a third of workers belonged to one. By 1997, only 14.1 percent of Americans belonged to a union. By 2008, that number had gone down to 12.4 percent. From the 1970s onward, news outlets laid off most of their labor reporters, and by the late 1990s, the most notable thing about labor was its absence from public discourse. Unions, it was widely assumed, were a twentieth-century relic.

Or, as Carrie told Charlotte on a 1999 episode of *Sex and the City*, "It's the millennium, sweetie. We don't say things like 'working class' anymore."

A FEW MONTHS after I had that first Frappuccino, my seventh-grade American history class had a unit on the Progressive Era. One of the topics was labor unions. I had to do some homework assignment and, as usual, I was procrastinating. My mom was trying to get me started.

"Unions are BORING," I told her.

To me, unions were from another time. Nobody I knew in Falls Church, Virginia, in the year 2001 worked for a steel mill or a shirtwaist factory or a railroad. To me, the universal story of twenty-first-century labor was the story of my own family. I assumed everyone's grandparents, like mine, had started out in a working-class Jewish neighborhood in Brooklyn (or whatever their version of a working-class Jewish neighborhood in Brooklyn was), gotten advanced degrees, and moved into the professional managerial class, which—as far as I understood—didn't need organized labor. This was, in some sense, the journey of Howard Schultz himself. It was the new millennium now, and everyone had a house and a stock portfolio and health insurance.

And if they didn't, well, they had just made bad choices. They should have gotten good grades so they could go to a good college so they could get a good job. You know, a real job. Because service jobs weren't real jobs. They were low-skilled labor. They were for people who were stupid or lazy or both. "What you earn depends on what you can learn," said Bill Clinton on the 1992 campaign trail, explaining, basically, why we couldn't give fast-food workers benefits or a living wage. It was the End of History, and everything was as balanced and fair as it would ever be. In *You've Got Mail* there are two separate instances where Tom Hanks yells at two different immigrant service workers and you're supposed to laugh.

In March 1985, a majority of employees at Starbucks' original stores and plant voted to join Local 1001 of the United Food and Commercial Workers. Their 1986 union contract brought significant gains, including health care coverage, sick leave, and paid vacation for part-time employees, as well as a seat at the table of a company on the cusp of a major expansion.

But in *Pour Your Heart into It*, Howard Schultz tells this as a story of betrayal.

"I wanted people to feel proud of working at Starbucks, to believe in their hearts that management trusted them and treated them with respect," Schultz wrote. "I was convinced that under my leadership, employees would come to realize that I would listen to their concerns. If they had faith in me and my motives, they wouldn't need a union."

The trouble is, faith isn't legally binding. A union contract, however, can guarantee that employees will be treated with the trust and respect Schultz says he values. Companies—especially publicly traded ones—have a fiduciary duty to maximize profits. This is done in large part by saving on labor costs—otherwise known as paying workers as little as possible. This is the case whether or not the company's CEO is a cool guy or a huge asshole, and whether or not the company's culture is about, as Starbucks says, "being good to people, being good to the world."

There were a lot of anti-union myths around at the turn of the twenty-first century. Most important was that unions were old-fashioned. They were rigid. They kept workplaces from becoming dynamic and flexible enough to compete in the New Economy. These ideas were brewing in 1987, when a Starbucks employee named Daryl Moore began an effort to decertify the company's union. Moore had worked at Starbucks since 1981, first as a clerk, then in the warehouse. He left the company to try his hand at entrepreneurship. Failing that, he returned to work as a barista. Moore wrote a letter requesting that Starbucks end their relationship with United Food and Commercial Workers and carried it around to local stores collecting signatures from his coworkers. According to Schultz, Moore "did some research on his own" and engaged in "philosophical debates" with his coworkers and the union representative.

By January 1988, Moore had collected enough signatures to submit the letter to the National Labor Relations Board, and the union was decertified. Four years later, in 1992, the union representing employees at Starbucks' warehouses and roasting plant was also decertified. Freed from the democratic constraints of union ownership, Schultz could go public and push profits into the stratosphere.

"Although he comes from a blue-collar family, Daryl didn't see the need for a union as long as Starbucks managers were responsive to employee concerns," Schultz wrote approvingly.

I don't know where Daryl Moore's family worked. But I do know that, statistically, it very well may have been Boeing. During the 1970s, Seattle experienced the "Boeing Bust" following the 1969 closure of the region's largest employer, an aircraft factory full of unionized jobs. By 1971, the unemployment rate in the region was nearly 14 percent (compared to a national unemployment rate of around 4.5 percent), and the city was known as "the food stamp capital" of America.

The Boeing Bust was an early example of a trend that was happening across the country during the 1970s and '80s: the offshoring of jobs in unionized heavy industry and the growth, instead, of lower-paying, non-union service jobs (like Starbucks barista). During the 1980s, the United States added almost 19 million jobs, but 76 percent of job growth was in the (traditionally non-union) service and retail sectors. That trend continued into the 2000s. According to the Pew Research Center, this was part of "the implicit contract between workers and employers . . . loosening." Pew noted that "the earnings of workers overall have lagged behind gains in labor productivity since the 1970s."

In 2004, the Industrial Workers of the World tried to make Starbucks a union company once again. Unionizing Starbucks seemed patently absurd, both because union strength was at an all-time low and because there was a widespread belief even by union supporters that jobs like those at Starbucks—service and retail jobs at multinational corporate chains—simply couldn't be unionized. The union drive seemed like it would go about as well as that scene in season 6 of *The Sopranos* where Patsy Parisi tries to get protection money out of a Starbucks-like chain coffee shop.[*]

Unsurprisingly, the IWW did not win Starbucks workers an NLRB-recognized union. But the organizing efforts brought attention to poor working conditions, and perhaps planted a seed in the public imagination that service workers deserved more than what they were getting, especially when they were a growing portion of the New Economy. The IWW's organizing efforts also threatened to tarnish the brand's image as a place for discerning and ethical consumers. In response, the company instituted modest improvements in pay, scheduling, and safety protections.

---

[*] In one of the show's best one-liners, the scene ends when Patsy leaves the store unsuccessfully, muttering, "It's over for the little guy!" by which he means not just independent coffee shops but also the mafia.

"Starbucks is selling an image more than coffee," an East Village barista involved in the campaign told *New York* magazine. "That's a very vulnerable point for them."

MEANWHILE, THE YEAR 2004 was the high-water (milk foam?) mark of the "latte liberal" discourse. A poll found that Americans associated Democratic presidential challenger John Kerry with the brands Starbucks and BMW, while President George W. Bush was associated with Folgers and Ford. John Kerry and the Democrats were for snooty professionals with disposable income. George Bush and the Republicans were for regular, everyday Americans who made plain coffee at home. The Bush administration, the Republican Party, and conservative news media ran with this image, insinuating that Kerry was not only out of touch, but also possibly gay and European. No man who drank coffee with whipped cream and chocolate syrup had the stomach to do a troop surge in Iraq.

As the 2000s marched on, most of the metrics went up for Starbucks. By 2005, they had over 10,000 stores. In 2007, their stock price was at $17 a share. By 2008, there were over 16,000 locations. Despite their stock price falling significantly during the recession, the company recovered and continued to grow, reaching over 36,000 locations by 2022, with their stock price rising 13 percent in six months to $99 a share. They opened outposts at rest stops and gas stations, on cruise ships and in remote Fairbanks, Alaska. The *Simpsons* joke about the total saturation of Starbucks really happened. By 2014, half of the island of Manhattan was within four blocks of a Starbucks.

This saturation expanded the company's clientele. The warm

lighting, the brown-striped banquettes, and the seasonally changing coffee-spiked milkshakes (especially the pumpkin spice latte)
became precious parts of the exurban identity. Starbucks became
associated in the public imagination with the "basic," with a provincial, high-carbon lifestyle popular among SUV-driving, heavily
made-up women and pickup truck–driving men that was coded
as—in a pivot from 2004—conservative. But the relationship of
the American conservative with the brand remains uneasy, and
Starbucks continues to operate as a focus for their anxieties and
fixations.

Starbucks launched their red cup Christmas season promo-
tion in 1997. It was a cute idea, and became extremely popular,
especially after Starbucks introduced the seasonal pumpkin spice
latte in 2003. Over the years, the red cups featured holiday motifs like Christmas trees and snowmen, and the release of each
year's unique design (usually in November) marked the start of
the company's lucrative seasonal menu.

In 2015, though, the red cups prompted a conservative meltdown. That year's design was minimalist: solid red with no additional art. For conservatives, this small change was evidence of
the war on Christmas. Fox News commentators threw hissy fits.
Rant videos were uploaded.

"Do you realize that Starbucks wanted to take Christ and Christ-
mas off of their brand-new cups?" asked an adult man named
Joshua Feuerstein in a 2015 video. "In fact, do you realize that
Starbucks isn't allowed to say merry Christmas to their customers?"

Prior to the 2016 election, Starbucks released a limited-edition
cup intended to promote "unity" in an increasingly divided country. The cup was green, and was covered with twee line drawings
of a diverse group of people. Conservatives freaked out again, this
time accusing Starbucks of trying to convert customers to Islam.

These twin reactions were warnings, I think, of where conservative culture was headed. The Starbucks cup freak-outs were similar (albeit smaller in scope) to QAnon and other culture-war conspiracy theories. All include a belief that major corporations are transmitting malign secret messages in an attempt to undermine American values. This is obviously both bigoted and ridiculous, but I think it stems from an increasing sense of powerlessness in the face of large corporations; a sense that Starbucks, in some way or another, is antidemocratic.

Following the election, conservative patrons attempted to start a micro trend by saying their name was "Trump" so puzzled baristas would have to yell out the name of the forty-fifth president. And in recent years, conservatives have threatened Starbucks locations for putting up Pride Month decorations, claiming that the company is an arm of what they call "woke capital." All of this is a scaldingly reheated version of the original latte-liberal discourse.

In the political center, Howard Schultz pondered running for president as an independent in 2020.

"Imagine if our country were more united," he mused in *USA Today* in 2019. "Imagine if more elected leaders collaborated, unselfishly put country over party, and were only beholden to the best ideas that serve the interests of more Americans. . . . The intentions of Starbucks reflect the business of our country, which has long been to try to balance humanity and prosperity."

Schultz has been speaking more or less this way since *Pour Your Heart into It*. He positions himself as a CEO who is in touch with his feelings, who wants to take all the good parts of the 1960s West Coast counterculture, clean them up, and repackage them to run a wildly profitable publicly traded corporation. He does not recognize any fundamental conflicts—either in national politics or within his own company—that cannot be resolved with a heart-to-heart talk. He and Starbucks are the essence of post-politics, of the end of history; like if you took all that Y2K-Era ideology and refined it into a flavored syrup.

TASTES ARE CHANGING, though, at least in certain circles. After the Great Recession in 2008, a lot of people craved something different. And so—seventeen years after the Wobblies tried to reunionize Starbucks in 2004—another group of workers would try again. In December 2021, employees at a store in Buffalo, New York, voted to join the Service Workers International Union, calling themselves Starbucks Workers United. Inspired by the success, other stores followed. By 2023, over three hundred stores had successful union elections.

In response, Starbucks has undertaken what Senator Bernie Sanders called, in 2023, "the most aggressive and illegal union-busting campaign in the modern history of our country." NLRB judges determined that Starbucks violated labor law 130 times, including firing employees for unionizing, promising increased pay and benefits for workers who voted against the union, conducting illegal surveillance, and relocating union leaders to other stores to interfere with upcoming union elections. One Starbucks barista told *Newsweek* that the company retaliated by removing anti-slip mats from the kitchen. A Starbucks spokesperson disputed this claim, telling *Newsweek* that the mats were in poor condition and were replaced.

Schultz appears to have taken the unionization efforts quite personally.

"I think unions have served an important role in American business for many years," he said during a 2023 Senate hearing on the company's labor practices. "In the '50s and '60s, unions generally were working on behalf of people in a company where people haven't been treated fairly. We do not believe that we are that kind of company. We do nothing nefarious. We put our people first."

These words might have reassured in the Y2K Era. But to many people now—especially those, like me, who entered the workforce after the Great Recession—they ring hollow. Schultz sounds like every boomer boss who made you work unpaid overtime, who paid you badly and refused you a raise, who laid you off, who told you to manage your workplace stress through meditation. Starbucks has come to stand for a young, diverse American labor movement, which took up a cause that had been dormant for decades and made it their own. And Starbucks stands, too, for the forces that oppose it.

I can't, of course, tell you which side will win. But we shouldn't turn away. As goes Starbucks, so goes the nation.

Closing Time

I T WAS SPRING 1998, AND WE WERE RENOVATING OUR kitchen. Contractors had been coming in and out for weeks, parking their pickup trucks in our driveway, spreading their tarps on our floors. Their work made an indoor soundscape of power tools, boot steps, and cuss words. I couldn't believe they said "shit" and "dammit" and even "fuck." I was in fourth grade, so I knew all my cuss words, but I usually didn't say them.

We were all eating dinner when my mom let slip that tomorrow, the biggest change yet would be made. Tomorrow, they would be installing skylights.

"Finally we're getting some natural light in here," my dad said, reaching across the table for more lentil salad.

Absurdly, I started to cry. My dad scowled with confusion, then laughed a little bit.

"What's this all this about?" he said. "Huh?"

"Oh, sweetie," my mom offered.

I got up and ran outside, slamming the kitchen door behind me. I rode the swing in the sweet gum tree in the side yard until the sun started to set, hot tears rolling down my cheeks. I didn't understand why we were cutting holes in the roof of our small ranch house, why the white laminate countertops weren't good enough, why we ordered gray-speckled Corian and cream-colored backsplash tiles cast in Italy. This was the end, it seemed, my very last day in the house I loved because it was the only house I had known for the decade I'd been alive.

All that summer changes were made. Paint swatches were looked at and looked at again, little rough squares of peach or beige or palest sage painted on the wall so they could be observed in the light of the morning, midday, golden hour, and evening. The hardwood floors were buffed and revarnished. Avocado-green appliances were swapped for contemporary stainless steel. Our house was built in 1968 and if these weren't the original appliances they were close. The unreliable coil range was taken to the dump and replaced with a sleek glass-top stove that could only be cleaned with a special liquid called Cerama Bryte that came in a little bottle. The new dishwasher was German and quiet. Out went the brown composite cabinets with their broken handles. In went blond maple cabinets in an Arts and Crafts style with brushed-steel hardware. Recessed lighting was installed in the ceiling. Our kitchen was too small for a kitchen island but our designer created what she jokingly referred to as a kitchen peninsula, complete with an auxiliary sink my mom used to water her bonsai.

By that fall, I grew to love it. The kitchen was clean and contemporary and, just as my dad had predicted, filled with light. I noticed that the people on TV also had our kind of countertops, our kind of cabinets, had two sinks just like we did. They even had skylights. This reassured me, that our house might be good enough for a TV family to live in. I started to realize that what my dad said was right: our old kitchen had been *ugly*, had looked *dated*, was really, as he pronounced it, *hahr-ible*.

Before the new kitchen, it never occurred to me that my parents might be capable of unhappiness. That they might want their own things the way I wanted CDs or Dippin' Dots or a silver inflatable chair. That they might sometimes feel cheated, disappointed, or maybe even powerless. That kitchen made them both so happy. Which meant that, before, they must have been unhappy. Especially my dad.

My dad worked all the time. He still does, even though this year he'll be seventy. He'd be downstairs in his office, marking up blueprints, writing proposals, modeling SCIFs and condos and conference rooms in AutoCAD. He'd drive around DC and Maryland and Virginia, taking meetings, doing on-site measurements, supervising construction, having disagreements with architects. I learned, early on, that architects and engineers don't get along. That's how I first learned the word *asshole*.

When my dad wasn't working, he'd drink his coffee or his cabernet sauvignon at the kitchen table while reading the *New York Times*. On the weekend we'd share the paper: he'd read the architecture section and give me the fashion section. He'd ask what I was learning in school, then quiz me on math and physics and music theory. He'd read his classical music magazines: *BBC Music*, *American Organist*, *The Strad*. He'd tell me which operas had the best mad scenes and I'd ask him what he thought about blink-182. He didn't like them, but he thought they sounded like the Buzzcocks, who he did like.

He'd tell me that, if I kept practicing trumpet for three hours a day, if I stayed first chair at school and top-ranked in my district, I might get a music scholarship at a good college—like Stanford, like Amherst. Between that and the 50 percent tuition reimbursement he got from his teaching job at Johns Hopkins, and of course my college fund with its large contribution from Uncle Paul, I could easily afford to graduate with no student debt. When my dad spoke of Uncle Paul, there was gratitude, yes, but there was also a note of resentment. Uncle Paul, said my dad, got lucky. He didn't have to work hard *like everybody else*, by which he mostly meant himself.

Then I'd show him a photo in the paper of a funny outfit from a Thierry Mugler show, and we'd laugh about it together.

This is what the kitchen means in America: a place to unwind and relax, to be with your family. When Americans are awake we mostly work, our backs knotted with stress. If we work for someone else, we can be let go *at will*, a legal term meaning "for no reason at all." Maybe we're lucky like my dad and we work for ourselves. But then there's the constant chase: the next gig, the last paycheck. The fear will come for you one way or another.

Because there's nothing to catch you below. It's this fear that keeps us working, working longer and harder than people in just about any other developed country. That kept us, through the '90s and the 2000s, working even longer and even harder than we were before.

In the kitchen, you can forget the fear. This is the place of unconditional love, where your time belongs only to you. It's the heart in a heartless world, where, if you're lucky, you can express yourself through your interior design choices. If not now, then in some bright future where you have saved up the money or—more likely—applied for a home equity loan. The kitchen is what's supposed to make the fear worthwhile.

They work less in Europe. And in Europe they have fancy kitchens, too. But most Americans don't know that. And anyway, the only metric most Americans have for measuring quality is size, and the kitchens in America generally *are* bigger, because the houses in America generally are bigger, flouting their energy inefficiency like the SUVs in their driveways. In America, the way the story goes is this: If you work very, very hard and you're very, very lucky, your suffering, too, can be remunerated. You, too, can remodel your kitchen.

IN 1994, TELEVISION executives Kenneth Lowe and Frank Gardner launched HGTV. Now a basic cable mainstay, the idea of an entire channel devoted to unscripted shows about people renovating, decorating, buying, or selling houses was unprecedented.

"Home building [and] home design 20 years ago was this deep, dark mystery," Lowe said. "People just didn't understand it."

In 1999, the channel aired its first episode of *House Hunters*, which followed a Los Angeles couple as they looked for a new home. The show later settled into its well-known formula, in which the house hunter presents a checklist of seemingly opposing musthaves (this is, of course, played up if it's a couple, a family, or, in one episode, a throuple). Three homes are looked at, the attributes of each are compared, and then one is selected in the end.

House Hunters quickly became one of the most popular shows on cable, spawning more than a dozen spin-offs, starting with *House Hunters International* in 2006. Other networks vied for a piece of the real-estate-show market. TLC aired *Trading Spaces* in 2000, and ABC debuted *Extreme Makeover: Home Edition* in 2004. Both of these shows are focused on redecorating existing homes: tearing down walls with sledgehammers, ripping out carpeting, building decks and staircases and kitchen islands, transforming modest houses into turreted faux castles.

The look preferred on TV was not the edgeless, hypermodernist Y2K aesthetic. It was a throwback, a mixture of rococo and Louis XIV and Georgian and Tuscan and Tudor and French provincial. There were columns and multiple pediments and circular driveways. There were vaulted ceilings and open floor plans, with grand staircases curving down two-story foyers. There were chef's kitchens with Sub-Zero appliances, tile backsplashes, marble and granite countertops, wine fridges. There were walk-in closets and walk-in pantries and in-home theaters and game rooms and snack bars and swimming pools and gyms. There were garages big enough to fit multiple SUVs. There were Jack and Jill baths and multiple guest bedrooms. There were elaborate window treatments and fake wrought iron and recessed lighting and big leather couches. Everything was sponge-painted and beige and white and cream and brown and gray. Maybe it was also gold and dark green and dark red, the colors of royalty as seen by a person who thinks themselves a king, though they don't know European history and barely leave their American suburb.

Or, as Jia Tolentino wrote, "The world looked like long granite countertops and lamplit stucco." You could see these houses everywhere: on *MTV Cribs*, where celebrities showed you their bedrooms and the contents of their refrigerators. They were the backdrops of reality TV, of *Newlyweds* and *The Flavor of Love* and *Rock of Love* and *Bad Girls Club* and *Big Brother*, and of all the pornography you watched on the internet. Every Sunday night between 1999 and 2007, viewers of *The Sopranos* watched Tony exit the Lincoln Tunnel in his Chevy Suburban, smoking his cigar through the Meadowlands and strip malls before pulling up his driveway to one of these houses.

I could see these houses where I lived, first in the DC suburbs and then, to a lesser extent, in the Baltimore suburbs, where historic preservation rules in our neighborhood put a limit on new construction. There would be a patch of forest that had always been there, and then one day a For Sale sign would go up, and then another sign would go up, announcing that it had been purchased by Toll Brothers or Ryan Homes. And then the oaks and the beeches and the maples would all be cut down, the forest floor regraded, the land parceled off into too-small yards planted with non-native Bradford pear and arborvitae. The houses were built quickly, wrapped in Tyvek before they were finished with fake stucco and vinyl siding. Sometimes, these flourishes would get added to, say, a pre-existing split-level ranch. When the contractors left, it looked like two separate homes had been grafted together.

My dad hated these houses. He said they were tacky and cheap and poorly built. He knew; he had worked on some. Every time we'd pass one he'd tell me how things used to be, with more trees and more animals and the houses on appropriately sized lots. And there was a word he'd always say with derision: "McMansion."

"The simplest way to define a McMansion is: a poorly designed, poorly executed, oversized house," wrote my friend, the architecture critic Kate Wagner, in 2017. "But there's something more to them than looming entryways, vinyl siding, and mismatched windows that causes the knee-jerk hatred they rouse in so many. In part, the wounds are historical: as the 2008 crash unfolded, McMansions became the symbols of aspirational hubris, of excess, of wanting too much and borrowing too much to get it."

Kate runs a blog called *McMansion Hell*, scouring Zillow and traveling the country to document these strange and ubiquitous houses, which started showing up in America in the 1980s, rising in popularity as the old economy turned into the New Economy. She argues that McMansions—despite their traditional pretensions—fail to adhere to traditional architectural principles of balance, rhythm, and proportion. McMansions don't care about the history they reference. They're just interested in mashing together as many signifiers of wealth as possible. They're made with cheap materials and shoddily constructed. Unlike other new homes,

McMansions will show signs of wear in a few years. But who cares? If McMansions are merely a backdrop for an eternal, televised present, aren't giant foyers more important than structural integrity?

"What's interesting about the McMansion and what's not commonly noticed is that in some ways it became a multi-racial phenomenon, often along the lines of transgression," she told me.

The McMansions in Falls Church, Virginia, were inhabited not just by white families but also by nonwhite ones, from El Salvador and Bolivia and Lebanon and Vietnam. And in Black areas of Baltimore County, I saw McMansions as well, mixed in among the mid-century tract housing. Kate notes that many of the celebrities featured on *Cribs* were rappers like Nelly and Lil Wayne, and McMansions featured prominently in Spanish-language telenovelas.

The McMansion became a scapegoat for the housing bubble. For many commentators, it was these foolish (mostly nonwhite) people who trashed the economy by using subprime mortgages to buy houses (McMansions) they couldn't afford. That's what former bond trader Rick Santelli said in a viral rant in February 2009.

"Why don't you put up a website to have people vote on the Internet as a referendum to see if we really want to subsidize the losers' mortgages," he told CNBC in a video clip that would arguably launch the Tea Party. "Or would we like to at least buy cars and buy houses in foreclosure and give them to people that might have a chance to actually prosper down the road, and reward people that could carry the water instead of drink the water? How many of you people want to pay for your neighbor's mortgage that has an extra bathroom and can't pay their bills? Raise their hand."

Kate thinks this is nonsense. According to her, the people who lost their homes due to subprime mortgages and a plunge in housing values "are victims of the predatory lending and mortgage fuckery that landed everyone in this mess." And anyway, she argues, the McMansion is a cultural phenomenon, not an economic one.

"Its role in the 2008 crisis is greatly exaggerated."

Nonetheless, the McMansion is a great symbol: a shoddily built consumer product with underlying structural deficiencies.

WHEN MY UNCLE got rich in the dot-com bubble, one of the first things he did was look at real estate. He already had an apartment in San Francisco, which appeared in *Architectural Digest* after extensive renovations. He bought a house in Sarasota, Florida. He and his wife became "bicoastal," traveling between their two homes while scouting out real estate in Italy and London and Sonoma.

I remember sitting by the pool at the Sarasota house in March 2002 in my first bikini, a coral-colored floral string bikini from American Eagle, hands covering the stomach I thought wasn't flat enough. I was sunburned, with chunky orange highlights in my hair. Out there by the pool and the hot tub that overlooked the long private dock and the boat, the yard shaded by banana trees and grapefruit trees and palms and hibiscus and plumeria that every week, at least, the crew of brown men came to maintain, my uncle said what he wanted. What he wanted was an infinity pool tiled black, "like a black monolith." He wanted to redo the hexagonal foyer with the grand staircase. I thought Uncle Paul was so rich he didn't want for anything. But even he was redoing his house!

There was a tub in one of the bathrooms there where you could spread out all the way. I took a bath there and read an issue of *Seventeen* with Keri Russell on the cover. I wondered if she had a house this big. There were eight bedrooms and eight bathrooms even though it was just my uncle and aunt and sometimes their grown-up daughter. In the basement there was a theater with a real movie screen and a dozen leather seats bolted to the floor. I watched MTV2 down there. I pretended I was in *Cribs*. I remember hearing that the house cost $4.5 million. That's over $7 million today.

A DECADE LATER, it was 2012. Uncle Paul no longer had the Florida house. I had just graduated college, and unemployment was at 8 percent nationally. I was subletting the smallest bedroom in a cockroach-infested apartment off the Hewes JMZ subway stop in Brooklyn. After months of unemployment and living at home with my parents, I was working a low-level media job that didn't pay me enough to cover my basic expenses. I was racking up credit card debt. The next year, I got a slightly better-paying job at a different media company, but there was no clear way to advance and my bosses screamed at everyone. I started to develop debilitating panic attacks. After a year there I quit and moved back in with my parents again, to regroup and figure out what to do next.

Before I left New York and especially after, I became obsessed with history. And when I say "history," what I really mean is a very specific tradition on the political left that uses history to explain economic, political, technological, and cultural conditions. In the Y2K Era, this tradition was pronounced dead (it's what Francis Fukuyama meant when he said we were at the End of History). But in the wake of the 2008 financial crisis, it seemed I had completely misunderstood the world, and I wanted to know what really happened. Most of all, I wanted to know how I fit into that story.

So I read and I read and I read. I became friends with scholars and activists who told different stories than the ones I heard growing up. (I met Kate, in fact, through Democratic Socialists of America.) I began piecing together my own narrative:

In America, it's always gone back to real estate.

Before he won the Revolutionary War, and before he became our first president, George Washington got rich as a land speculator. He wasn't the only one. Colonists crossed the Alleghenies to stake their claims, even though the Iroquois, Choctaws, Chickasaws, and Seminoles already lived there. In 1763, the British crown passed a law forbidding American colonists from settling Indian territory west of the mountains. Most likely it was this proclamation that really caused the Revolutionary War, not the Stamp Act or the Tea Act.

"We have now lands enough to employ an infinite number of people in their cultivation," Thomas Jefferson enthused to John Jay in 1785, two years after American independence. That same year, in *Notes on the State of Virginia*, Jefferson argued that "those who labor in the earth are the chosen people of God." The writers Richard Barbrook and Andy Cameron talk about this in their 1995 essay "The Californian Ideology," arguing that the values of Silicon Valley were just a modern, digital update of the Jeffersonian ideal.

Of course, as Barbrook and Cameron understood, Jefferson wasn't exactly doing his own farming. While the people he enslaved worked the land at Monticello, he sat around drinking opium tinctures and fancy French wines, researching agriculture, and building weird clocks. For him, freedom was predicated on property rights, on owning land and people. Most of the time when Jefferson talked about freedom, he meant that other people had to be unfree, like Sally Hemings and her family.

The Industrial Revolution got going in the early nineteenth century, first in England, then in mainland Europe and Eastern American cities. In Europe, all the land had been settled, and so workers were forced into factories by economic necessity. They rebelled, going on strike and breaking their machines. They founded labor parties, then elected candidates who passed laws to limit working hours and institute safety precautions. Eventually, these parties passed laws that guaranteed housing and vacations and health insurance.

But in America, things were different. There was, as Jefferson said, "infinite" land, which meant that if you didn't want to work in a factory, you could just go west, where you didn't need unions or labor parties to protect you. Out on the plains, in the mountains, the plateaus, and even the deserts, opportunity was there for the taking, as long as you were white and willing to kill some Indians. So we marched to California and called it progress. Some of my dad's ancestors took this journey, traveling from Pennsylvania to settle in the Central Valley and around San Diego. There's no evidence that we killed anyone, but there's no evidence that we didn't.

Word spread around the world of this great nation with supposedly infinite land and infinite wealth, this nation where the rules did not apply. My mom and Uncle Paul's side were Jews fleeing persecution in Poland and Ukraine. America became the repository for every problem, from poverty to pogroms. The blood of the Indians proved remarkably absorbent.

By the end of the nineteenth century, America looked out at the Pacific Ocean. There was no more land to take. So we looked abroad, to the Philippines, Puerto Rico, Cuba, and Guam. We looked to Haiti and Hawaii and all of the Americas. Later, we looked to Vietnam, and then, by the time I was a teenager, to Iraq. It was our growing military that let us skirt the rules, that let us never be brought to account, that let us provide more and more stuff to calm everyone down without ever having to address the fundamental problems that were making them so upset in the first place.

In 1929, the Great Depression arrived. Americans were losing their houses, so as part of the New Deal, the Roosevelt administration got the federal government involved, for the first time, in financing home ownership. During World War II, the G.I. Bill was passed, which opened up home ownership to even more Americans, with the government-sponsored enterprise Fannie Mae giving special mortgages to returning veterans.

But this deal wasn't open to all Americans. The federal government and private real estate interests invented a series of racially discriminatory practices that kept most nonwhite people from cashing in on the great American home equity bonanza of the twentieth century. Many remained renters. Others were able to secure mortgages, but got stuck with extortionate rates, and could only buy real estate in segregated neighborhoods.

It was during the Cold War that American homeownership policy became focused on the suburbs. Cities were seen as places where people from different walks of life might meet and get scary ideas. Communist ones, maybe. The suburban American lifestyle was deliberately homogenous, focused on the nuclear family, car ownership, and shopping. Home ownership was thought to give Americans a stake in the economy, to prevent them from getting disaffected and turning left.

"No man who owns his own house and lot can be a communist," said real estate developer William Levitt. "He has too much to do."

In the 1970s, the booming American economy ground to a halt. A miasma of stagflation, oil crises, and deindustrialization enveloped the country. Wages stagnated, inequality grew, and the living standard of most Americans stalled or dropped. And of course, there were the (mostly nonwhite) Americans whose living standards were pretty bad to begin with, who had futilely set the cities on fire a few years before to demand their piece of the American dream. The bad times got worse, first under President Jimmy Carter—whose Federal Reserve chief Paul Volcker deliberately created a recession through interest rate hikes in an attempt to tame inflation—and then under President Ronald Reagan and his policy of supply-side economics.

For most Americans—starting in the '80s, but increasing in the '90s and 2000s—credit began to make up for wages, the real value of which was decreasing by the day. Personal debt went through the roof. And speaking of roofs, it was at this time that home ownership became a kind of substitute social safety net. A home—as most Americans' largest and increasingly only asset—could serve as collateral for the loans they needed to keep living normally. With the loss of defined-benefit pensions, a home could help finance your retirement. A home could put your kids through college. A home was the legacy you could leave them after you died. To renovate your home became a kind of economic maintenance, like managing your 401(k) (at the time a new product, replacing said defined-benefit pensions). Housing values had to go up, because American life depended on it.

In the 1980s, just before my great-grandparents died, they sold the ten-acre avocado farm they owned outside San Diego. They had done well for themselves, and their children had done well for themselves, and their grandchildren—my dad and his sister—had done well for themselves. How could they not sell? The price of land in Southern California was only rising. So the land was bought and parceled off. The avocado trees were razed and McMansions were built in their place. I feel sad when I think about all those dead trees. But alongside my Nokia stock, those McMansions helped put me through college.

In 1994—a year before the dot-com bubble would start to inflate—President Clinton launched National Partners in Home-ownership. This initiative brought together banks, construction firms, securities firms, the National Association of Realtors, government agencies, and private nonprofits to focus on helping more Americans buy homes. Specifically, they were trying to help more nonwhite Americans buy homes, those same Americans who had been deliberately kept out of the housing market for decades. Home ownership, President Clinton said, was "the heart of what it means to harbor, to nourish, to expand the American dream." The plan worked. During the president's first three years in office, home-purchase loans rose by 36 percent for Latino Americans and 48 percent for Black Americans. The president bragged that "the government . . . appears to be succeeding in helping ensure that creditworthy low-income and minority borrowers are not overlooked." In 2002, President Bush announced a similar program to increase home ownership among minorities* by 5.5 million, stating that "part of economic security is owning your own home." The dot-com bubble had burst two years before, but the economy was still doing well overall, since most of the losses in that bubble were stocks owned by rich people, and thus there was no broad effect on consumer spending. And now, another bubble was beginning to inflate: the housing bubble. That bubble, when it burst, would be much more consequential, as it would largely affect people who could least afford to absorb losses.

In the Y2K Era, the financial sector was becoming a major part of the global economy. Markets were becoming increasingly complex, international, and interconnected. A sector growing particularly fast was derivatives: investments whose value is tied

---

* The term used at the time.

to the price of other assets, be they orange juice or Treasury bonds. The star of the moment was a product called mortgage bonds: individual mortgages that were packed into bonds by investment bankers and then bought by institutional investors like retirement funds. Some mortgage bonds contained risky subprime loans, which were extended to poorer (and disproportionately nonwhite) buyers, thanks in part to the policies of Clinton and Bush. Or, in the words of an affidavit from a federal lawsuit against Wells Fargo, subprime loans were "ghetto loans" for "mud people."

Some financial experts were getting worried. The very foundations of the American-led global economy were shaky, and a series of crises in the late '90s—in Asia, in Latin America—did not bode well for the future. Brooksley Born—chair of the Commodity Futures Trading Commission under President Clinton—was concerned. In the wake of these crises, she gave a stern warning "about the unknown risks that the over-the-counter derivatives market may pose to the US economy and to financial stability around the world."

But Larry Summers and Alan Greenspan and all the other smart people in the room said no. We couldn't constrain "today's quicksilver market place." So it all kept going. In 1999 the government repealed the New Deal–era Glass-Steagall Act, which separated commercial and investment banking. There would be no limits on the economy in the Y2K Era. Limits, after all, are what our country was founded on transcending.

WHEN I GRADUATED high school in 2006, economic indicators looked better than ever. America had just been through three straight years of over 3 percent growth. Exports were up by more than 8 percent. Unemployment was down to 4.6 percent. Both housing prices and corporate profits were at record highs.

But by early 2007, things were starting to go south. Residential investment was down by 22 percent, and a lot more subprime borrowers were defaulting than most finance people had predicted. Rating agencies started to downgrade risky new securities, cooling the market. The real estate investment company New Century Financial collapsed. Ben Bernanke—who had just started his new job running the Federal Reserve—warned that Fannie Mae and Freddie Mac could cause major instability. By August 2007, Treasury Secretary Hank Paulson was trying to tamp down the emergency, taking hourly phone calls with Bernanke, Wall Street CEOs, and overseas finance ministers.

By early 2008, the global markets were in rough shape. In March, the investment bank Bear Stearns was about to go bankrupt. To prevent a domino effect on the global economy, the Federal Reserve oversaw a leveraged buyout of the bank by J.P. Morgan. See, this was the problem now. The entire global financial system had become so interconnected that if Bear Stearns went bust, people driving buses for the Los Angeles Transit Authority could lose their retirement savings. Pension funds around the world lost $5.4 trillion, or 23 percent of their value. American real estate had come full circle: from igniting the Revolutionary War to tanking the entire global economy.

On September 15, 2008, Lehman Brothers fell. It was the biggest bankruptcy in US history. Maybe you've seen the infamous photos of stone-faced people in office clothes carrying bankers boxes down the New York City sidewalks. Or maybe you've seen the photos of traders in the pit with anguished expressions, pulling at their hair as they watch the ticker when, two weeks later, the Dow Jones fell by 777.68 points, a single-day point drop bigger than the one that started the Great Depression. Though regulators tried to act like things were under control, they were freaking out. This series of events had no precedent. Company after company was collapsing. Ben Bernanke said privately that twelve out of thirteen of the country's most important financial institutions were "at risk of failure within a period of a week or two." The Great Recession, Bernanke would later admit, was the worst financial crisis that had ever occurred. It was—and I do not mean this hyperbolically—apocalyptic.

Many people think, incorrectly, that "apocalypse" means "the end of the world." The Greek word *apokálypsis*—from which it is translated—means "a revelation," "a disclosure," or "an unveiling." In an apocalypse, as it is commonly understood, a world is destroyed violently. But more important, an apocalypse means an era of false living is over. An apocalypse gives us the ability to see things as they really are. The Christian Bible begins with Genesis and ends with a story in which the sinful Earth is beset by plague, fire, and political turmoil. But then a better world is revealed, with a river "bright as crystal" and "the tree of life, with its twelve kinds of fruit; and the leaves for the healing of the nations." In this story, change is possible, but only if things can be looked at honestly. This is a common narrative across faith traditions, throughout art and literature, and in my own adopted political tradition. Even Semisonic sang, in 1998, that "every new beginning comes from some other beginning's end."

From 1997 through 2008 we lived dishonestly. In fact, it was a kind of dream state. We dreamt we were ascending into the future, leaving history and all its complications behind on the ground. Up and up we went into the sky. Now everyone could get rich on the stock market, drive a Hummer, own a McMansion. There was only one way for girls to be, and that was thin and young and white, with blond hair and tan skin and straight, bleached teeth. We floated through the air amid speculations and scams and just plain trash, from dot-com IPOs to subprime mortgages to flag T-shirts. Up there, torture was acceptable and mass incarceration wasn't a problem. A lot of us were sexist and racist and homophobic. A lot of us denied that anything could be learned from others, or from the American past. We acted like we lived outside of history, like we could stay up there forever.

In 2008, we awoke in our beds, drenched in sweat.

The full scope of the tragedy would unspool over the coming months. American households lost $14 trillion in net worth and 15.4 million people were out of work, bringing the total unemployment rate to 10 percent. Around 3.8 million households lost their homes in foreclosure, many of them Black or Latino households "integrated" into home ownership and financial markets through subprime mortgages. Instead of playing FDR and throwing homeowners and unemployed people a line, President Obama listened to Tim Geithner and "foamed the runway" for the banks, giving them bailouts while letting millions of Americans lose their biggest asset. Obama brought on Larry Summers as a top economic adviser, despite the fact that Summers's previous work helped create the crisis in the first place (not to mention helping trash Russia's economy in the '90s).

The recession went on and on and on, even after the government claimed it was over in 2009. I graduated in 2011 and I couldn't find paying work for months because no one could. Lawyers were working at Starbucks. Employers for entry-level office jobs were demanding multiple unpaid internships on your résumé before they'd consider hiring you. Jobs were posted and you'd apply to dozens and dozens and dozens and never hear back from one, not even to confirm that your résumé had been received, not even after you had uploaded it and retyped all the information into the shitty online portal.

If this was the employment landscape, why the hell had everyone been told to go to college if they wanted to get a good job? My newly issued degree wasn't doing me much good getting *any* kind of job, let alone one that paid more than minimum wage. And I didn't even have student debt. I knew people with $40,000 of debt, $80,000 of debt, $150,000 of debt. And that debt just kept growing because the interest kept compounding in a fucked-up reversal of the way I'd watched my college fund grow since age eleven.

I saw people I knew start doing sex work, drive for a new app called Uber, and move back in with their parents. I saw them go to food banks and pay their electric bill on their credit card. I saw them go to graduate school because at least that was something to do for the next few years. I saw them kill themselves on purpose and by accident. I saw ads encouraging people to sell their plasma and join the military and get paid to volunteer as medical test subjects. All the while, the amount of carbon in the atmosphere went up and up and up even though Obama signed the Paris Accords. There were fires and hurricanes and heat waves and bomb cyclones. There was a wildfire during a pandemic. And still we were at war in Afghanistan and the prison stayed open at Guantánamo Bay. And still austerity reigned, and public services were cut, and bridges collapsed and roads crumbled. This wasn't the bright future I had predicted in my 1999 elementary school time capsule.

And that's how, apprehensively, I found my way to politics.

To tell the story of the Y2K Era is, in some way or another, to tell the story of the millennial left during the decade that followed: Occupy Wall Street, *Jacobin*, the Bernie campaign, Chapo Trap House, the Democratic Socialists of America. It is to tell the story of Black Lives Matter and MeToo, of the increasingly visible trans rights and disability rights and immigrant rights movements, of body positivity, of Standing Rock, of Starbucks unions and the movement for climate justice. It is to explain why, suddenly, so many millennials were calling themselves socialists and making podcasts about historical materialism and tweeting profanity at *New York Times* columnists. A generation raised to believe that history's biggest questions were settled and the future would be awesome felt they had been lied to. We were pretty angry about it.*

Politics, to use a piece of contemporary millennial slang, was a cope. Another cope was nostalgia. Nostalgia is always a form of self-soothing, but for millennials in the wake of the recession, it took on the quality of trauma-induced age regression. BuzzFeed rose to popularity with listicles like "29 Things Only 90's Kids Will Remember." By the end of the 2010s, "nostalgia influencers" were creating TikToks about Y2K aesthetics. Now the nostalgia cycle is in full swing. Low-rise jeans, baby tees, platform shoes, and tattoo chokers are back in style. The Backstreet Boys did a Downy commercial. Eminem performed in a Super Bowl halftime show. *Mean Girls* was remade. In some ways, this is no different from the way that, in the Y2K Era, flared jeans and peasant blouses got popular and Led Zeppelin licensed their music for Cadillac ads targeted at boomers.

But millennial nostalgia feels different from boomer nostalgia. When boomer nostalgia was at its peak, its target audience was aging (a scary prospect for a generation whose identity was predicated on youth), but the world seemed, overall, to be improving.

---

* Some of that anger yielded different forms of politics: right-wing populism, white nationalism, tradcaths, conspiracy theories. All of these ideologies are a reaction to the failures of the Y2K Era political order. After the 2008 crisis, very few people could say with a straight face that neoliberal capitalism was working great or that it was the best of all possible systems.

Their stock portfolios were growing, at least, and they had comfortable careers and housing equity and families of their own. (This experience, by the way, explains why the boomer cohort largely became more conservative with age.) The end of the Cold War brought about unprecedented peace and prosperity. The internet promised both personal wealth and societal progress. Millennials are aging now, too, but in a far more violent, precarious, and uncertain world. And so we look to the past for our hope, because hope in the future feels so hard to come by.

Nostalgia is, in many ways, the opposite of politics. Politics may look to the past for context, but it offers us a chance to shape the future. Nostalgia is a surrender to the world as it is. I vacillate between both. When I'm in a nostalgic mood, I retreat to the world of my childhood. I escape into visions of silver eyeshadow and glittery lip gloss, of dELiA*s catalogs and butterfly hair clips. My happy place is the sleek chrome of a Ron Norsworthy video set, with its promise of the wonderful future to come.

It's an afternoon in October 2000. I've just come home from seventh grade, and I throw my Jansport on the floor in the rec room. I turn on *TRL*, where Christina Aguilera gyrates in the "Come On Over Baby" video. She has rhinestones around her belly button, and her hair has red underlights. I want red underlights, I think. Throughout the video, little windows pop up and other teenagers scream that they love Christina, that they voted for her to be on *TRL* today, that they want her to beat Britney. The video ends, and we cut back to Carson in the studio. I do not particularly care about politics, except to vote for Al Gore in our school's mock election.

What I care about is logging onto AIM. I double click the icon and I hear the dial tone, then the beeping, the up and down tones, the static. I'm LilAlien2. I wonder if Danny will be online, though I'm usually too scared to IM him. I'm just happy to know we're both online at the same time. He looked really hot today in the cafeteria. He wore an army jacket and a Green Day T-shirt and a silver ball chain necklace. Hannah will probably be on, and I can't wait to tell her about it.

The home page loads. I check my Buddy List. There's Koala-Gurl88, drinkyourslurpee, XxBigDevxX, natnat182. Just a few random people, and no one I really talk to. Danny is starlight711, and he isn't on yet. Hannah is HaPpY23ChIcA, and she isn't on yet either. Her bus must have been late, I think. I go to the kitchen for some Doritos 3D. I bring the bag back to the computer with me even though I'm not supposed to. I eat a handful, licking cheese dust off my fingertips. There are ads on TV: for Herbal Essences and Gatorade and PlayStation and *The Real World: New Orleans*. I crunch some more Doritos 3D.

Then, from the tinny computer speaker, there's the sound of an opening door.

Acknowledgments

I've wanted to write this book, in some form or another, since the Y2K Era. I am so grateful I finally got the opportunity.

Book writing is a team effort, and many people made it possible. First, I want to thank you, the reader. I hope you enjoyed spending time in my brain.

Next, I need to thank my agent, Erik Hane, who has stuck by my side since 2020. You helped me come up with the original idea for *Y2K* back in spring 2022. When I joked that Larry Summers caused my eating disorder, you encouraged me to turn that joke into the essay that got me this book deal. You continue to be among my biggest boosters, and I can't wait to see what the future holds for us.

Thank you to my editor, Stuart Roberts, for taking a chance on a genre-bending proposal by a first-time author. You transformed my rantings and ramblings into something coherent to a general audience. Sometimes you knew what I was trying to say before I knew it myself. I got really lucky with you.

Thank you to Chelsea Herrera for your time, input, and care as an editorial assistant.

Thank you to the rest of the team at Dey Street Books: Andrew Jacobs for legal review, Amanda Hong for production editing,

Ploy Siripant and Patrick Barry for design, Karen Richardson for copyediting, Kelsey Hess-O'Brien for content management, Jamie Keenan for the gorgeous cover. Thank you to Kelly Cronin for publicity and Kelly Dasta for marketing.

Thank you to Varsha Venkatasubramanian for research assistance, fact-checking, and compiling my citations.

Thank you to all my teachers over the years who helped me develop my talents. To my fifth-grade teacher, Mrs. Hathaway: I'm so glad you had us write those time capsule letters! Thank you to Mr. Hohner, my high school creative writing teacher. It was in your class that I first began to engage with some of the themes in this book. To Philip Baruth, my undergraduate writing professor at the University of Vermont, thank you for encouraging me to pursue writing as a career, and for teaching me that essays could be as fun to write as fiction.

Thank you to the crew at Red Emma's for giving me a place to work, and for giving me book recommendations that refined my political analysis.

Thank you to those who fight for a more livable future, particularly the climate justice movement and the labor movement.

Thank you to the following friends and acquaintances who provided subject-specific expertise, editing advice, general input, and at times emotional support: Will Anderson, Erik Baker, Lindsay Ballant, Tim Barker, Gabriela Barkho, Nellie Beckett, Stefan Borst-Censullo, Evan Collins, Matt Christman, Daniel Denvir, Margaret Eby, Cullen Enn, Liza Featherstone, Dave Heilker, Joe Henderson, Doug Henwood, Chase Madar, Colin Moynihan, Dharna Noor, Osita Nwanevu, Molly Phelps, Lester Spence, Kate Wagner. Margaret, thank you for coining the phrase "the fear" to describe work in the US. Thank you to Evan and the Consumer Aesthetics Research Institute for introducing me to the terms "Y2K aesthetic," "global village coffee house," and "McBling." Your work created a basis for me to write much of this book. Thank you to Lauren Cerand for the dinners and publicity advice. Thank you to Noah McCormack for believing in me from the beginning.

I must, of course, thank my family. Mom, you read to me every night and taught me to love language. You even helped me write my first book (*The Mystery of the Cat*) when I was four. I hope you like this one better. Dad, you taught me to love birds, opera, architecture, and coffee. To my brother, thanks for putting up with me. Thank you, Nana, for being a strong female role model, and for telling me stories about Brooklyn, the foreign service, and the early days of computing. I love that we share the same birthday. To my uncle, thanks for sharing your memories of Stanford, the counterculture, and the dot-com bubble, and for making me walk all over San Francisco (it's only three blocks).

I absolutely have to thank my husband, Lyle Jeremy Rubin. When we first met I had quit writing publicly. I said I'd never publish again; you told me I'd write a book. I'm glad you were right and I was wrong. Thank you for helping me think through the history of US militarism as it pertains to this book, and for your daily support and love. And I am so grateful to all the Rubins for welcoming me into your big, beautiful family.

Notes

Introduction

xv *In July 1997:* Peter Schwartz, "The Long Boom: A History of the Future, 1980–2020," *WIRED*, July 1, 1997, https://www.wired.com/1997/07 /longboom/.

xv *In 1991, the Soviet Union:* Serge Schmemann, "End of the Soviet Union; The Soviet State, Born of a Dream, Dies," *New York Times*, December 26, 1991, sec. World, https://www.nytimes.com/1991/12/26 /world/end-of-the-soviet-union-the-soviet-state-born-of-a-dream-dies .html.

xv *Political scientist Francis Fukuyama:* James Atlas, "What Is Fukuyama Saying? And to Whom Is He Saying It?" *New York Times*, October 22, 1989, sec. Magazine, https://www.nytimes.com/1989/10/22/magazine/what-is -fukuyama-saying-and-to-whom-is-he-saying-it.html; Francis Fukuyama, *The End of History and the Last Man*, 1st edition (New York: Free Press, 1992).

xvi *That same year back in America:* "1992 Democratic Party Platform | The American Presidency Project," The American Presidency Project, July 13, 1992, https://www.presidency.ucsb.edu/documents/1992- democratic-party-platform; Michael Kelly, "The 1992 Campaign: Clinton Says He's Not Leaning Left But Taking a New 'Third Way,'" *New York Times*, September 26, 1992, sec. National, https://www.nytimes.com/1992/09/26 /us/1992-campaign-democrats-clinton-says-he-s-not-leaning-left-but -taking-new-third.html.

xvii *The internet, it was assumed:* Doug Henwood, *After the New Economy: The Binge . . . And the Hangover That Won't Go Away*, reprint edition (New York: The New Press, 2005).

xvii *All this wealth:* Juliana Menasce Horowitz, Ruth Igielnik, Rakesh Kochhar, "Trends in Income and Wealthy Inequality," *Pew Research Center—U.S. Politics & Policy* (blog), January 9, 2020, https://www .pewresearch.org/social-trends/2020/01/09/trends-in-income-and-wealth -inequality/.

xviii *In 1997:* Ismail Muhammad, "1997 | Mo Money Mo Problems by Notorious B.I.G.," *American Experience,* PBS, August 4, 2017, https://www .pbs.org/wgbh/americanexperience/features/songs-of-the-summer-1997/.

xviii *The video, directed by Hype Williams:* "The Notorious B.I.G. feat. Puff Daddy and Mase," 1997, https://www.imdb.com/title/tt7352380/.

xviii *The video is undercut:* Bill Pennington, "Four Days That Changed Golf," *New York Times,* April 4, 2022, sec. Sports, https://www.nytimes .com/2022/04/04/sports/golf/tiger-woods-1997-masters.html.

xviii *In "The Rain (Supa Dupa Fly)":* "Missy Misdemeanor Elliott: The Rain (Supa Dupa Fly)," 1997, https://www.imdb.com/title/tt6723074/.

xix *"Your love is":* Aaliyah, "One in a Million," 1996, https://genius.com /Aaliyah-one-in-a-million-lyrics.

xix *Jennifer Lopez's 1999 video:* Jennifer Lopez, "If You Had My Love" (Sony Legacy, 1999).

xix *That same year:* TLC, *FanMail* (Sony Legacy, 1999).

xx *The 1999 Backstreet Boys album:* Backstreet Boys, *Millennium* (Sony Legacy, 1999).

xx *In a 2000 issue:* "AG Time Capsule," *American Girl Magazine,* January/February 2000: p. 3.

xx *In the words of:* Karim Rashid, "Technorganics," evolution (New York: Universe, 2004): p. 205.

xxi *The Volkswagen New Beetle:* "Y2K Aesthetic," Consumer Aesthetics Research Institute, accessed February 18, 2024, https://cari.institute /aesthetics/y2k-aesthetic.

xxii *A popular country song:* Toby Keith, "Courtesy of the Red, White, and Blue (the Angry American)," 2002, https://genius.com/Toby-keith -courtesy-of-the-red-white-and-blue-the-angry-american-lyrics.

xxiii *The Dow Jones:* Vikas Bajaj and Michael M. Grynbaum, "For Stocks, Worst Single-Day Drop in Two Decades," *New York Times,* September 29, 2008, sec. Business, https://www.nytimes.com/2008/09/30/business /30markets.html.

xxiii *US unemployment:* Sharada Dharmasankar, Bhash Mazumder, "Have Borrowers Recovered From Foreclosures during the Great Recession?," Federal Reserve Bank of Chicago, Chicago Fed Letter, No. 370, 2016,

https://www.chicagofed.org/publications/chicago-fed-letter
/2016/370.

xxiii *Around the world:* Edward Whitehouse, "Pensions During the Crisis:
Impact on Retirement Income Systems and Policy Responses," *The Geneva
Papers on Risk and Insurance. Issues and Practice* 34, no. 4 (2009): 536–47.

xxiv *"Men make their own history":* Karl Marx, *The Eighteenth Brumaire
of Louis Bonaparte* (International Publishers, 1926).

xxiv *And it hurts:* Smash Mouth, *"All Star,"* 1999, https://genius.com
/Smash-mouth-all-star-lyrics.

Only Shooting Stars Break the Mold

2   *He got into smoking:* Terry Gross and Stephen Kinzer, "The CIA's
Secret Quest for mind control: Torture, LSD, and a 'Poisoner in Chief,'"
Fresh Air, NPR, September 19, 2019, https://www.npr.org/transcripts
/758989641.

3   *On August 6, 1991:* "A Short History of the Web," CERN,
January 25, 2024, https://www.home.cern/science/computing/birth-web
/short-history-web; Josie Fischels, "A Look Back At The Very First Website
Ever Launched, 30 Years Later," NPR, August 6, 2001, https://www.npr.org
/2021/08/06/1025554426/a-look-back-at-the-very-first-website-ever
-launched-30-years-later.

3   *But it was in 1995:* "Americans Going Online . . . Explosive Growth,
Uncertain Destinations," *Pew Research Center—U.S. Politics & Policy* (blog),
October 16, 1995, https://www.pewresearch.org/politics/1995/10/16
/americans-going-online-explosive-growth-uncertain-destinations/.

3   *On August 9:* "Netscape Is Fast out of the Gate," *Tampa Bay Times*,
August 10, 1995, https://www.tampabay.com/archive/1995/08/10/netscape
-is-fast-out-of-the-gate/.

3   *"It was the spark":* Adam Lashinsky, "Remembering Netscape: The
Birth of the Web," CNNMoney, July 25, 2005, https://money.cnn.com
/magazines/fortune/fortune_archive/2005/07/25/8266639/.

4   *The late '90s gave us:* Malcolm Harris, *Palo Alto: A History of
California, Capitalism, and the World,* first edition (New York: Little, Brown,
and Company, 2023); Doug Henwood, *After the New Economy: The Binge . . .
And the Hangover That Won't Go Away,* reprint edition (New York: The New
Press, 2005).

4   *That year, online pet goods retailer:* "Amazon.Com Announces
Investment in Pets.Com," Amazon Press Center, March 29, 1999, https://

press.aboutamazon.com/1999/3/amazon-com-announces-investment-in
-pets-com.

4   *In January 2000:* David Goldman, "10 Big Dot.Com Flops—
Pets.Com," CNNMoney, March 10, 2010, https://money.cnn.com/
galleries/2010/technology/1003/gallery.dot_com_busts/index.html; "The
Sock Puppet—Tribble Agency," March 26, 2007, https://tribbleagency.com
/en/the-sock-puppet/; Tom McNichol, "A Startup's Best Friend? Failure,"
Business 2.0, February 28, 2007, https://web.archive.org/web/20070303063805
/http://money.cnn.com/magazines/business2/business2_archive/2007/03
/01/8401031/?postversion=2007022807.

4   *The dog mascot:* Joshua Bote, "Pets.Com Was an SF Sensation. It
Collapsed Months after Going Public," SFGATE, July 18, 2023, https://
www.sfgate.com/tech/article/pets-dot-com-sock-puppet-look-back
-18205346.php.

4   *Former US surgeon general:* "10 Big Dot.Com Flops—Drkoop.com,"
CNNMoney, March 10, 2010, https://money.cnn.com/galleries/2010
/technology/1003/gallery.dot_com_busts/8.html; "Auditors Doubt Future
Health of Drkoop.Com Site," *Los Angeles Times*, March 31, 2000, https://
www.latimes.com/archives/la-xpm-2000-mar-31-fi-14460-story.html.

4   *Profits spilled over from tech:* Malcolm Harris, *Palo Alto: A History
of California, Capitalism, and the World*, first edition (New York: Little,
Brown, and Company, 2023).

5   *The internet came to my house:* "Americans Going Online . . .
Explosive Growth, Uncertain Destinations," *Pew Research Center—U.S.
Politics & Policy* (blog), October 16, 1995, https://www.pewresearch.org
/politics/1995/10/16/americans-going-online-explosive-growth-uncertain
-destinations/.

8   *"The US economy":* Doug Henwood, "Age of the Unicorn: How the
Fed Tried to Fix the Recession, and Created the Tech Bubble," September 3,
2015, https://www.thenation.com/article/archive/age-of-the-unicorn-how
-the-fed-tried-to-fix-the-recession-and-created-the-tech-bubble/.

9   *In his 1989 book:* George Gilder, *Microcosm: The Quantum
Revolution in Economics and Technology*, reprint edition (New York: Free
Press, 1990).

9   *When the Dow crossed 10,000:* "10,000 at Last," CNNMoney,
March 29, 1999, https://money.cnn.com/1999/03/29/markets/marketwrap/.

9   *"1999 Goes into the Record Book":* Tom Petruno, "1999 Goes
Into the Record Book on Wall Street," *Los Angeles Times*, January 1, 2000,

https://www.latimes.com/archives/la-xpm-2000-jan-01-fi-49732-story
.html.

9   *It seemed like the stock market:* James K. Glassman and Kevin A.
Hassett, *Dow 36,000: The New Strategy for Profiting from the Coming Rise
in the Stock Market,* 1st edition (New York: Three Rivers Press, 2000).

9   *"The Californian Ideology":* Richard Barbrook and Andy Cameron,
"The Californian Ideology," *Science as Culture* 6 (January 1, 1996): 44–72,
https://doi.org/10.1080/09505439609526455.

10   *In 1999, Smash Mouth:* Smash Mouth, *Astro Lounge* (Interscope
Records, 1999).

11   *Aliens were everywhere: The Journey of Allen Strange* (Lynch
Entertainment, Nickelodeon Network, 1997).

11   *The United States Postal Service:* National Postal Museum,
"Exhibitions: Stampin' the Future," May 23, 2001–June 17, 2002, https://
www.si.edu/es/exhibitions/stampin-future:event-exhib-4515.

12   *In "Home":* Smash Mouth, "Home," 1999, https://genius.com/Smash
-mouth-home-lyrics.

12   *In "I Just Wanna See":* Smash Mouth, "I Just Wanna See," 1999, https://
genius.com/Smash-mouth-i-just-wanna-see-lyrics.

13   *Even "All Star":* Smash Mouth, "All Star," 1999, https://genius.com
/Smash-mouth-all-star-lyrics.

14   *The dot-com bubble:* Mark Kowlakowski, "How the Next Recession
May Look Like the 2001–2002 Dotcom Bust," *Investopedia,* June 25, 2019,
https://www.investopedia.com/how-the-next-recession-may-look-like-the
-2001-dotcom-bust-4584237.

14   *Nokia retained blue-chip:* Kenji Explains, "What Happened to
Nokia? The rise and fall of the world's largest phonemaker," The Startup,
August 10, 2020, https://medium.com/swlh/what-happened-to-nokia
-2a920b622d52#:~:text=By%201998%2C%20Nokia%20overtook%20
Motorola,25%25%20of%20global%20market%20share; Kevin Curran,
"Chart of the Day: A Timeline of Nokia's Rise and Fall," TheStreet's Real
Money Pro, February 7, 2019, https://realmoney.thestreet.com/stocks
/chart-of-the-day-a-timeline-of-nokia-s-rise-and-fall-14859219.

Global Village, Crying Eagle

16   *"They're boycotting Nike":* "The Saipan Workers Lawsuit," ecommons
at Cornell, accessed April 26, 2024, https://ecommons.cornell.edu/server

/api/core/bitstreams/b758d5dd-5060-4b64-8615-136651668052/content;
Michael Ellison, "Fashion Favorites Named in Sweatshop Lawsuit," *The
Guardian*, January 5, 1999, https://www.theguardian.com/world/1999/jan
/15/michaelellison; Jeff Ballinger, "Nike Chronology," University of
Washington Center for Civic & Community Engagement, accessed
April 26, 2024, https://depts.washington.edu/ccce/polcommcampaigns
/NikeChronology.htm.

18   *There was a specific look:* VENUSSTADT, "globalism and its
aesthetics: part one," April 28, 2023, https://www.youtube.com/watch
?v=Ku3lHHjLh4g; VENUSSTADT, "globalism and its aesthetics: part two,"
May 26, 2023, https://www.youtube.com/watch?v=aUXlJUV7V8A.

19   *The anti-sweatshop movement:* "Ending the Business of Injustice:
Anti-Sweatshop Activism at the University of Michigan, 1999–2007,"
United Students Against Sweatshops, accessed February 21, 2024, https://
michganintheworld.history.lsa.umich.edu/antisweatshop/exhibits/show
/exhibit/origins/usas.

19   *In 1992,* Harper's: Jeffrey Ballinger, "The New Free-Trade Heel: How
Big Tech Is Losing the Wars of the Future," *Harper's*, accessed February 21,
2024, https://harpers.org/archive/1992/08/the-new-free-trade-heel/.

20   *In 1996, the labor activist:* Stephanie Strom, "A Sweetheart Becomes
Suspect; Looking Behind Those Kathie Lee Labels," *New York Times*,
June 27, 1996, https://www.nytimes.com/1996/06/27/business/a-sweetheart
-becomes-suspect-looking-behind-those-kathie-lee-labels.html.

20   *In 1997, they agreed:* Paul Blustein, "Apparel industry reaches
agreement to end sweatshops in U.S. and abroad," *The Washington Post*,
April 10, 1997, https://www.washingtonpost.com/archive/politics/1997
/04/10/apparel-industry-reaches-agreement-to-end-sweatshops-in-us
-and-abroad/34b24a0b-f308-4352-aadd-45b72c9e02c3/?_pml=1.

20   *Starting in 1998:* "United Students Against Sweatshops Exhibit
Ending the Business of Injustice: Anti-Sweatshop Activism at the
University of Michigan, 1999–2007," Michigan in the World, accessed
February 29, 2024, https://michiganintheworld.history.lsa.umich.edu
/antisweatshop/exhibits/show/exhibit/origins/usas.

20   *November 30, 1999:* David Moberg, "How the Battle in Seattle
Changed Everything," *In These Times*, November 30, 2020, https://inthesetimes
.com/article/seattle-world-trade-organization-labor-protests-wto-trade.

21   *One pointed toward: This Is What Democracy Looks Like* (Big Noise
Films, Independent Media Center, 2000).

21 *"The Battle in Seattle":* Margot Hornblower, "The Battle in Seattle," CNN, November 22, 1999, https://edition.cnn.com/ALLPOLITICS/time /1999/11/22/seattle.battle.html.

21 *The opening ceremony:* Jim Brunner, "50,000 Protesters, Tear Gas—and Madeleine Albright Trapped in Her Hotel: How the 1999 WTO Protests Changed Seattle," *Seattle Times*, November 30, 2019, https://www .seattletimes.com/seattle-news/wto-seattle-protests-20-years-later-do -they-matter/; "Day Two: November 30, 1999," The WTO History Project, The University of Washington, accessed April 30, 2024, https://depts .washington.edu/wtohist/day2.htm.

21 *For a few hours:* Daniel Denvir, "Today's Socialist Revival Began on the Streets of Seattle 20 Years Ago," accessed February 21, 2024, https:// jacobin.com/2019/11/seattle-world-trade-organization-protests-socialism.

22 *The City of Seattle:* Gregory Scruggs, "20 Years Ago, Seattle Redefined the Modern Protest," Bloomberg.com, November 29, 2019, https://www.bloomberg.com/news/articles/2019-11-29/what-seattle-s -wto-protests-mean-20-years-later; "World Trade Organization Protests in Seattle," Seattle City Archives, accessed February 21, 2024, https://www .seattle.gov/cityarchives/exhibits-and-education/digital-document -libraries/world-trade-organization-protests-in-seattle.

22 *The WTO meeting:* "The Third WTO Ministerial Conference," December 3, 1999, https://www.wto.org/english/thewto_e/minist_e/min99_e /min99_e.htm.

22 *Even President Clinton:* David E. Sanger, "The Overview: In Stormy Seattle, Clinton Chides World Trade Body," *New York Times*, December 2, 1999, https://archive.nytimes.com/www.nytimes.com/library/world/global /120299wto-talks.html.

23 *Most youth entertainment:* "The Merchants of Cool: Media Giants," *Frontline*, February 27, 2001. https://www.pbs.org/wgbh/pages/frontline /shows/cool/giants/.

25 *This phenomenon:* "The Merchants of Cool," *Frontline*, February 27, 2001; Malcolm Gladwell, "The Coolhunt," *The New Yorker*, March 10, 1997, https://www.newyorker.com/magazine/1997/03/17/the-coolhunt; Naomi Klein, *No Logo: 10th Anniversary Edition with a New Introduction by the Author* (New York: Picador, 2009).

26 *"Today, our fellow citizens":* George W. Bush, "Statement by the President in His Address to the Nation," Office of the Press Secretary, September 11, 2001, https://georgewbush-whitehouse.archives.gov/news

/releases/2001/09/20010911-16.html#:~:text=THE%20PRESIDENT%3A
%20Good%20evening.,and%20dads%2C%20friends%20and%20neighbors.

26   *In his book* The Nineties: Chuck Klosterman, *The Nineties: A Book*
(New York: Penguin Press, 2022).

26   *Ten days after:* Edward Rothstein, "Attacks on the US Challenge
the Beliefs of Postmodern True Believers," *New York Times*, September 22,
2001, https://www.nytimes.com/2001/09/22/arts/connections-attacks-us
-challenge-perspectives-postmodern-true-believers.html.

26   Vanity Fair *editor:* Eric Randall, "The 'Death of Irony' and its
Many Reincarnations," *The Atlantic*, September 9, 2011, https://www
.theatlantic.com/national/archive/2011/09/death-irony-and-its-many
-reincarnations/338114/.

26   *The September 28 issue: Entertainment Weekly*, September 28, 2001.

28   *The band was at the peak:* wookubus, "Limp Bizkit's Wes Borland
Says 9/11 Put an End to 'Rollin'' Music Video," Theprp.com, August 14,
2015, https://www.theprp.com/2015/08/14/news/limp-bizkits-wes-borland
-says-911-put-an-end-to-rollin-music-video/.

28   *On September 10:* "The Bizarre Letter Limp Bizkit Received a Day
Before the 9/11 WTC Attacks," Headbangerz Club, September 11, 2001,
https://headbangerzclub.net/news/the-bizarre-letter-limp-bizkit-received
-a-day-before-the-9/11-wtc-attacks.

28   *Two days after 9/11:* Chris Krovatin, "The 164 Songs That Were
Banned from American Radio after 9/11," Kerrang! September 10, 2021,
https://www.kerrang.com/here-are-the-164-songs-that-were-banned
-from-american-radio-after-9–11.

28   *"Learn to Fly":* Steven Wishnia, "Bad Transmission: Clear Channel's
Hit List," archive.ph, October 24, 2001, https://archive.ph/OgdL0.

30   *For example, P!nk's video:* P!nk, "Get This Party Started," October 9,
2001, https://www.youtube.com/watch?v=mW1dbiD_zDk.

31   *Even though the president:* George W. Bush, "At O'Hare,
President Says Get on Board," Office of the Press Secretary, September
27, 2001, https://georgewbush-whitehouse.archives.gov/news/
releases/2001/09/20010927-1.html.

31   *George W. Bush:* David Moore, "Bush Job Approval Highest in
Gallup History," Gallup.com, September 24, 2001, https://news.gallup.com
/poll/4924/Bush-Job-Approval-Highest-Gallup-History.aspx.

31   *And the attacks elevated:* "Oprah Talks to Rudy Giuliani," O, *The
Oprah Magazine*, January 2002, https://www.oprah.com/omagazine/oprah
-interviews-with-rudy-giuliani/all.

31   Time *magazine:* Nancy Gibbs, "Person of the Year 2001: Rudy Giuliani," *Time,* December 31, 2001.

31   *In an address on September 20:* "President Declares 'Freedom at War with Fear,'" White House of George W. Bush, September 20, 2001, https://georgewbush-whitehouse.archives.gov/news/releases/2001/09/20010920−8.html.

31   *When Susan Sontag wrote:* John Updike et al., "Tuesday, and After," *The New Yorker,* September 16, 2001, https://www.newyorker.com/magazine/2001/09/24/tuesday-and-after-talk-of-the-town.

32   *What's more, the United States:* Emily Stewart, "The history of US intervention in Afghanistan, from the Cold War to 9/11," *Vox,* August 15, 2021, https://www.vox.com/world/22634008/us-troops-afghanistan-cold-war-bush-bin-laden.

32   *We even invited a Taliban contingent:* The National Security Archive, "The September 11 Sourcebooks," National Security Archive Electronic Briefing Book No. 97, https://nsarchive2.gwu.edu/NSAEBB/NSAEBB97/index.htm#:~:text=On%20December%208%2C%201997%20Taliban,to%20fund%20crop%20substitution%20programs.

32   *When he suggested one evening:* "Maher Apologizes for 'Cowards' Remark," ABC News, September 24, 2001, https://abcnews.go.com/Entertainment/story?id=102318&page=1.

32   *"I have to catch a flight to California":* "The NY Friars Club Roast of Hugh Hefner," November 4, 2001, https://www.imdb.com/title/tt0300261/; Gilbert Gottfried, "Gilbert Gottfried on His Infamous 9/11 joke and 'Too Soon,'" *Vulture,* February 2, 2016, https://www.vulture.com/2016/02/gilbert-gottfried-on-his-911-joke-too-soon.html.

33   *Reading the room:* The Strokes, *New York City Cops,* 2001, https://genius.com/The-strokes-new-york-city-cops-lyrics.

33   *"The band stands by":* Billboard Staff, "Strokes Pull NYPD-Themed Song from Album," *Billboard,* September 20, 2001, https://www.billboard.com/music/music-news/strokes-pull-nypd-themed-song-from-album-78359/.

33   *A year and a half later:* Billboard Staff, "Protesters Destroy Dixie Chicks CDs," *Billboard,* March 17, 2003, https://www.billboard.com/music/music-news/protesters-destroy-dixie-chicks-cds-71953/.

34   *Because of 9/11, the government:* Safia Samee Ali and Halima Abdullah, "Did the PATRIOT Act Change US Attitudes on Surveillance?" NBC News, September 8, 2016, https://www.nbcnews.com/storyline/9−11-anniversary/did-patriot-act-change-us-attitudes-surveillance-n641586.

34   *Because of 9/11, the very definition of terrorism:* "Surveillance Under the USA/PATRIOT Act," *American Civil Liberties Union* (blog), October 23, 2001, https://www.aclu.org/documents/surveillance-under-usapatriot-act.

34   *Because of 9/11, Guantánamo Bay:* "Timeline: 22 Years of Guantanamo Bay Prison," *Al Jazeera,* January 10, 2022, https://www.aljazeera.com/news /2022/1/10/timeline-20-years-of-guantanamo-bay-prison.

34   *Because of 9/11, the administration started talking:* Ed Pilkington, "'The Forever Prisoner': Abu Zubaydah's Drawings Expose the US's Depraved Torture Policy," *The Guardian,* May 11, 2023, sec. Law, https:// www.theguardian.com/law/2023/may/11/abu-zubaydah-drawings -guantanamo-bay-us-torture-policy.

34   *Moral relativism didn't matter:* Moustafa Bayoumi, "Disco Inferno," *The Nation,* December 26, 2005, https://www.thenation.com/article/archive /disco-inferno/.

Get Naked

37   *In September 2000:* Ludacris (featuring (Shawnna), "What's Your Fantasy," 2009, https://www.youtube.com/watch?v=mq-Ru6kQhE4.

37   *She recited some of it:* Ludacris (featuring Shawnna), "What's Your Fantasy," 2000, https://genius.com/Ludacris-whats-your-fantasy-lyrics.

39   *In "Come On Over Baby":* Christina Aguilera, "Come On Over Baby (All I Want Is You)," 2000, https://genius.com/Christina-aguilera-come-on -over-all-i-want-is-you-lyrics.

40   *"Know what I mean?":* 112, "Peaches & Cream," 2001, https://genius .com/112-peaches-and-cream-lyrics.

40   *The song and video for "One Minute Man":* Missy Elliott (featuring Ludacris), "One Minute Man," 2001, https://genius.com/Missy-elliott-one -minute-man-lyrics.

40   *The most profane video I saw:* Methods of Mayhem (featuring Lil' Kim, Tommy Lee, and Fred Durst), "Get Naked," 1999, https://www .youtube.com/watch?v=23A16kpAL1A.

40   *And then there was the 2001 video:* Christina Aguilera, Lil' Kim, Mýa, P!nk, "Lady Marmalade," (Interscope Records, 2002), https://www .youtube.com/watch?v=RQa7SvVCdZk&ab_channel=CAguileraVEVO.

43   *Sexual content was popular:* Samantha Cole, "ASCII Porn Predates the Internet but It's Still Everywhere," *Vice* (blog), January 14, 2019, https:// www.vice.com/en/article/nepapk/ascii-pr0n-porn-predates-the-internet -but-its-still-everywhere-rule-34.

43   *Journalist David Friend:* David Friend, *The Naughty Nineties: The Triumph of the American Libido,* 1st edition (New York: Twelve, 2017).

43   *Porn sites pioneered:* David Kushner, "A Brief History of Porn on the Internet," *WIRED,* April 3, 2018, https://www.wired.com/story/brief -history-porn-internet/.

43   *Her swift success:* WIRED staff, "The Brains Behind the Boobs," *WIRED,* accessed February 21, 2024, https://www.wired.com/1999/01/the -brains-behind-the-boobs/.

43   *In 1997, a website called Eyescream:* "Yahoo! Top 200 Search Words," accessed February 21, 2024, http://web.archive.org/web/19970502094027 /http:/www.eyescream.com/yahootop200.html.

46   *If you stayed up late:* Adrian Horton, "'Lives Were Being Ruined': The Dark History of Girls Gone Wild," *The Guardian,* April 22, 2022, sec. Television and Radio, https://www.theguardian.com/tv-and-radio/2022 /apr/22/joe-francis-girls-gone-wild-documentary.

48   *Girls Gone Wild was forced:* Eriq Gardner, "'Girls Gone Wild' Company Declares Bankruptcy," *Hollywood Reporter,* February 28, 2013, https://www.hollywoodreporter.com/business/business-news/girls-gone -wild-company-declares-425226/.

48   *The very first one:* David Friend, *The Naughty Nineties: The Triumph of the American Libido,* 1st edition (New York: Twelve, 2017).

49   *Kim sued Vivid in 2007:* Lorenzo Benet, "Kim Kardashian Sues Over Sex Tape," February 21, 2007, https://people.com/celebrity/kim -kardashian-sues-over-sex-tape/.

49   *Family friend Joe Francis:* Daisy Hall, "Joe Francis Alleges Kim Kardashian and Ray J Leaked Their Own Sex Tape," *Grazia,* October 6, 2023, https://graziadaily.co.uk/celebrity/news/joe-francis-kim-kardashian-sex-tape/.

52   *The president's administration:* "Bush Pushes Questionable Abstinence Programs," NBC News, March 22, 2005, https://www.nbcnews .com/id/wbna7221243; Marcella Howell and Marilyn Keefe, "The History of Federal Abstinence-Only Funding," Advocates for Youth, July 2007, https://www.advocatesforyouth.org/wp-content/uploads/storage//advfy /documents/fshistoryabonly.pdf.

53   *There was little to no discussion:* Emily St. James, "The Sexual Abuse Scandal Rocking the Southern Baptist Convention, Explained," *Vox,* June 7, 2022, https://www.vox.com/culture/23131530/southern-baptist -convention-sexual-abuse-scandal-guidepost.

53   *Tens of thousands:* "How effective are abstinence pledges?" BBC, June 29, 2004, http://news.bbc.co.uk/2/hi/uk_news/magazine/3846687.stm.

53   *The nonprofit organization:* Rachel Hart, "The Silver Ring Thing," *American Civil Liberties Union* (blog), February 23, 2006, https://www.aclu.org/news/reproductive-freedom/silver-ring-thing.

54   *Described as "a comprehensive":* "Our Whole Lives: Lifespan Sexuality Education," Unitarian Universalist Association, accessed February 21, 2024, https://www.uua.org/re/owl.

55   *I actually started to envy:* Clyde Haberman, "How an Abstinence Pledge in the '90s Shamed a Generation of Evangelicals," *New York Times*, April 6, 2021, sec. U.S., https://www.nytimes.com/2021/04/06/us/abstinence-pledge-evangelicals.html.

55   *Kids who do comprehensive sex ed:* The American Academy of Pediatrics, "The Importance of Access to Comprehensive Sexual Education," February 15, 2024, https://www.aap.org/en/patient-care/adolescent-sexual-health/equitable-access-to-sexual-and-reproductive-health-care-for-all-youth/the-importance-of-access-to-comprehensive-sex-education/#:~:text=Instead%2C%20comprehensive%20sex%20ed%20is,an%20increase%20in%20condom%20use.

57   *In fact, most Americans:* Rachel Martin, "Church Tries Its Hand at Sex Education," NPR, March 13, 2007, sec. Religion, https://www.npr.org/2007/03/13/7867316/church-tries-its-hand-at-sex-education.

58   *"UU parents should feel proud":* Cynthia Kuhn, "Don't Just Say No," *UUWorld*, August 14, 2005, https://www.uuworld.org/articles/dont-just-say-no.

Larry Summers Caused My Eating Disorder

59   *It opens with the only:* Laird Borrelli-Persson, "Inside the Making of *Vogue*'s 'Alice in Wonderland' Shoot with Annie Leibovitz and Grace Coddington, on Episode 6 of *In Vogue*: The 2000s," *Vogue*, October 12, 2021, https://www.vogue.com/article/in-vogue-the-2000s-podcast-episode-6.

60   *Four years earlier:* Krista Smith, "A Fashion Fairy Tale," *Vanity Fair*, July 17, 2014, https://www.vanityfair.com/news/2005/01/natalia-vodianova-story; Hannah Kane, "Natalia Vodianova: Supermodel Supernova," CNN, May 5, 2009, https://www.cnn.com/2009/TRAVEL/05/05/vodianova.biog/index.html.

61   *"Voronezh, Karaganda":* Peter Pomerantsev, *Nothing Is True and Everything Is Possible: The Surreal Heart of the New Russia,* 1st edition (New York: PublicAffairs, 2014).

61   *"If you catch the girl": Girl Model,* 2012.

62   *These policies were helped along:* Janine R. Wedel, "The Harvard Boys Do Russia," May 14, 1998, https://www.thenation.com/article/world/harvard-boys-do-russia/.

63   *The advice from the Harvard Boys:* The Associated Press, "Harvard Agrees to Settlement in Complaint Over Investments," August 4, 2005, *New York Times,* https://www.nytimes.com/2005/08/04/education/harvard-agrees-to-settlement-in-complaint-over-investments.html.

63   *"The people in Russia":* Lucy Komisar, "Interview with Joseph Stiglitz," Progressive.org, June 16, 2000, https://progressive.org/%3Fq%3D news/2000/06/5088/interview-joseph-stiglitz/.

70   *A 2003 paper:* Anne M. Morris and Debra K. Katzman, "The Impact of the Media on Eating Disorders in Children and Adolescents," *Journal of Paediatrics and Child Health* 8, no. 5 (2003): 287–89.

70   *A 2004 study:* Mia Foley Sypeck, James J. Gray, and Anthony H. Ahrens, "No Longer Just a Pretty Face: Fashion Magazines' Depictions of Ideal Female Beauty from 1959 to 1999," *International Journal of Eating Disorders* 36, no. 3 (November 2004): 342–47, https://doi.org/10.1002/eat.20039; Nicole Hawkins et al., "The Impact of Exposure to the Thin-Ideal Media Image on Women," *Eating Disorders* 12, no. 1 (2004): 35–50, https://doi.org/10.1080/10640260490267751.

70   *During the period from 2000 to 2018:* Marie Galmiche et al., "Prevalence of Eating Disorders over the 2000–2018 Period: A Systematic Literature Review," *American Journal of Clinical Nutrition* 109, no. 5 (May 1, 2019): 1402–13, https://doi.org/10.1093/ajcn/nqy342.

71   Lean *is part of:* John Patrick Leary, *Keywords: The New Language of Capitalism* (Chicago: Haymarket, 2019).

71   *When the photographer Terry Richardson:* Jenna Sauers, "Exclusive: More Models Come Forward With Allegations Against Fashion Photographer," *Jezebel,* March 18, 2010, https://www.jezebel.com/exclusive-more-models-come-forward-with-allegations-ag-5495699; "Supermodel Rie Rasmussen SLAMS Fashion Photographer Terry Richardson, Calls Him a Coward," *Huffington Post,* May 12, 2010, https://www.huffpost.com/entry/supermodel-rie-rasmussen_n_496491.

72   *In 2017, Condé Nast International:* Jessica Testa, "Terry Richardson Accused of Sexual Assault in Two New Lawsuits," *New York Times,* November 22, 2023, sec. Style, https://www.nytimes.com/2023/11/22/style/terry-richardson-sexual-assault-lawsuit.html.

73   *In 2021, artist Precious Okoyomon:* Group Think, "The American Apparelification of Life," Substack newsletter, *Groupthink* (blog), March 16, 2021, https://groupthink.substack.com/p/the-american -apparelification-of.

74   *"The return of low-rise":* Rachel Rabbit White, "Miu Miu Mini Skirts, Kim Kardashian & The 'End of the BBL,'" NYLON, February 20, 2024, https://www.nylon.com/entertainment/miu-miu-mini-skirts-kim -kardashian-end-of-bbls.

75   *On the post-left podcast:* Ann Merlan, "What is Red Scare and Am I Exempt From Caring About It?" Jezebel, July 11, 2019, https://www .jezebel.com/what-is-red-scare-and-am-i-exempt-from-caring-about -it-1836221532.

They Misunderestimated Me

78   *And in 2004, Democratic:* Jodi Wilgoren, "Kerry on Hunting Photo-Op to Help Image," *New York Times*, October 22, 2004, https://www .nytimes.com/2004/10/22/politics/campaign/kerry-on-hunting-photoop -to-help-image.html.

80   *The inaugural Netroots Nation:* "History," Netroots Nation, accessed April 27, 2024, https://www.netrootsnation.org/about/history/.

82   *"We've been too often disappointed":* Guy Raz and Walter Cronkite, "Final Words: Cronkite's Vietnam Commentary," All Things Considered, NPR, July 18, 2009, https://www.npr.org/2009/07/18/106775685/final-words -cronkites-vietnam-commentary.

82   *And the* New York Times: "From the Editors: The Times and Iraq," *New York Times*, May 26, 2004, https://www.nytimes.com/2004/05/26 /world/from-the-editors-the-times-and-iraq.html; Pien Huang, "20 years on, remembering the mess of misinformation that propelled the Iraq War," All Things Considered, NPR, March 18, 2023, https://www.npr .org/2023/03/18/1164565624/20-years-on-remembering-the-mess-of -misinformation-that-propelled-the-iraq-war.

82   *Thomas Friedman:* "Thomas Friedman," Charlie Rose, May 30, 2003, https://charlierose.com/videos/26893.

82   *Leading up to the March 2003:* Stefaan Walgrave and Dieter Rucht, "Introduction," *The World Says No to War: Demonstrations against the War on Iraq*, Vol. 33, p. xiii (Minneapolis: University of Minnesota Press, 2010).

84   *At least $138 billion:* Anna Fifield, "Contractors Reap $138B from Iraq War," CNN, March 9, 2013, https://www.cnn.com/2013/03/19 /business/iraq-war-contractors/index.html.

84   *During the court's Lochner Era:* Andrew Prokop, "The Supreme Court's Infamous 'Lochner Era' Ended in the 1930s. Rand Paul Wants It Back," *Vox,* January 17, 2015, https://www.vox.com/2015/1/17/7628543 /rand-paul-lochner.

84   *Before that, in 1857: Dred Scott v. Sandford,* 1857, *National Archives,* https://www.archives.gov/milestone-documents/dred-scott-v-sandford.

85   *In 2001, they attempted:* "About Us | ACS," *American Constitution Society* (blog), January 12, 2018, https://www.acslaw.org/about-us/.

85   *"It's difficult to find":* Ryan D. Doerfler and Samuel Moyn, "The Constitution Is Broken and Should Not Be Reclaimed," *New York Times,* August 19, 2022, sec. Opinion, https://www.nytimes.com/2022/08/19 /opinion/liberals-constitution.html.

86   *Bill Clinton continued:* Lauren-Brooke Eisen, "The 1994 Crime Bill and Beyond: How Federal Funding Shapes the Criminal Justice System," Brennan Center for Justice, September 9, 2019, https://www.brennancenter .org/our-work/analysis-opinion/1994-crime-bill-and-beyond-how-federal -funding-shapes-criminal-justice; Arloc Sherman, "After 1996 Welfare Reform Law, a Weaker Safety Net and More Children in Deep Poverty," Center for Budget and Policy Priorities, August 9, 2016, https://www.cbpp .org/family-income-support/commentary-after-1996-welfare-law-a-weaker -safety-net-and-more-children-in.

86   *Then came the plaintive:* Andrew Prokop, "Read the letter the FBI sent Martin Luther King to try to convince him to kill himself," *Vox,* January 15, 2018, https://www.vox.com/xpress/2014/11/12/7204453/martin -luther-king-fbi-letter.

87   *In 2007, the* Washington Post: Glenn Kessler, "About the Fact Checker," *Washington Post,* February 22, 2024, https://www.washingtonpost .com/politics/2019/01/07/about-fact-checker/.

87   *"I never understood wind":* Richard Luscombe, "'I never understood wind': Trump goes on bizarre tirade against wind turbines," *The Guardian,* December 24, 2019, https://www.theguardian.com/us-news/2019/dec/23 /trump-bizarre-tirade-windmills.

88   *"Rarely is the question asked":* Jacob Weisberg, "W's Greatest Hits," Slate, January 12, 2009, https://slate.com/news-and-politics/2009/01/the -top-25-bushisms-of-all-time.html; "Top 10 Bushisims," *Time,* accessed

April 27, 2024, https://content.time.com/time/specials/packages/article
/0,28804,1870938_1870943_1870961,00.html.

89 *But perhaps the most glaring example:* Brian Krassenstein, Ed
Krassenstein, Benny Rahdiana, *How the People Trumped Ronald Plump*
(Herndon, VA: Mascot Books, Inc., 2018).

90 *The precedent for* Ronald Plump*:* Andy, "Bedtime for Bush," Galleycat,
May 27, 2008, https://archive.ph/20130128093555/http://www.mediabistro
.com/galleycat/authors/bedtime_for_bush_85483.asp.

90 Good Night Bush*:* Joanne Kaufman, "The Secret to Success in
Publishing: Bash Bush, With Nods to a Classic," *New York Times*, June 16,
2008, sec. Business, https://www.nytimes.com/2008/06/16/business
/16goodnight.html.

91 *On NPR, they talked:* Rebecca Leung, "Abuse of Iraqi POWs by GIs
Probed," CBS News, April 27, 2004, https://www.cbsnews.com/news/abuse
-of-iraqi-pows-by-gis-probed/; Seymour M. Hirsh, "Torture at Abu Ghraib,"
The New Yorker, April 30, 2004, https://www.newyorker.com/magazine
/2004/05/10/torture-at-abu-ghraib.

92 *In the photo, Ali Shallal al-Qaisi:* Osama Bin Javaid, "Abu Ghraib
survivor: Taking the hood off 20 years after Iraq War," Al Jazeera, March 20,
2023, https://www.aljazeera.com/news/2023/3/20/reporters-notebook
-taking-the-hood-off-20-years-later.

92 *According to a 2015 article:* Noah Bierman, "Few Have Faced
Consequences for Abuses at Abu Ghraib Prison in Iraq," *Los Angeles Times*,
March 17, 2015, https://www.latimes.com/nation/la-na-abu-ghraib-lawsuit
-20150317-story.html.

[Remix]

93 *In 1999, the video:* B.G. (featuring Big Tymers and Hot Boys),
"Bling Bling," 1999, https://www.youtube.com/watch?v=2FnRnKHS5ds.

94 *In 2003, the* Oxford English Dictionary*:* MTV—*Bling Bling*, 2004,
https://www.youtube.com/watch?v=9FUaPpb9ees.

94 *The Houston-based graphic design firm:* Will Stephenson, "Letter of
Recommendation: Pen & Pixel," *New York Times*, July 6, 2016, sec. Magazine,
https://www.nytimes.com/2016/07/10/magazine/letter-of-recommendation
-pen-pixel.html; "Pen & Pixel," University of Houston Digital Collections,
accessed April 27, 2024, https://digitalcollections.lib.uh.edu/collections
/mg74qn10n.

95 *In 1986, Run-D.M.C.'s:* Richard Harrington, "Run-DMC and the Rap Flap," *Washington Post*, August 28, 1986, https://www.washingtonpost.com/archive/lifestyle/1986/08/29/run-dmc-and-the-rap-flap/552172c5-eef3-48f3-b700-028ef4bcd28f/.

95 *In the Bling Era:* Bakari Kitwana, *Why White Kids Love Hip Hop: Wankstas, Wiggers, Wannabes, and the New Reality of Race in America* (New York: Basic Books, 2006).

98 *The market for crack:* Eloise Dunlap and Bruce D. Johnson, "The Setting for the Crack Era: Macro Forces, Micro Consequences (1960–1992)," *Journal of Psychoactive Drugs* 24, no. 4 (1992): 307–21.

99 *"The prison":* Loïc J.D. Wacquant, *Prisons of Poverty* (Minneapolis: University of Minnesota Press, 2009).

100 *In 2011, he published:* Lester K. Spence, *Stare in the Darkness: The Limits of Hip-Hop and Black Politics* (Minneapolis: University of Minnesota Press, 2011).

100 *A "takeover":* Alex Frew McMillan, "The Year of Hostile Mergers," CNNMoney, December 9, 1999, https://money.cnn.com/1999/12/09/personalfinance/q_hostiledeal/.

101 *In 1996, the president:* Office of the Press Secretary, "Remarks by the President at the Signing of the Personal Responsibility and Work Opportunity Reconciliation Act" (The White House of Bill Clinton, August 22, 1996), https://clintonwhitehouse6.archives.gov/1996/08/1996-08-22-president-remarks-at-welfare-bill-signing.html.

101 *Standing next to the president:* Victoria M. Massie, "Lillie Harden Was Bill Clinton's Welfare Reform Success Story. Welfare Reform Failed Her," *Vox*, August 22, 2016, https://www.vox.com/2016/8/22/12583376/welfare-reform-history-clinton-lillie-harden; Gene Demby, "The Black Mothers Who Fought To Radically Reimagine Welfare," June 9, 2019, Code Switch, NPR, https://www.npr.org/sections/codeswitch/2019/06/09/730684320/the-mothers-who-fought-to-radically-reimagine-welfare#:~:text=At%20the%20Rose%20Garden%20ceremony,former%20welfare%20recipient%20from%20Arkansas.

102 *In 2002, she had a stroke:* Nathan J. Robinson, "It Didn't Pay Off," October 1, 2016, *Jacobin*, https://jacobin.com/2016/10/clinton-welfare-reform-prwora-tanf-lillie-harden.

102 *50 Cent's:* 50 Cent, *Get Rich or Die Tryin'* (Shady/Aftermath/Interscope, 2003).

102 *A 2019 study at the University of Wisconsin:* Autumn Fearing et al., "Is Hip-Hop Violent? Analyzing the Relationship Between Live Music Performances and Violence," *Journal of Black Studies* 49, no. 3 (April 1, 2018): 235–55, https://doi.org/10.1177/0021934718754313.

102 *A 2014 study from the* Journal*:* Jeffrey Podoshen, Susan Andrzejewski, and James Hunt, "Materialism, Conspicuous Consumption, and American Hip-Hop Subculture," *Journal of International Consumer Marketing* 26 (June 20, 2014): 271–83, https://doi.org/10.1080/08961530.2014.900469.

103 *Since the 1970s, women:* Janet Yellen, "The History of Women's Work and Wages and How It Has Created Success for Us All," Brookings, May 2020, https://www.brookings.edu/articles/the-history-of-womens-work-and-wages-and-how-it-has-created-success-for-us-all/.

104 *A 2007 study:* Michael D. Cobb and William A. Boettcher III, "Ambivalent Sexism and Misogynistic Rap Music: Does Exposure to Eminem Increase Sexism?" *Journal of Applied Social Psychology* 37, no. 12 (2007): 3025–42, https://doi.org/10.1111/j.1559–1816.2007.00292.x.

104 *The "triple cocktail" treatment:* Interview with David Ho | The Age Of Aids | *Frontline*," PBS, May 30, 2006, https://www.pbs.org/wgbh/pages/frontline/aids/interviews/ho.html.

104 *In 2000, Vermont:* Jason Szep, "Vermont Becomes 4th U.S. State to Allow Gay Marriage," Reuters, April 7, 2009, sec. United States, https://www.reuters.com/article/idUSTRE53648V/.

104 *In 1998, Matthew Shepard:* Julie Bindel, "The Truth Behind America's Most Famous Gay-Hate Murder," *The Guardian*, October 26, 2014, sec. World News, https://www.theguardian.com/world/2014/oct/26/the-truth-behind-americas-most-famous-gay-hate-murder-matthew-shepard.

104 *In a skit:* Gollum MTV Awards, 2003, https://www.youtube.com/watch?v=bXI-Jrg9_T4.

104 *"Last I heard":* DMX, "Where the Hood At?" 2003, https://genius.com/Dmx-where-the-hood-at-lyrics.

104 *Lil Wayne cast aspersions:* Lil Wayne (featuring Mannie Fresh), "Go D.J.," 2004, https://genius.com/Lil-wayne-go-dj-lyrics.

104 *Eminem kept it short:* Eminem, "Criminal," 2000, https://genius.com/Eminem-criminal-lyrics.

104 *On the outro of his 2002 song:* Cam'ron (featuring Jay-Z and Juelz Santana), "Welcome to New York City," 2002, https://genius.com/Camron-welcome-to-new-york-city-lyrics.

105 *"With me, 'no homo'":* "Cam'ron Trolls Wikipedia Over 'No Homo' Origin Story," *Crumpe* (blog), May 29, 2020, https://www.crumpe.com /2020/05/camron-trolls-wikipedia-over-no-homo-origin-story/.

105 *As Martin Luther King noted:* Martin Luther King Jr., "Beyond Vietnam: A Time to Break Silence," April 4, 1967, www2.hawaii.edu /~freeman/courses/phil100/17.%20MLK%20Beyond%20Vietnam.pdf.

106 *"N–– I'm the colonel":* Master P (featuring Fiend, Mia X, Mystikal, and Silkk the Shocker), "Make 'Em Say Uhh," 1997, https://genius.com /Master-p-make-em-say-uhh-lyrics.

107 *B.G. had a 1999 song:* B.G., "Cash Money Is an Army," 1999, https:// genius.com/Bg-cash-money-is-an-army-lyrics.

107 *B.G's group the Hot Boys:* B.G., "Cash Money Is an Army," 1999, https://www.youtube.com/watch?v=z1o16s0gs4s; Hot Boys, *Guerrilla Warfare* (Cash Money Records, 1999).

107 *"This is the army":* Hot Boys, "Boys at War," 1999, https://genius .com/Hot-boys-boys-at-war-lyrics.

107 *On "Takeover":* Jay-Z, "Takeover," 2001, https://genius.com/Jay-z -takeover-mtv-unplugged-lyrics.

107 *"See Cash Money":* Destiny's Child (featuring Lil Wayne and T.I.), "Soldier," 2004, https://genius.com/Destinys-child-soldier-lyrics.

108 *"Hey, who I'm is?":* T.I., "Rubber Band Man," 2003, https://genius .com/Ti-rubber-band-man-lyrics.

109 *A popular series:* Michelle Garcia, "DJ's Appeal: Kill the Whiteness Inside," *Washington Post*, August 26, 2005, https://www.washingtonpost .com/wp-dyn/content/article/2005/08/25/AR2005082501818.html.

110 *"Blackface minstrels":* David R. Roediger, Priyamvada Gopal, and Kathleen Cleaver, *The Wages of Whiteness: Race and the Making of the American Working Class*, 4th edition (London, New York: Verso, 2022).

111 *In 1885, a fifteen-year-old boy:* "Howard Cooper," MSA SC 3520– 13733," Archives of Maryland, accessed February 26, 2024, https://msa. maryland.gov/megafile/msa/speccol/sc3500/sc3520/013700/013733 /html/13733bio.html; Alexander Ormond Boulton, "The Lynching of Howard Cooper," *Maryland Historical Magazine*, Vo. 106, No. 3, Fall 2011, 293-315, https://msa.maryland.gov/megafile/msa/speccol/sc3500 /sc3520/013700/013733/pdf/MHMFall2011_Howard%20Cooper.pdf.

112 *In his 2005 book:* Bakari Kitwana, *Why White Kids Love Hip Hop: Wanksters, Wiggers, Wannabes, and the New Reality of Race in America* (New York: Basic Books, 2006).

113 *And yet, Kitwana:* Ibid.

They're Just Like Us!

115 *An exclusive 2000 photo:* Claudia Rosenbam, "How the Fast Times of the Paparazzi Came to a Screeching Halt," BuzzFeed News, October 15, 2015, https://www.buzzfeednews.com/article/claudiarosenbaum/downfall -of-the-paparazzi.

115 *A 1997 photo:* Kristyn Burtt, "This Paparazzi Photo of Princess Diana & Her Lover Sold for $6 Million," SheKnows, November 17, 2020, https://www.sheknows.com/entertainment/articles/2371707/princess -diana-paparazzi-photo/.

116 *It was a forerunner:* William Turvill, "Perez Hilton Interview: How Hollywood's 'Most Hated' Sacrificed Clicks (and Ad Revenue) for His Conscience," *Press Gazette* (blog), October 14, 2021, https://pressgazette .co.uk/news/perez-hilton-interview/.

116 *By 2007, the* New York Times*:* Mireya Navarro, "Perez Hilton: A Bad-Talking Blogger Celebs Love to Hate," *New York Times*, July 31, 2007, sec. Arts, https://www.nytimes.com/2007/07/31/arts/31iht-hilton .1.6917096.html.

119 *"Of all the girls in gossip land":* Nancy Jo Sales, "Hip Hop Debs," *Vanity Fair*, September 1, 2000, https://www.vanityfair.com/culture /2000/09/hiltons200009.

120 *She invented: Paris: The Memoir* (New York: Dey Street Books, 2023).

121 *The Consumer Aesthetics Research Institute:* "McBling," Consumer Aesthetics Research Institute, https://cari.institute/aesthetics/mcbling.

123 *"She's become the face":* The Fabulous Life of . . . Lindsay Lohan, The Fabulous Life of . . . 2005, https://www.imdb.com/title/tt0847289/releaseinfo/.

130 *The pictures would be decorated:* Ben Cost, "Perez knows he made Britney Spears' life a living hell," *New York Post,* February 15, 2021, https:// nypost.com/2021/02/15/perez-hilton-expresses-remorse-over-britney -spears-coverage/.

132 *In 2021, the* New York Times*:* Framing Britney Spears, New York Times, November 2, 2021, sec. Universal, https://www.nytimes.com/article /framing-britney-spears.html.

132 *In Paris Hilton's 2020 documentary:* This Is Paris (The Intellectual Property Corporation (IPC), 2020); Paris Hilton, *Paris: The Memoir* (New York: Dey Street Books, 2023).

132 *In her 2020 memoir:* Jessica Simpson, *Open Book* (New York: Dey Street Books, 2020).

132 *Lena Dunham and Alissa Bennett's:* Lena Dunham and Alissa Bennett, "Lindsay Lohan, Part 1," *The C-Word,* September 8, 2022; Lena Dunham and Alissa Bennett feat. Naomi Fry, "Lindsay Lohan, Part 2," *The C-Word,* September 15, 2022.

134 *As Natasha Stagg:* Natasha Stagg, *Sleeveless: Fashion, Image, Media, New York 2011–2019* (South Pasadena, CA: Semiotext, 2019).

Stupid Ugly Vehicles

137 *In the 1990s, environmentalism:* Dan Nosowitz, "How the Save the Rainforest Movement Gave Rise to Modern Environmentalism," *Vox,* September 16, 2019, https://www.vox.com/the-goods/2019/9/16/20863152/save-the-rainforest-environmentalism-conservation.

137 *The Rainforest Cafe:* Justine Jones, "Why We're Still Obsessed with the Rainforest Cafe," *Eater,* February 22, 2023, https://www.eater.com/twin-cities/23598371/rainforest-cafe-history-appreciation-mall-of-america.

138 *Over 3 million SUVs:* "An Analysis of the Impact of Sport Utility Vehicles in the United States," U.S. Department of Energy Office of Scientific and Technical Information, August 1, 2000, https://www.osti.gov/biblio/763236.

139 *"Number one, the earth is warmer":* Madelein Ostrander, "Thirty Years Warmer," Slate, July 2, 2018, https://slate.com/technology/2018/07/james-hansens-1988-climate-change-warning-30-years-on.html.

139 *In the 1860s:* "Who Discovered the Greenhouse Effect?" Royal Institution, May 17, 2019, https://www.rigb.org/explore-science/explore/blog/who-discovered-greenhouse-effect.

139 *"Coal consumption":* "Coal Consumption Affecting Climate," *Rodney and Otamatea Times, Waitemata and Kaipara Gazette,* August 14, 1912.

139 *In 1977, a scientist:* Neela Banerjee, "Exxon's Own Research Confirmed Fossil Fuels' Role in Global Warming Decades Ago," *Inside Climate News* (blog), September 16, 2015, https://insideclimatenews.org/news/16092015/exxons-own-research-confirmed-fossil-fuels-role-in-global-warming/.

140 *According to a subsequent internal memo:* Jason M. Breslow, "Investigation Finds Exxon Ignored Its Own Early Climate Change Warnings," *Frontline,* September 16, 2015, https://www.pbs.org/wgbh/frontline/article/investigation-finds-exxon-ignored-its-own-early-climate-change-warnings/.

140 *Recent increases in global temperature:* Neela Bannerjee, Lisa Song, and David Hasemyer, "Exxon's Own Research Confirmed Fossil Fuels' Role in Global Warming Decades Ago," Inside Climate News, September 16, 2015, https://insideclimatenews.org/news/16092015/exxons-own-research -confirmed-fossil-fuels-role-in-global-warming/.

141 *Francis Bacon argued:* Carolyn Merchant, "The Scientific Revolution and the Death of Nature," *Isis* 97, no. 3 (2006): 513–33, https://doi.org /10.1086/508090.

141 *In 2004, BP released:* Rebecca Solnit, "Big Oil Coined 'Carbon Footprints' to Blame Us for Their Greed. Keep Them on the Hook," *The Guardian*, August 23, 2021, sec. Opinion, https://www.theguardian.com /commentisfree/2021/aug/23/big-oil-coined-carbon-footprints-to-blame -us-for-their-greed-keep-them-on-the-hook.

141 *Or the fact that human civilization:* Naomi Klein, *This Changes Everything: Capitalism vs. the Climate* (New York: Simon & Schuster, 2014).

144 *There is a famous chart:* Jeff Berardelli, "2,000 years of Earth's climate in one simple chart—and the copycat that isn't what it seems," CBS News, January 20, 2020, https://www.cbsnews.com/news/climate-change -2000-years-of-earths-temperatures-in-one-simple-chart-and-copycat -misinformation/.

145 *Its top-selling years:* "Hummer H2 Sales Figures, Good Car Bad Car," accessed April 27, 2024, https://www.goodcarbadcar.net/hummer-h2 -sales-figures-usa-canada/.

146 *In 2006, Al Gore: An Inconvenient Truth* (Lawrence Bender Productions, Participant, 2006).

146 *It received standing ovations:* Mignon Khargie, "An Oral History of 'An Inconvenient Truth,'" Grist, May 20, 2016, https://grist.org/feature/an -inconvenient-truth-oral-history/.

147 *"The aesthetics of fossil fuels":* Cara Daggett, "Petro-Masculinity: Fossil Fuels and Authoritarian Desire," *Millennium* 47, no. 1 (September 1, 2018): 25–44, https://doi.org/10.1177/0305829818775817.

149 *Or in 1995:* Mike Thomas, "How 739 People Died in a Chicago Heat Wave," *Chicago Magazine*, June 29, 2015, https://www.chicagomag.com /Chicago-Magazine/July-2015/1995-Chicago-heat-wave/.

149 *Other people:* Research Institute of Medicine (US) Roundtable on Environmental Health Sciences, "Hurricane Katrina: Challenges for the Community," in *Environmental Public Health Impacts of Disasters: Hurricane Katrina: Workshop Summary* (National Academies Press [US], 2007), https://www.ncbi.nlm.nih.gov/books/NBK54237/.

150 *Inside the Orleans Parish Prison:* "New Orleans: Prisoners Abandoned to Floodwaters," *Human Rights Watch* (blog), September 21, 2005, https://www.hrw.org/news/2005/09/21/new-orleans-prisoners-abandoned-floodwaters.

151 *According to one climate scientist:* Damien Carrington, "Earth 'well outside safe operating space for humanity,' scientists find," *The Guardian*, September 13, 2023, https://www.theguardian.com/environment/2023/sep/13/earth-well-outside-safe-operating-space-for-humanity-scientists-find.

151 *A 2023* New York Times *article:* J. L. Chen et al., "Rapid Ice Melting Drives Earth's Pole to the East," *Geophysical Research Letters* 40, no. 11 (2013): 2625–30, https://doi.org/10.1002/grl.50552.

151 *A recent study:* William Ripple et al., "2023 state of the climate report," Potsdam Institute for Climate Impact Research, *BioScience*, 73, 12, 841–50, https://publications.pik-potsdam.de/pubman/faces/ViewItemOverviewPage.jsp?itemId=item_28924_1.

151 *Which means that the younger:* Andrea Thompson, "How Climate Change Will Hit Younger Generations," *Scientific American*, February 1, 2022, https://www.scientificamerican.com/article/how-climate-change-will-hit-younger-generations/.

152 *In 2021,* The Lancet: Caroline Hickman et al., "Climate Anxiety in Children and Young People and Their Beliefs about Government Responses to Climate Change: A Global Survey," *The Lancet Planetary Health* 5, no. 12 (December 1, 2021): e863–73, https://doi.org/10.1016/S2542-5196(21)00278-3.

It's Definitely About Coffee, but It's About a Lot More Than Coffee

159 *Starbucks was founded:* "Our Founders: Starbucks Coffee Company," accessed April 29, 2024, https://archive.starbucks.com/record/our-founders.

160 *According to Starbucks:* "Our Name: Starbucks Coffee Company," accessed April 29, 2024, https://archive.starbucks.com/record/our-name.

160 *The logo has changed:* The Evolution of Our Logo: Starbucks Coffee Company," accessed April 29, 2024, https://archive.starbucks.com/record/the-evolution-of-our-logo; ibid.

161 *"I hope when people":* Michelle Flandreau, "Who is the Starbucks Siren?" *Starbucks Stories & News*, December 23, 2016, https://stories.starbucks.com/stories/2016/who-is-starbucks-siren/.

161 *As he describes:* Howard Schultz, *Pour Your Heart Into It: How Starbucks Built a Company One Cup at a Time* (New York: Hyperion, 1997).

162 *In 1987, Baldwin:* Sheila Farr, "Starbucks: The Early Years," History Link.org, February 15, 2017, https://www.historylink.org/File/20292.

162 *The privately held:* Starbucks Corporation, "Starbucks Stories & News: Timeline," 2020, https://stories.starbucks.com/uploads/2019/01 /AboutUs-Company-Timeline-1.6.21-FINAL.pdf.

163 *Starbucks had its initial:* "Starbucks: 32 Year Stock Price History," Macrotrends, accessed April 29, 2024, https://www.macrotrends.net /stocks/charts/SBUX/starbucks/stock-price-history; John Cziszar, "How much would you have today if you invested your coffee money in Starbucks IPO?" *Yahoo Finance*, June 28, 2021, https://finance.yahoo .com/news/much-today-invested-coffee-money-150029874.html ?guccounter=1&guce_referrer=aHR0cHM6Ly93d3cuZ29vZ2xlLmNvb S8&guce_referrer_sig=AQAAAFysKeC0I0gqpmSdZwHWCQIY-GxYPT2 iaSJ0moJ3pYeZni7dHTAE9xtA2OqCeZ7klPx7jzEpRvGB93l3CORx51F2Gf 3watXWnA3q-jIKX0K40EmR3n3yqwhKaj4sBFuP-tKlKLBGjzcib2ImlH -WQDFXIpOb6F29CTyEQwsxZ9X2.

163 *The IPO raised:* Howard Schultz, *Pour Your Heart Into It: How Starbucks Built a Company One Cup at a Time* (New York: Hyperion, 1997).

163 *The stock rose steadily:* "Starbucks: 32 Year Stock Price History," Macrotrends, accessed April 29, 2024, https://www.macrotrends.net /stocks/charts/SBUX/starbucks/stock-price-history.

164 *"Is it impossible":* Denis Leary: *Lock 'N Load* (Apostle, 1997).

164 *"The whole purpose":* You've Got Mail (Warner Bros., 1998).

164 *In the 1998 Simpsons:* "Simpson Tide," *The Simpsons*, March 29, 1998.

165 *In the 1999 film:* Austin Powers: *The Spy Who Shagged Me* (New Line Cinema, Gratitude, Moving Pictures [I], 1999).

165 *The company permitted Fincher:* Fight Club (Fox 2000 Pictures, New Regency Productions, Linson Films, 1999).

166 *By 1997, only 14.1 percent:* Stuart Silverstein, "Slight Membership Gain in State Fails to Brighten Outlook for Labor Unions," *Los Angeles Times*, February 14, 1999, https://www.latimes.com/archives/la-xpm-1999 -feb-14-fi-8079-story.html.

166 *By 2008, that number:* "Union Members in 2008," January 28, 2009, United States Department of Labor, Bureau of Labor Statistics, https:// www.bls.gov/news.release/archives/union2_01282009.pdf.

166 *From the 1970s onward:* "How the Mainstream Media Abandoned the Working Class," On the Media, April 16, 2021.

167 *Or, as Carrie:* "The Caste System," *Sex and the City*, August 8, 1999.

168 *In March 1985:* Matthew Sellers, "Starbucks Fires Union-Launching Employee," HRD America, April 3, 2023, https://www.hcamag.com/us /specialization/industrial-relations/starbucks-fires-union-launching -employee/441628.

168 *There were a lot of anti-union:* "Popular Anti-Union Talking Points and How to Combat Them," *Citations Needed*, episode 177, March 15, 2023.

169 *According to Schultz:* Howard Schultz, *Pour Your Heart Into It: How Starbucks Built a Company One Cup at a Time* (New York: Hyperion, 1997).

169 *By 1971, the unemployment rate:* Sharon Boswell, "Lights out, Seattle," *Seattle Times*, November 3, 1996, https://special.seattletimes .com/o/special/centennial/november/lights_out.html; Libby Denkmann and Hans Anderson, "What Can Seattle's 1970s 'Boeing Bust' Teach Us about Recent Tech Layoffs?" KUOW, March 7, 2023, https://www.kuow .org/stories/what-can-seattle-s-boeing-bust-teach-us-about-tech-layoffs.

170 *During the 1980s:* Lois Plunkett, "The 1980's: A Decade of Job Growth and Industry Shifts," *Monthly Labor Review* 3, no. 113 (1990).

170 *According to the Pew Research Center:* "Changes in the American Workplace," *Pew Research Center's Social & Demographic Trends Project* (blog), October 6, 2016, https://www.pewresearch.org/social-trends /2016/10/06/1-changes-in-the-american-workplace/.

170 *The union drive:* *The Sopranos* (HBO, Brillstein Entertainment Partners, 1999).

171 *"Starbucks is selling":* Anya Kamenetz, "Baristas of the World, Unite!" *New York Magazine*, May 19, 2005, https://nymag.com/nymetro/news /features/12060/.

171 *Despite their stock price:* "Starbucks Stock Up 13% Over Last 6 Months: What's Next?" March 15, 2023, NASDAQ https://www.nasdaq .com/articles/starbucks-stock-up-13-over-last-six-months.-whats -next.

173 *"Imagine if our country":* Howard Schultz, "Howard Schultz: US Needs Third-Party Independent Like Me in 2020 Race," *USA Today*, January 30, 2019, https://www.usatoday.com/story/opinion/2019/01/29 /howard-schultz-2020-third-party-independent-centrist-starbucks- column/2701143002/.

174 *In December 2021:* Matt Bruenig, "The Starbucks Union Has Now Won 300 Elections," People's Policy Project, May 11, 2023, https://www .peoplespolicyproject.org/2023/05/11/the-starbucks-union-has-now-won -300-elections/.

174 *NLRB judges determined:* "HELP Majority Staff Report on Starbucks," U.S. Senate Committee on Health, Education, Labor & Pensions, March 26, 2023, https://www.help.senate.gov/chair/newsroom /press/news-help-majority-staff-report-on-starbucks.

174 *"I think unions":* Dee-Ann Durbin, "Starbucks leader grilled by senate over anti-union actions," *Associated Press*, March 29, 2023, https:// apnews.com/article/starbucks-bernie-sanders-howard-schultz-union-94ab 6a1e4e1302d5808f600f19a99085.

Closing Time

181 *They were the backdrops: Rock of Love with Bret Michaels* (51 Minds Entertainment, Mindless Entertainment, 2007); *Newlyweds: Nick and Jessica* (MTV Productions, 2003); *Flavor of Love* (51 Minds Entertainment, 2006); *Cribs* (MTV Productions, 2000); *Big Brother* (Evolution Film & Tape, Arnold Shapiro Productions, CBS, 2000); *Bad Girls Club* (Bunim-Murray Productions, 2006).

182 *"The simplest way":* Kate Wagner, "McMansion, USA," *Jacobin*, November 9, 2017, https://jacobin.com/2017/11/mcmansions-housing -architecture-rich-people.

182 *Kate runs a blog:* Kate Wagner, *McMansion Hell* (blog), accessed February 26, 2024, https://mcmansionhell.com/.

185 *I had just graduated:* "Regional and State Unemployment—2012 Annual Averages" (US Bureau of Labor Statistics, March 1, 2013), https:// www.bls.gov/news.release/archives/srgune_03012013.pdf.

186 *In 1763, the British:* Greg Grandin, *The End of the Myth: From the Frontier to the Border Wall in the Mind of America*, 1st Edition (New York: Metropolitan Books, 2019).

186 *That same year:* Thomas Jefferson, "Notes on the State of Virginia, Query 19, 164–65," 1784, https://press-pubs.uchicago.edu/founders /documents/v1ch4s9.html.

188 *During World War II:* "A Brief History of the Housing Government Sponsored Enterprises," Federal Housing Finance Agency, accessed April 29, 2024, https://www.fhfaoig.gov/Content/Files/History%20of%20the%20 Government%20Sponsored%20Enterprises.pdf .

188 *Others were able:* Keeanga-Yamahtta Taylor, *Race for Profit: How Banks and the Real Estate Industry Undermined Black Homeownership* (Chapel Hill: The University of North Carolina Press, 2019).

190 *In 1994—a year before:* Frederick J. Eggers, "Homeownership: A Housing Success Story," *Cityscape* 5, no. 2 (2001): 43–56.

190 *In 2002, President Bush:* "Bush Push on Housing," CBS News, June 17, 2002, https://www.cbsnews.com/news/bush-push-on-housing/.

190 *In the Y2K Era, the financial:* Sam Gindin and Leo Panitch, *The Making of Global Capitalism: The Political Economy of American Empire* (London; Brooklyn, NY: Verso Books, 2013).

191 *Or, in the words of an affidavit:* Michael Powell, "Bank accused of pushing mortgage deals on Blacks," *New York Times*, June 6, 2009, https://www.nytimes.com/2009/06/07/us/07baltimore.html.

191 *In the wake of these crises:* "Testimony of Brooksley Born," Committee on Banking and Financial Services, House of Representatives, (Washington DC, October 1, 1998), https://www.cftc.gov/sites/default/files/opa/speeches/opaborn-35.htm.

191 *We couldn't constrain:* Sam Gindin and Leo Panitch, *The Making of Global Capitalism: The Political Economy of American Empire* (London; Brooklyn, NY: Verso Books, 2013).

191 *In 1999 the government:* Neil Irwin, "What Is Glass-Steagall? The 82-Year-Old Banking Law That Stirred the Debate," *New York Times*, October 14, 2015, sec. The Upshot, https://www.nytimes.com/2015/10/15/upshot/what-is-glass-steagall-the-82-year-old-banking-law-that-stirred-the-debate.html.

192 *In March, the investment bank:* Laura Rodini, "What Happened to Bear Stearns? Who Bought It?" TheStreet, July 21, 2023, https://www.thestreet.com/personal-finance/bear-stearns.

192 *Pension funds:* Edward Whitehouse, "Pensions During the Crisis: Impact on Retirement Income Systems and Policy Responses," *The Geneva Papers on Risk and Insurance. Issues and Practice* 34, no. 4 (2009): 536–47.

192 *Or maybe you've seen:* Alexandra Twin, "Stocks Crushed," CNNMoney, September 29, 2008, https://money.cnn.com/2008/09/29/markets/markets_newyork/.

193 *Even Semisonic sang:* Semisonic, "Closing Time," 1998, https://genius.com/Semisonic-closing-time-lyrics.

194 *American households:* Sam Gindin and Leo Panitch, *The Making of Global Capitalism: The Political Economy of American Empire* (London; Brooklyn, NY: Verso Books, 2013), 318.